Forgiveness from a Feminist Perspective

Forgiveness from a Feminist Perspective

KATHRYN NORLOCK

LEXINGTON BOOKS
Lanham • Boulder • New York • London

Published by Lexington Books
An imprint of The Rowman & Littlefield Publishing Group, Inc.
4501 Forbes Boulevard, Suite 200, Lanham, Maryland 20706
www.rowman.com

6 Tinworth Street, London SE11 5AL

British Library Cataloguing in Publication Information Available

Library of Congress Cataloging-in-Publication Data

Norlock, Kathryn, 1969-
  Forgiveness from a feminist perspective / Kathryn Norlock.
     p. cm.
  Includes bibliographical references and index.
  ISBN: 978-0-7391-0857-4 (cloth: alk. paper)
  ISBN: 978-1-4985-9121-8 (pbk. : alk. paper)
  1. Forgiveness. 2. Feminist theory. I. Title.
  BJ1476.N67 2009
  179'.9-dc22   2008031565

♾™ The paper used in this publication meets the minimum requirements of American
National Standard for Information Sciences—Permanence of Paper for Printed Library
Materials, ANSI/NISO 239.48–1992.

Printed in the United States of America

To my parents, who have always been surprisingly forgiving

Contents

Preface

When I first wrote this book, some scholars still described research on forgiveness as in its infancy, and feminism was not a common topic on social media and in public discourse. Since the first edition was published in December 2008, the literature on forgiveness has expanded remarkably, and social media movements have moved discussions of misogyny, feminism, and gendered harm into everyday conversation, especially when some accused of sexual misconduct issue public apologies. How anyone, including and not limited to direct victims, should respond to apologies in gendered and sexualized contexts is a common subject in public discourse today, to an extent I had not anticipated. My early efforts to suggest that the power relations and gender relations between wrongdoers, victims, and witnesses should be taken into account in considering refusal to forgive or extensions of forgiveness might be easier to establish now, as I can point to such a prominently covered cultural example as film producer Harvey Weinstein's reported sexual misconduct toward actresses over whom he enjoyed power. That gender matters in analyzing responses to apology is no longer a difficult case to make.

In 2018, more writers are raising questions as to what comes *after* calling someone out. One recent and widely reprinted column in the press is headlined, "In age of #MeToo, can there be forgiveness, second chances?"[1] The author describes public forgiveness on the part of a victim of sexual harassment:

> After comedy writer Megan Ganz called out her former boss, Harmon, on the sitcom *Community* for sexually harassing her, she got more than a simple "I'm sorry." Harmon, in an episode of his podcast in January 2018, acknowledged specific things he did to her. Ganz called it "master class" in how to apologize. "He's not rationalizing or justifying or making excuses. He doesn't just vaguely acknowledge some general wrongdoing in the past. He gives a full account," she wrote on Twitter. She publicly forgave him. (Smith 2018)

As I discuss in the chapters to follow, public expressions of forgiveness are only one dimension of forgiveness, and sometimes only the beginning of a social process. That process, in the social media age, includes varieties of scrutiny and criticism of the forgiveness of victims in public. After Dylann Roof shot and killed black Americans gathered for a prayer meeting at a church in Charleston, South Carolina, in 2015, survivors and relatives of the victims publicly forgave him; as philosophers Luke Brunning and Per-Erik Milam observe, their choice to forgive was controversial to some, and the oppressive circumstances in which they faced an unrepentant killer create obstacles and complexities to their forgiving and to public receptions of their forgiveness.[2] Milam and Brunning argue that "by systematically legitimizing and normalizing violence, hatred, discrimination, and other dimensions of oppression, a society can systematically undermine the ability of the oppressed to forgive" (Brunning and Milam 2015).

It is my hope that the chapters that follow normalize *recognition* of dimensions of oppression, and contribute to identifying some of those complexities that undermine the capacities for victims to respond and that work against their recognition by others as aptly responsive. The short answer to Smith's titular question is that even wrongs commonly described as unforgivable have been forgiven by someone, but that what is possible is not coextensive with what is right or best, especially in gendered and oppressive contexts. Political events in the United States since this book was first published have also provided all too many occasions for discussions of division, despair, and anger. This book went to press before press and social media attention to the deaths of black Americans at the hands of police officers gave rise to Black Lives Matter, before the global refugee crisis that would result in the most displaced people since measures of refugees first started tracking human displacement after World War Two, and before divisive elections in many countries that gave rise to new policies surrounding the treatment of migrants seeking amnesty at national borders. A better book today would address intersectionality of identities as crucial to articulation of the multiple meanings of forgiveness for victims of serious harm in circumstances of oppression and marginalization that are not comparable, but that call for a relational and feminist approach with attention to power dynamics and a plurality of ethical responses. I was too ignorant of the scholarship of intersectionality when I completed this first attempt, and overtly feminist approaches to forgiveness have been slow to follow.

Having said that, it is a pleasure to reflect that philosophical work on forgiveness has expanded so much in the decade since I wrote this book. My comments in the chapters on self-forgiveness, speech acts of forgiveness, and third-party forgiveness that philosophers rarely engage with these topics are now happily inaccurate. More broadly, philosophers of forgiveness are more likely today to build accounts of forgiveness that consider empirical information in moral psychology and the narratives of victims and wrongdoers in complicated contexts of oppression or violence. Multidimensional accounts of forgiveness and advancement of arguments for degrees of forgiveness or standing to forgive are increasingly the norm instead of the exception. Wider interest in nonideal theory motivates some of these changes; if conceptual analyses of forgiveness in the early days of the boom in philosophical attention were idealized conceptions, the focus of more recent scholarship is to the importance of, as Glen Pettigrove (2012) says, getting the phenomenology right. More, philosophers taking nonideal approaches tend to argue that experiences with forgiving ought to inform better theorizing. As Alice MacLachlan (2017) says, "A philosophical account should distill those features and functions that are central to the concept as it emerges from everyday practices and develop a rational or regulative ideal that best reflects them. If these cannot be unified into a single, universal paradigm, it is better to sit with complexity than to deny the phenomenology of moral experience" (138).

In the original preface to the first edition, I mentioned two motivating reasons for the monograph, that no other book-length treatment of forgiveness in philosophy considered the extents to which forgiveness is gendered or brought an explicitly feminist perspective to bear on analyses of forgiveness. That has not changed, but the field, which was already well-populated with outstanding scholars, includes many more, to whom I owe new acknowledgments. Gratitude is owed to Alice MacLachlan, Barrett Emerick, David McNaughton, Myisha Cherry, Per-Erik Milam, and Brandon Warmke, all of whom gave generously of their time and thoughts in these intervening years when I needed to work out approaches to forgiveness, helped me think more than they may realize, and drew me into new appreciation of the complexities of forgiving.

My continued gratitude for help in the preparation of this monograph goes to those mentors who encouraged my project and assisted me with it long after I ceased to be their student or even a resident of the same state. Claudia Card read and encouraged my work even in her last year of life. Paula Gottlieb, Lester Hunt, and Dan Hausman read early versions of many portions and provided detailed comments. Mike Byrd posed difficult questions that forced me to better articulate the distinction between forgiveness and reconciliation, prompting my realization of my own position that forgiveness is not necessary to relationships, and we carry on many of our longest relationships without ever forgiving some wrongs.

The first and third chapters benefited greatly from the audiences at meetings of the Society for Analytical Feminism and the Society for Women in Philosophy at conferences over several years. I count myself as unreasonably lucky to have received such thorough review of many chapters from my friends and colleagues, including Dave Concepcion, Andrea Veltman, and Stephen Schulman.

I owe a great deal to Robert Enright and everyone at the International Forgiveness Institute for their numerous reading suggestions, the research materials they made available to me and the opportunity to sit in on their stimulating Friday sessions for a year, in order to gain a better understanding of their work on forgiveness in psychotherapy. Bob Enright was the first to utter that invaluable phrase, "when you write your book," allowing the possibility of authorship to bloom in my mind for the first time, and he was unfailingly encouraging of my efforts to bring psychology to bear on philosophy, and vice versa.

Faculty at St. Mary's College of Maryland are thanked for their enthusiastic reception to my presentations of my project. I owe a special debt to Michael Taber for editing and commenting on the initial proposal for this work, and to Katharina von Kellenbach for comments and criticisms on an early draft of the first chapter. St. Mary's College of Maryland awarded pre-tenure leave in Fall 2004 and sabbatical for the 2007–2008 school year, which afforded me the precious stretches of quiet time necessary to writing and revising this work.

My students at both Trent University and St. Mary's College of Maryland have contributed greatly to my understanding of philosophy, forgiveness, and feminism. Zach Dunn and Megan McGrew were heaven-sent student assistants during my tenure track who provided daily care in the form of menial tasks, manual labor, and a variety of the kinds of support a writer needs.

I remain grateful to the encouraging and patient staff at Lexington Books. Thanks especially to Jana Hodges-Kluck, senior acquisitions editor for Philosophy, Classical Studies, and Linguistics, for first discussing with me the release of a paperback edition.

I thank my husband for loving and supporting me every day. As ever, this book is dedicated to my parents; I thank the parent that is gone and the parent that remains for continuous love and forgiveness.

References

Brunning, Eric, and Per-Erik Milam. 2015. "Forgiving Hate Crimes: The Case of Dylann Roof." International Network for Hate Studies (INHS). Accessed June 22, 2018. www.internationalhatestudies.com/forgiving_hate_crimes/.

MacLachlan, Alice. 2017. "In Defense of Third-Party Forgiveness." In *The Moral Psychology of Forgiveness*, edited by Kathryn J. Norlock, 135–59. London and New York: Rowman & Littlefield International.

Pettigrove, Glen. 2012. *Forgiveness and Love*. Oxford: Oxford University Press.

Smith, Michelle R. 2018. "Can there be forgiveness, second chances in the age of #MeToo?" *Associated Press News*. Accessed June 20, 2018. www.apnews.com/c69e3a82417f4af280376fdc10cf8651.

Notes

1. The article, by Michelle R. Smith for Associated Press, April 15, 2018, is frequently reprinted with the slightly different headline front-loading forgiveness rather than the social movement: "Can there be forgiveness, second chances in the age of #MeToo?" (The original essay is available at the following URL and last accessed June 22, 2018: www.apnews.com/c69e3a82417f4af280376fdc10cf8651.)

2. The excellent blog post, "Forgiving Hate Crimes: The Case of Dylann Roof," appears at the blog of the International Network for Hate Studies (INHS) (at www.internationalhatestudies.com/forgiving_hate_crimes/). In line with the mission of the INHS, the authors attend to the fact that the survivors and victims are racial minorities. They do not attend to the genders of those who took part in the public delivery of forgiveness, and one has to look elsewhere to learn that all identified speakers were black women: a daughter, a mother, a granddaughter, a sister (see Elahe Izadi, "The powerful words of forgiveness delivered to Dylann Roof by victims' relatives," *The Washington Post*, June 19, 2015, available at www.washingtonpost.com/news/post-nation/wp/2015/06/19/hate-wont-win-the-powerful-words-delivered-to-dylann-roof-by-victims-relatives/?utm_term=.598ddae15862).

Chapter One

Forgiveness Is Gendered

Theorizing about forgiveness is philosophically important. Many have offered compelling reasons for its significance. Donald Shriver and Margaret Urban Walker describe forgiveness as indispensable to human relationships.[1] Desmond Tutu famously suggests there can be no future without forgiveness.[2] And Hannah Arendt argues similarly that "trespassing is an everyday occurrence . . . and it needs forgiving, dismissing, in order to make it possible for life to go on."[3] Jeffrie Murphy and Charles Griswold cite Bishop Joseph Butler's sermons, in which he says forgiving our trespassers reduces to "no more than that we should not indulge a passion which, if generally indulged, would propagate itself so as almost to lay waste the world."[4] These are not exhaustive of the reasons forgiveness is a worthy subject of study. I choose them as representative of the most influential philosophical accounts, by which I mean those most widely read and often cited.

Perhaps not coincidentally, a common feature of mainstream accounts of forgiveness is that they do not take gender as central to the meaning or practice of forgiving.[5] That forgiveness is gendered goes without saying. I intend that claim in at least two senses. For some philosophers who study forgiveness, that it is gendered is obvious. For others, the ways in which forgiveness is gendered are unaddressed, or discussed briefly in ways that imply gender is not a central matter to questions of forgiveness. Most philosophers belong in the latter camp; brief or no attention to gender has prevailed in the more influential works on forgiveness. This is not to say that the gender-neutral accounts of forgiveness are written by philosophers with no sensitivity to gender issues. Margaret Urban Walker, Trudy Govier, and Claudia Card are feminist or feminist-friendly authors who have written extensively on forgiveness and take up, or at least mention, the subject of women's forgiveness in the course of their work, and Robert Enright's work in psychology heavily influences my own feminist work in philosophy.[6] However, neither do authors such as the above center the claim with which I began, that forgiveness is gendered. Feminist contributions to a fuller

1

conception of forgiveness have been increasing in number, but don't yet seem to be a part of a common discourse; both treatments of forgiveness as gendered, and gender-neutral treatments are insightful and informative, but there seem to be few conversations or connections between these two approaches.[7]

For the purposes of discussing forgiveness, I proceed with an understanding of forgiveness which connects the multiplicity of gendered and neutral definitions of forgiveness. As most theorists of forgiveness note, forgiveness is complex; any identifications of its features will serve more as a model and a mirror of the theorist's priorities than a perfectly applicable definition with necessary and sufficient conditions. Yet in pursuing the connections between gender-conscious and gender-neutral views, I find a few features helpfully recur and admit of the following conception. Forgiveness is held to be a moral, and therefore at least partially deliberative, action or set of actions, which functions as a remedy in responding to blame or condemnation, releasing offenders from the fullness of their blameworthiness, in relational contexts which therefore require considerations of power between relata. In describing forgiveness as one or more *actions* in differing accounts, I intend to capture both the dominant conception of forgiveness as a change of heart and/or forswearing of resentment, as well as the decisive quality of forgiveness in those accounts which describe it as a process involving recommitment to a relationship or a determined reviewing of someone in a new light. For some authors the essence of forgiveness is in the change in one's internal states, for others the communication of forgiveness to offenders, and for still others the forward-looking activities involved in repair and rebuilding; I venture to describe all these as actions, that is, as the moral actions of moral agents. Authors of process-conceptions of forgiveness may be the least satisfied with this account, but as it is hard to think of a process which doesn't involve actions, I suggest that processes are adequately characterized by my account. Ultimately, I advance a multi-dimensional account of forgiveness, precisely because I consider many types of acts to "count" as forgiveness.

I grant that I take more liberties with characterizing forgiveness, across accounts, as relational, yet I wish to emphasize those occasions on which relational features are common between accounts. Moreover, insisting that forgiveness is relational does not preclude self-forgiveness, as long as one can be held to stand in relationship to one's self, or selves. In later chapters, I defend the conception of a multiplicity of selves in detail. For now, I am merely drawing up a conception of forgiveness with which to proceed, and a relational model brings theorists together most effectively. Even the most dyadic accounts involve at least two persons at the same time that they overlook possibilities for self-forgiveness, and so the relational nature of forgiveness seems appropriate to emphasize. The function of forgiveness as somehow releasing wrongdoers from the fullness of condemnation or blameworthiness is true across all the accounts I consider, although I grant that my provisional model here covers a great deal of variety with respect to the meaning of "release." Most theorists establish clear differences between forgiving and condoning, excusing, or refraining from punishing, a project I both appreciate and resist, for reasons which will become clear.

Last, my working model of forgiveness, as moral action(s) releasing offenders in relationships, includes consideration of power; considerations of relationality and power include considerations of gender. Power is an element which, surprisingly, is not explicit in most of the accounts I'm connecting, and which I add for feminist reasons. Walker provides a refreshing exception to the general tendency to ignore power relations. She notes, "I think that to understand the moral content of forgiveness, we need to understand the content of moral relations," and she reminds us, importantly, that to the extent moral relationships involve trust and vulnerability to others, they inevitably involve differences in vulnerabilities and power.[8] Many accounts approach discussing the role of power in relationships, and all the accounts I've encountered provide thought-experiments involving particular relationships in ways which obliquely consider power. I do not find it a coincidence that philosophers with the most gender-neutral accounts are also the philosophers least likely to discuss power imbalances within relationships.

Gender Matters

Why do many theorists discuss forgiveness in the absence of considerations of gender? One answer may be inferred from Walker's recent analysis of feminist philosophy's uneasy place in the wider profession. Walker noted that (1) women have contributed to philosophy for millennia, and yet (2) women in philosophy do not yet make up half the profession or even a "tipping point" of more than thirty-five percent, at which minority cultures are more likely to affect majority cultures.[9] "What happens at that point is that gender as a category of analysis, a subject matter, and a principle of locating suspiciously neglected subject matters . . . becomes a part of the standard equipment of scholars in the field."[10] My own research in forgiveness has often led me to parallel observations. Women and feminists (which are not coextensive sets, of course) have contributed notably to philosophies of forgiveness. Although I feel that as a feminist philosopher of forgiveness, I benefit from the excellent company of those who have already called attention to gender matters, I also see that a dominant discourse holds fast. Just as gender is not a central organizing category of analysis in philosophy on the whole, it also does not organize or take a central role in philosophical analyses of forgiveness. This is evident when we consider that in a leading philosophical database, one can find 293 citations of philosophical work related to forgiveness, but only eight of these are written from explicitly feminist perspectives; all eight are journal articles or chapters, not monographs, and these are not (yet) considered the most influential works in forgiveness.[11]

The striking genderlessness of the dominant discourse moves me to point out that gender is central to forgiveness. Accounts of forgiveness which do not center gender and women's experience are accounts which develop a deceptively universal conception of forgiveness, and therefore miss some opportunities to capture further complexities and multiple meanings of forgiveness. That forgiveness admits of multiple meanings is evident from the rich accounts developed so far in many disciplines, and as I argue in later chapters, I believe it is more accurate and more productive to speak of multiple meanings than to quest for a single, monistic definition of genuine or true forgiveness. I immediately identify with Nick Smith when he writes of his own work on the nature of apology, "My own attempts to provide a definition of apologies collapsed under a barrage of questions;" although he credits the great value of previous definitional work, Smith pointedly "shifts the focus from the definition of the term to its value within our lives."[12] Walker says similarly, "Let's ask what it *means* for individuals, or for a group or society collectively, to declare an act unforgivable. What is the moral power of that declaration?"[13] The importance and value of practical acts of forgiveness, as described by practitioners, guide my attempts at definition, rather than the other way around.

Following Alison Jaggar, I suggest that a feminist perspective would not merely add to the information about forgiveness, but would importantly widen and deepen the scope of philosophy of forgiveness.[14] Like Smith, I do not intend to show that philosophers who proceed from their own methods are therefore wrong about the aspects of forgiveness on which they focus, any more than I would wish to show that someone who lifts fingerprints from a crime scene is wrong about the contents of the fingerprints; I hope rather to suggest other fruitful ways of looking for clues. Yet a purportedly neutral and genderless approach is, at times, infused with gender bias, in a way which certainly distracts from other methods of considering information about forgiveness. In saying this I presume that accounts from Kantian, Aristotelian, or other canonical frameworks are not themselves objective, and that indeed no framework is objective in the sense of being value-neutral or free from a perspective or bias; as Karen Warren has argued, depending on one's purpose, one's definitional work may simply be "better-biased."[15]

The assumption in prevailing accounts of forgiveness that they are objective may have informed the blank response of some theorists to whom I've suggested that forgiveness is a traditionally feminine virtue. Vicky Davion has saliently observed that the existence of the gender roles "masculine" and "feminine" as we know them presupposes the context of patriarchy and sexism.[16] If so, she provides a possible reason that the major works on forgiveness do not address gender; if one's analysis of forgiveness is not overtly sexist, if one aspires to operate in a manner free of patriarchal influence or sexist bias, then critiquing gender roles in the course of theorizing about forgiveness may seem unnecessary, because there are no genders where there is no bias or patriarchy, or at the least, gender is as irrelevant as eye color. I proceed from the position that no account is unbiased, and in later chapters, will argue for prioritizing personal narrative and inevitably biased experience, although doing so, I grant, comes with epistemological risks.

I suggest that the fascinating complexity of forgiveness is best appreciated when studied from a feminist perspective that prioritizes the gendered history and meanings of forgiveness, and attends in much more focused ways to the experience of women. Gender matters are central to the meanings, values, and practices of forgiveness because, as Jaggar says, "gender operates as a set of socially instituted expectations that regulate every aspect of our lives," and I would add that this is especially true of our interpersonal moral experiences.[17] I am not the only feminist philosopher to arrive at this conclusion, and will draw on the work of predecessors and contemporaries, integrating their observations to develop a multidimensional account of forgiveness. My intention is to contribute to the presence of feminist analyses in philosophy of forgiveness, in the hopes of moving philosophy closer to the tipping point.

Despite whatever integration I may employ for my ends, feminist philosophy is by no means monolithic. Feminists have points of difference between them, and as so many feminists have aptly observed, there is no one short definition or established method of feminism, any more than there is one definition or established method of philosophy.[18] My analysis of what it means to say an object of inquiry is gendered, therefore, will consider definitional candidates and advance a possible interpretation, but will not be exhaustive of the possibilities, and should not be taken to be representative of the viewpoint of feminism simpliciter. Instead, this chapter continues the conversations I've had with helpful feminist philosophers about forgiveness in particular; in later chapters, I incorporate the views of feminist philosophers about, more generally, the purposes of writing from a feminist perspective, especially the goal of showing that gender is central to understanding many objects of philosophical importance. I do not consider my own the definitive picture, and in this, I'm heavily influenced by Walker's observation: "There is no reason to think that anyone individually could imagine the full gamut of representational techniques for mapping, and of critical devices for testing, our differentiated and multilingual moral-social worlds."[19] I will not argue, then, that accounts of paradigm forgiveness are incomplete whereas mine is complete. Rather, I recognize that mainstream accounts rectify the previous neglect of forgiveness as a philosophical topic, but tend to proceed in an ahistorical and acontextual manner that misses valuable sources of knowledge which would contribute to a more robust understanding of the functions and values of forgiveness. Since I find that forgiveness is strongly associated with gender ideals of femininity in Euro-American culture, the experiences of women are particularly important to my analysis, but I do not solely rely on the experiences of women. I do not believe women have a wholly separate reality from men or that women always have more in common with each other than they do with men of their own races, classes and institutions.[20] Having said that, I do proceed on the assumption that women's experiences with a trait many consider feminine – forgivingness – will be revealing of the functions and value forgiveness can have, particularly for men and women in American culture.

To the study of forgiveness, of course, one could take gender to be relevant without believing it necessitates analysis from a feminist perspective. Therefore, before I go further with justification of a particular feminist method, I should address the more basic objection that forgiveness may not be gendered at all. Philosophers have used the term "gendered" in more than one sense; indeed, I'm sure I've used it in multiple ways in the same written piece, myself. Below I take up a few candidates for the definition of "gendered," and consider the ways in which philosophers have argued for similar claims, testing their applicability to accounts of forgiveness. While no one possible meaning below will be sufficient to account for all the uses of the term, taken together they provide compelling reasons to see gender as a fundamental organizing concept in forgiveness theory. Throughout this chapter, I rely on evidence from psychology and the social sciences to support my position, for the excellent reason that fundamental claims of philosophy should be well supported and contextualized within actual social practices.[21]

In what follows, then, I explore three senses in which forgiveness is gendered. In light of cultural stereotypes and social realities, I argue that (1) forgiveness as a practice is expected of women more often than men, and this expectation is a shared cultural assumption reported by both men and women. Next, I move to tracing the ways in which, conceptually and historically, (2) forgiveness, and the trait of being a forgiving person, is associated with femininity, which requires some elaboration of what I mean by the feminine. I consider a few ways in which (3) in predominantly Kantian and individualistic accounts, sexist biases affect the most basic conceptions we bring to forgiveness as a field of study, including our assumptions about the natures of individuals, rationality and moral acts.

(1) Forgiveness is expected of women

First, full disclosure is in order; I brought the above hypothesis to my own study of forgiveness. My motivating intuition was that women as a group are expected to forgive more often. This is not to say that (a) women, in fact, have more occasion to forgive; I don't really believe we're wronged more often, although women may suffer from some kinds of wrongs more often than do men, and vice versa. Neither am I claiming that (b) women, on the whole and in practice, just are more forgiving (in nature or behavior). To make such a statement about all women without regard to race, class, sociopolitical power, religious commitments or personality seems preposterous. Further, it would be empirically impossible to show evidence for either (a) or (b) even if they happened to be true, although depending on how one tends to define forgiveness, (b) may be possible.

However, the widespread cultural *assumption* that, on the whole, women are more forgiving, is important, and potentially demonstrable. I add the caveat that its demonstrability is merely potential, because although psychologists have attended to the importance of gender to forgiveness better than philosophers, the body of evidence is still none too large. Varda Konstam, Miriam Chernoff and Sara Deveney, with many other psychologists, note that forgiveness has only recently received scientific study, and with many other theorists, they describe the literature as "sparse" and "in its infancy."[22] They observe that in a study of mental health counselors, the respondents reported that among their clients, "social expectations differed for men and women regarding forgiveness. It was perceived that the ability to forgive was acceptable—perhaps admirable and socially sanctioned—for women. In contrast, the ability to forgive was more likely to be associated with weakness for men. [Respondents] noted that women were expected to be more forgiving in our culture." [23]

Relatedly, women seem to demonstrate more interest in exploring forgiveness in counseling and educational settings, and more open to discussing it than men. In light of the perception above that women are generally expected to be more forgiving in our culture, it is intriguing when the psychological literature reflects surprise on the researchers' parts that women are more likely to take part in forgiveness-oriented studies. Of the Stanford Forgiveness Project, Frederic Luskin says,

> One interesting thing we learned . . . was that more women than men sign up for forgiveness experiments. This gender difference has been corroborated by other forgiveness studies and by my experience in teaching public classes. Eighty percent [of inquiring calls] were from women. We wanted to recruit an equal number of men and women to determine if forgiveness is different according to gender. As an interesting aside, we recruited more men when we changed our ads to ask for "people who held a grudge."[24]

Everett Worthington, more bluntly, says simply that "women seem more likely to forgive and certainly are more likely to participate in forgiveness research," but adds, "No studies have investigated gender differences in actual forgiveness."[25] He too notes the cultural expectation that women are more forgiving. Oddly, following his suggestion that gender is "potentially important," he concludes, "We very tentatively recommend that additional studies of gender effects be undertaken."[26]

Similar recommendations are endorsed less tentatively by other psychologists.[27] The aims of such recommendations apparently include establishing the differences in actual practice between men and women, but more meaningful to my thesis is the consensus among researchers that the cultural expectations on women to forgive (as opposed to cultural expectations upon men) persist and are shared by males and females. Sharon Lamb's related work in psychology argues that "this expectation that women will be more compassionate" is connected to women's perceived responsibility for relationships in general, and "traditional notions of what it means to be a 'good girl' or 'good woman.'"[28] Janice Haaken refers to the development of this cultural perception as "the feminizing of the capacity to forgive," and argues, "There also are long-standing cultural scripts aligning forgiveness, as an emotional state, with femininity."[29] Considering how forgiveness came to be associated with femininity is the task of the next section.

(2) Forgiveness is associated with femininity

Association of forgiveness with femininity has been explored very little in philosophical literature, especially compared with psychological literature on forgiveness. Feminist philosophers are more likely to proceed from this point than to elaborate their reasons for holding it, and it is considered at best contentious by many nonfeminist philosophers to whom I've expressed it. My initial response to denial of the association was surprise that my intuition of the association was not more widely shared, but the objection that forgiveness is not obviously ascribed to the feminine is itself revealing of the culture in which I live, a culture which is both predominantly Christian, and aims for gender neutrality as a corrective to past injustice, and in which, therefore, forgivingness is presumably a virtue for everyone. If I wish to show connections between feminist work on forgiveness and other philosophers' views, then some lengthy defense of (2) is in order.

Before I proceed, I wish to clarify that to say forgiveness is associated with the feminine in my culture is not yet to say anything about its worth. I do not proceed on the assumption that the feminine is bad, or that the association renders forgiveness as having only one particular value. As Margaret Walker has said, an analysis of this kind presents "a culturally embedded and socially situated ideal of character, a . . . normative self-conception [that] situates but does not morally evaluate" the object of study.[30] I study forgiveness in its associative context "so that we can begin to understand what moral understandings it makes available (and to whom), enforceable (and by whom), and both of these at what costs (and for whom)."[31] At this point, I intend merely to outline my reasons for the claim (which is, to some, controversial) that forgiveness is associated with femininity. I proceed to evaluation of the worth of forgiveness in later chapters.

I wish to further clarify that suggesting an association of forgiveness with femininity does not entail that therefore men forgive less or are inherently less capable than women of forgiving. As I use them, the terms *feminine* and *masculine* refer to cultural ideals and stereotypes of women and men, rather than to the traits of actual men and women, let alone desirable traits. It is for precisely this reason that each of the terms *feminine* and *masculine* can refer to a set of inconsistent and at times contradictory traits; precisely because they represent ideals that are amalgams of gender notions over time, they have come to represent complex and unattainable ideals. For example, depending on which conceptions of femininity we choose to consider, a woman fitting such an ideal might be physically weak and helpless in the face of needed home repairs, or a healthy, nurturing mother of multiple children and unbelievably competent in the management of house- and childcare. Rousseau famously said that in all things women must be pleasing to men, but what pleases men also changes over time, and from man to man, and new tastes often comfortably coexist alongside old ones in stereotypes and ideals.[32]

Hélène Cixous says relatedly, "It is not anatomical sex. . . . It is, on the contrary, history from which one never escapes, individual and collective history."[33] She notes that *feminine* and *masculine* refer to "a classical vision of sexual opposition between men and women," and the designations do not refer to actual men and women; Alan Schrift saliently observes that Cixous "cautions against the dangers of resorting to the classical binaries," but argues these designations are still useful, because "they . . . become socialized and metaphorized . . . a whole huge system of cultural inscription."[34] To use such terms, therefore, is not to essentialize. Rather, such designations contextualize our discussion in a shared cultural history.

When I use the term "feminine," I proceed from a cultural script that not every reader will necessarily share, but from which I provide elements, in what follows, so ensuing references to the feminine (and its "opposite") will be sufficiently sensible. Nevertheless, I expect that as is often the case in English-language philosophy, most of my readers will be, like me, white, American, and/or of European descent, college-educated and of Christian upbringing, middle-class, heterosexual, and with the feminist tag on the cover, many will be women, so the characterizations of femininity that follow will be all too familiar. Although America is a heterogeneous society, its ideals and stereotypes tend to be those of the dominant groups; therefore, nonwhite, non-Christian, nonwealthy and/or nonheterosexual readers will also be (somewhat) familiar with the "ideal" of femininity, even as (and precisely because) they're not well reflected in this account.

Yet even assuming a shared cultural history with my reader, I realize that cultural scripts are fissured and unstable.[35] Since I'm operating on the view that femininity is an evolving ideal, I have no single standard definition of femininity to appeal to and must instead note repeated themes in philosophy and history. Fortunately for my purposes, those repeated themes are often very clear. Femininity, as described by many philosophers today, is almost always modified with adverbs like 'classically,' 'traditionally,' 'historically.' Writers have reached as far back as Aristotle and Plato to demonstrate the persistence of ideals of masculinity and femininity as existing in opposition to each other. Nancy Tuana has argued at length that Aristotle and Plato differ in their bases for arguing women's difference and inferiority; Aristotle's is focused on "women's reproductive role and biological inferiority," and Plato's is based in difference in soul rather than body.[36] Both, however, contribute to the view of the male as truly human, reasoning, courageous and active. Women would, in contrast, be emotional, yielding, and passive, a view which would be "in turn used as the basis for justifying the exclusion of women from full participation in the state."[37] Stereotypes and ideals of women in the centuries that follow center on her role in domestic life, a harmonizer of the private sphere, and a less than fully rational agent. Philosophers including Kant and Rousseau would ascribe worth to women's beautiful (if not moral) acts and emotional acuity, but relegate their importance or functionality to the private sphere, the interpersonal and religious life of individuals and the family.[38]

Such perceptions of feminine versus masculine character were firmly held and well understood in American culture from the country's beginnings. This explains how women could be so easily excluded from participation in public life in early America even as the founding documents established the equal rights of citizens—that is, of European-American (and in most states, Christian) men of property.[39] The feminine as domestic harmonizer persists through our history; psychologist Janice Haaken, arguing that forgiveness, in particular, is "feminized," cites Barbara Epstein's description of the cult of domesticity, arguing that "the feminizing of the capacity to forgive in Western discourse is also related to the heightening of the division, particularly in the nineteenth century, between private and public life."[40] Haaken may be the only theorist working in forgiveness to explicitly draw connections between the persistent cultural perception that women are more forgiving, and the nineteenth-century view of middle-class women as "guardians of virtue, family togetherness, and emotional harmony . . . the embodiment of unconditional love, turning the other way when confronted with the infidelity of husbands."[41] She argues that "there are long-standing cultural scripts aligning forgiveness, as an emotional state, with femininity. . . . To forgive may be divine, but it is also thought of as a feminine spiritual craft."[42]

Haaken concludes that to say forgiveness is "feminized" is to say "it is associated with traditional female gendered attributes, for instance, yielding, empathy, responsiveness to others."[43] The three particular qualities Haaken chose to stress may be influenced by their inclusion in a list of feminine traits developed in the twentieth century by Sandra Lipsitz Bem. Bem began researching sex roles in the 1970s, and the Bem Sex Role Inventory (BSRI) first developed in 1971 "achieved instant celebrity within the field of psychology," and has become a widely discussed measure of gender role conformity.[44] Her method of developing the inventory is of particular interest, since it is indicative of the persistence of cultural perceptions of forgiveness that may otherwise be dismissed as ancient history.

> First, and perhaps most important, the masculine and feminine items on the BSRI were selected, not on the basis of how males and females describe themselves, but on the basis of what was culturally defined as gender appropriate in the United States in the early 1970s. Judges who screened the pool of items for the test were thus treated as "native informants" about the culture . . . rating each item not by how well it described themselves personally but by how desirable they thought it to be "in American society generally" for either a man or a woman. This procedure was designed to locate masculinity and femininity in the discourse of the culture rather than in the personality of the individual and itself constituted a challenge to [previous] reification of masculinity-femininity as a core dimension of the human personality.[45]

Bem concluded that America is a gendered culture, which "has a readiness to superimpose a gender-based classification on" otherwise genderless concepts, and described American culture as having "highly polarized definitions of gender appropriateness."[46] This method has been criticized in that it relies on mere stereotypes, and was, once again, the product of the perceptions of largely white, middle-class, college-educated "judges."[47] Yet the results are still instructive, and as argued above, the ideals and assumptions of the dominant group tend to be imposed on and familiar to members of a culture who may otherwise be marginalized in a variety of ways. The perceptions of femininity and masculinity today have slightly, but measurably, changed and become more liberal since the introduction of the Bem inventory, more so among women than men, but the ideals and stereotypes are still largely the same even among teens and young adults.[48]

This suggests that what Tuana calls our "metaphysical inheritance" has a persistence that transcends our abstract ideals of morality, justice or religious obligation.[49] Whether we're all to be self-respecting, or all to be forgiving, the test of what members of a culture think, in practice, reveals that traditional ideals and stereotypes influence our thinking as to who should, or who is expected, to really conform to such expectations. This is a greater problem than it may appear at first glance. One could set it aside with the observation that the contrast between our ideals and our imperfect selves is a perennial concern in moral philosophy, and not one that renders the ideals problematic. Yet the persistence of notions of femininity and their association with forgiveness suggest more than a point at which we fall short of universal ideals. It suggests a more intractable conflict between general rules, to which we will have to return.

The inevitability or desirability of gendered traits is a separate matter, and one thoroughly explored in moral philosophy centered on theories of caring as distinct from justice. Nel Noddings's work in philosophy of education describes caring as "a feminine approach," even as she makes a point of arguing that caring is a moral perspective and praxis available to men as well as women.[50] Many philosophers have argued for reevaluation of, and positively valuing, those aspects of the private sphere and domestic life previously relegated to women and therefore considered feminine, including relationships, affections, and emotions related to and including forgiveness.[51] Philosophical debates about the merits of investing traditionally feminine concerns with positive value often center on whether or not doing so perpetuates notions of femininity and "good women" in uncritical and problematic ways, and I will not attempt to resolve all the arguments here. The association of the feminine with forgiveness persists within philosophy, and without in the wider culture.

The above may be, for many, a routine rehearsal of arguments about what constitutes femininity in American culture. I explore its roots not to advance a novel conception of the feminine but to clarify my reasons for proposing that (a) forgiveness is associated with femininity and (b) gender concepts are persistent and powerful organizing categories of thought. Stereotypes of femininity and masculinity are generalizations which American philosophers since the mid-to-late twentieth century have routinely and understandably renounced in the interests of doing philosophy in ways that aim to be less distorted and presumably universally applicable to all human beings regardless of gender. Such an aspiration is certainly an improvement on the millennia-old tradition of explicitly endorsing "the classical binaries" and devaluing the feminine half. However, the decontextualized and nongendered discussions of forgiveness that have resulted from such aspirations still suffer from a legacy of biased methods of inquiry.

(3) Forgiveness is predominantly conceptualized from within biased frameworks.

So far I have considered two observable senses in which forgiveness is gendered, insofar as it's (1) expected of women and (2) associated with historical conceptions of femininity. Stereotypes and histories are certainly influential, many philosophers would grant. However, to the extent that they are arguably constructs and nonrational, they could be safely ignored or considered but set aside if our abstract theories could simply be sensitively applied to accommodate more reflective understandings of gender issues. On this argument, there's nothing inherently masculinist in most conceptions of forgiveness, even if gender is peripheral to philosophical treatments of the subject.

Yet the peripheral status of gender issues in philosophies of forgiveness should give us pause. In light of the prevalence of gender concepts throughout our metaphysical and cultural history, the resulting gendered influence on philosophers' (historically, men's) priorities in moral theory, and the obvious, global, varied ways in which gender inequalities persist and are lived, how do we ever theorize about forgiveness while ignoring gender? Why is its absence not shocking? A comparison with related work in psychology on forgiveness is illustrative; although psychologists acknowledge forgiveness is a fledgling field, gender increasingly appears as a variable and an organizing factor in data, frequently with little fanfare, because it is recognized as a valuable source of information regarding one's identity, experiences and context. How is it that philosophy so often avoids considering gender, which seems to affect the very meaning the term 'forgiveness' has for men and women?

For a discipline to allow engagement with forgiveness so robustly (of late), and with gender so marginally, it would seem to be systematic to the discipline that differences in identity, experience, and context seem either irrelevant or unaffected by gender. It is no longer news that presumably neutral philosophical accounts are infused with biased presumptions about such fundamental concepts, and this is true of some theoretical approaches more than others. Kantian approaches tend to predominate in philosophical treatments of forgiveness, especially in the well-known works of Jeffrie Murphy, Joram Haber and Margaret Holmgren. With the prevalence of Kantian accounts in the literature, we can turn to many excellent and renowned critiques of Kantian philosophy to aid in our investigation of their possible biases. Having said that, I wish to begin the discussion of particular theoretical treatments with a consideration of Joram Haber's Kantian framework, and his later analysis of his own account's limitations from a feminist point of view.[52]

I begin with a consideration of Haber's Kantian model, because to date he seems to be the only philosopher of forgiveness who, in a later work, entertains potential feminist criticism of his own view, insofar as he fails to take the moral agent's relational nature into account. In his first influential work on forgiveness, Haber argued for the necessary conditions of the victim's self-respect (and hence resentment) and the wrongdoer's repentance for forgiveness to be appropriate.[53] In making his ethical recommendations he noted in passing that "what is appropriate will depend on the nature of the relationship."[54] In his later article, "Forgiveness and Feminism," he observes that some feminist theorists hold "that relationships are morally and ontologically prior to the individuals who compose them," and therefore "it will not do to gloss over [the 'nature of the relationship'] in so facile a manner."[55]

In the course of reconsidering his position, Haber compares the likely outcomes of, first, a scenario in which two men in fairly equal positions of power in a formal relationship stand in the wrongdoer-victim relation, and second, a scenario in which a man and woman in financially and socially unequal positions of power in an intimate relationship stand in the wrongdoer-victim relation. His conclusion that the woman in the second case is more likely to forgive than is the man in the first case prompts him to reconsider what constitutes "the paradigm case of forgiveness."[56]

> In the present light, it now seems that my analysis of forgiveness . . . . tacitly assumed a male-based individualistic perspective in which solitary moral agents reasoned from a sense of justice whose primary value was some Kantian concern for self-respect. . . . The moral agents I identified in the paradigm case are self-interested, autonomous individuals seeking to further their own interests, whose sense of justice is aroused when a wrong threatens to undermine the victim's sense of self-respect.[57]

Haber notes, rightly, that the same criticism holds for other theorists who adopt a similar Kantian model, such as Jeffrie Murphy.[58] He represents feminist theories inadequately, however, when he observes that "a proclivity in women to forgive emanates from the kind of care-based considerations that typify a feminist approach to morality."[59] As said above, care-based considerations are controversial within feminist philosophy. To say that care-based considerations *typify* a feminist approach, when Noddings described care as explicitly feminine, is to tacitly assume that feminist accounts are likewise feminine. The above also reveals his assumption that women have such a proclivity to forgive, which I may share, but which I have argued is a pervasive and problematic view of the feminine rather than a justifiable generalization about women in practice.[60] Haber concludes that it may be more enlightening to take the intimate relationship as the paradigm occasion for forgiveness.

The solitary and individualistic approach Haber identifies is a much-discussed limitation, especially in feminist interpretations of Kant. By the same token, Kantian theorists arguing for traditional models of forgiveness can also be guilty of seeing us as all-too-constituted by our relations. For example, Jeffrie Murphy, even as he's taking pains to reject the idea that one can forgive a wrongdoer for wrongs to others (hereafter called third-party forgiveness), argues that at the same time, a mother can forgive someone for doing morally culpable injury to her son, saying, "Sometimes, of course, I will psychologically identify *with* [emphasis mine] some persons and will see injuries to them as in some sense injuries to me."[61] He later adds, "Parents can resent harms done to their children, but this is the kind of exception that proves the rule . . . Resentment only seems possible for the parents because they regard their children as somehow an extension of themselves."[62] And Joram Haber similarly notes, "This is because the relationship between mother and son is such that an injury to the son is an injury to the mother, so that the mother's forgiveness is really for her own injury."[63]

Worth keeping is the important insight by both Murphy and Haber that we psychologically identify with some others and in these cases, resentment and forgiveness may be logically possible, even morally appropriate, on the other's behalf. But the language used above, in seeing the injury to the son as just an injury to the mother, seems to take her relation as one of identification as, rather than identification with, her son. In the context of Murphy's theory, especially, this is understandable; his thesis is that only the direct victim of injury can forgive, and therefore he wishes to describe the mother of the injured as a direct victim, herself.[64] Yet this move turns out to do too much work, since psychological identification with another now seems to consist in taking on their subjectivity as one's own. It calls to mind Noddings's related notions of femininity, including her ideas that true caring between intimates involves the "motivational displacement" and "engrossment" of the one-caring in the person cared for, so that we enter into their perspective and experience injuries from their point of view, see through their eyes.[65]

For Murphy and Haber to appeal to an idea so like Noddings's ideas of displacement and engrossment seems only to add to the difficulty already inherent in Kantian models of being perceived as atomistic and unrelated to others who suffer injury; the new problem is that some moral agents are described as disappearing into some of their relations. For women this is not an obviously preferable addendum to the otherwise "male-based individualistic perspective," for the same reasons that Noddings has been subject to criticism for her similar arguments. Claudia Card argues that "with a capacity for 'motivational displacement'—receiving others into oneself—but lacking integrity one is in danger of dissolving into a variety of personalities, changing one's colors (values) like a chameleon . . . . Women know this danger intimately."[66] In saying the harm to her son is a harm, quite simply, to the mother, Murphy and Haber argue for something stronger than perhaps they intended, something more than we normally think identification with someone consists in. A better account of our relations is in order.

Trudy Govier offers a robust criticism of the individualist account, and refers to the position that only victims can forgive as a variety of skepticism.[67] She notes correctly that philosophers whose accounts rely on direct victims tend to assume rather than argue for their individualist and strict view; in contrast, Govier argues for the possibility that there are many kinds of victims.[68] With Donald Shriver, she suggests that fundamental moral notions including forgiveness and identity are falsely individualized, and urges a view of persons as relational, social and interdependent.[69] In doing so, she appeals explicitly to the concept of *ubuntu*, which has been famously articulated by Tutu; "It is to say, 'My humanity is caught up, is inextricably bound up, in yours.' . . . We say, 'A person is a person through other persons.'"[70] Feminist philosophers have eloquently elaborated on the concept of the self-in-relation in Euro-American philosophy as well, and regarding forgiveness in particular. This demands further attention, since such feminist contributions explicitly work to correct the dominant discourse of individualist and masculinist traditions, especially in American culture.[71]

I explore differing accounts of a relational self in later chapters; what these accounts have in common is a description of the self as the product of the psychological and dialogical connections we have with others. Annette Baier refers to us as "second-persons" insofar as our development is essentially dependent upon other persons, and our "personality is revealed both in [our] relations to others and" in our responses to our awareness of that dependence.[72] Carol Gilligan refers to relations as the attachments formed through discourses with the others in our lives whose interactions with us make us the persons that we are; Dana Jack argues with Gilligan against Cartesian and Kantian accounts of the self that exclude contingent psychological factors from the constitution of the autonomous subject; she suggests persons develop, or maldevelop, within the relations in which they are embedded.[73] Susan Hekman prefers to refer to this idea as the discursive self, arguing that our relations are constituted by the discourses we have with both intimate and distant others.[74] With many feminists, I refer to this idea as the relational self, and I argue that it can provide a more accurate account of individuals as both distinct and bounded; one's boundaries include one's relations of identification and what Ann Ferguson calls relations of disidentification with those to whom one's psychological connection is one of opposition.[75] Precisely because we are relational and interdependent, gender becomes a foundational feature of our understandings of forgiveness. Our interpersonal and political relations in a less than equitable world are critically connected to our gender, and affect our very conceptions of ourselves as agents and as victims. A nonrelational account presumes a variety of independence and self-sufficiency which turns out to be both falsely nongendered and simultaneously appropriate to a masculine ideal.

In addition to assuming a view of the moral agent as individualistic and rationally self-interested, paradigm and Kantian accounts of forgiveness tend to demand a robust sort of integrity, self-respect and autonomy, which precludes forgiving for reasons that seem to fall short of what self-respect is taken to require. Instead, many accounts that identify necessary conditions for forgiveness argue that common uses of the expression which do not meet their conditions are instances of pseudo-forgiveness, or not genuine forgiveness, or forgiveness only in a metaphorical sense.[76] This is especially notable in light of interpretations of forgiveness in many women's narratives, when they describe forgiving to end or avoid a conflict, or to avoid hurting others' feelings or incurring others' anger at being denied forgiveness.[77] Evidence that women do this to a greater extent than do men is set aside as description of 'forgiveness' by agents whose conceptions are at best mistaken or ethically suspect, at worst irrelevant and self-deluded on the part of those who think they are 'genuinely' forgiving. Walker notes the philosophical tendency to speak of "true," "real," or "genuine" forgiveness, and objects, "This can imply either that there is one real process that alone deserves the name, or that if there is more than one kind of forgiveness, one of them is the 'best' or 'truest' case of it. I have come to find it odd to think of there being a single correct idea of forgiveness."[78] Smith similarly resists "using 'genuine' because of its definition as either authentic in origin or motivated by sincere intentions," and describes such approaches to concep- tual analysis as "binary," splitting the set of moral acts into those which count as genuine, and those which do not.[79]

One example of such a binary approach is Jean Hampton's argument that a hypothetical woman who 'forgives' a boorish visiting father-in-law to preserve family peace is not engaging "in genuine 'forgiveness' [because] to drop that judgment and the angry feeling it engenders" is instead "con- donation."[80] As another example, Margaret Holmgren argues that forgive- ness is "genuine and true" only after one completes the task of responding to wrongdoing by working through the emotional processes involved in overcoming resentment.[81] She repeats this frequently in more recent work, stressing that many forms of what people may call forgiveness are "not genuine" because they do "not experience the true internal resolution of the issue that genuine forgiveness requires."[82] For accounts like Holmgren's and Hampton's, and there are many, Kantian self-respect is required for forgiveness to be, not just morally best, but sensibly referred to as forgive- ness at all. What some women describe as forgiving to avoid conflict is definitely in the non-genuine category on this analysis. "To forgive is not to refuse to recognize one's negative feelings toward the offender," Holmgren argues, at least "to the extent that it is incompatible with [one's] self- respect."[83]

It is important to clarify here what these authors mean by requiring 'genuineness,' even if the authors themselves are not always clear. I should note that what Murphy, Hampton and Holmgren, with others, find important is not merely that one believe one means it when one says, "I forgive you." My objection is not that their definitions require one not lie; as J.L. Austin would phrase it, moral expressions can be abused, or given in bad faith. Yet the examples above do not seem to be examples of forgivers who cross their fingers behind their backs when they perform the utterance. Hampton and Holmgren describe not reckless, willful liars, but agents with what may be moral conflicts or servile motives. Hampton's hypothetical woman seems to be in a position of trading off her righteous anger for the sake of the rela- tionships between all the family members. Holmgren's position is most charitably interpreted as a concern for a type of agent who may fail in a duty to oneself to see one's own negative reaction as justified.

Yet this seems to commit a larger leap than warranted, or at the least, it fails to do the desired work of excluding forgiveness which is given to avoid hard feelings. It is not obviously the case that avoiding conflict or rejecting negative feelings is condonation or incompatible with self-respect. Of course, Holmgren implies there's no problem with rejection of negative feelings in the presence of self-respect, but she doesn't seem to think the agent has achieved "true internal resolution" either. This seems to require robust self-reflection on one's resentment that day-to-day forgiveness may not allow for, and need not call for. It brings to mind Augustine's exhortation to forgive each other's wrongs as a kindness; "kindness is what you must practice, because sins abound."[84] Annette Baier says something similar about trust, that we live in (and ought to cultivate) a climate of trust wherein we largely refrain from hurting each other from day to day; Joram Haber has noted the importance of day-to-day forgiveness, in this climate of trust, for the routine sorts of wrongs of which we are all often guilty.[85] Jean Rumsey calls this kind of daily forgiveness "moral housekeeping," and says, "Forgiveness, in this narrow sense, has great value in managing the blunders and offenses in our daily lives, preventing their escalation to serious harms and making our lives more peaceful."[86] And Hannah Arendt argues that "trespassing is an everyday occurrence . . . within a web of relations, and it needs forgiving, dismissing, in order to make it possible for life to go on by constantly releasing men from what they have done unknowingly."[87]

Holmgren's argument that peacekeeping forgiveness is actually condonation seems guilty of overwork. Her position almost seems to amount to a false dilemma between forgiving from pure motives and condoning behavior in a way that involves ignoring one's own feelings. To drop one's judgment and its attendant feelings need not be the same as retracting it or believing oneself to be wrong, and if it requires additional moral work, it is more than merely writing an incident off; again we do not have good reasons to believe the daughter-in-law doesn't "really" forgive. Griswold notes, even as he defends the idea of "forgiveness at its best," that "forswearing resentment does not require giving up *every* negative feeling," describing forswearing as "an ultimate goal" involving commitments to future attitudes.[88] Moreover, the argument against preserving peace at the cost of one's own resentment implies that one's duty to oneself to engage in righteous anger is higher in some duty-hierarchy than are one's obligations to maintain relationships between many people, and as I suggest in more detail later, it is not clear that such a hierarchy is sensible or even morally good to many people, especially to many women.

The odd result is that going definitions in academic circles do not match up at all with the meanings and intentions of actual people who express forgiveness in daily life. The disconnect between philosophy and ex-

perience, at least in the study of forgiveness, stems in part from constructing conditions for conveying forgiveness in the utter absence of self-
defining narratives, or indeed any consideration of the socio-historical context in which forgiveness occurs, and then construing those narratives as
mistaken or not-genuine instances of the moral expression. As I have argued, the social and historical context of forgiveness in Euro-American and
predominantly Christian culture is a context in which gender plays a large
role, and so acontextual analyses of forgiveness also fail to take into account the different experiences with the expression that men and women
sometimes have.

As it stands, analytic and justice-based accounts of forgiveness seem
guilty of what Alasdair MacIntyre described when he said, "Analytic philosophers . . . seem to be determined to go on considering arguments as objects of investigation in abstraction from the social and historical contexts
of activity and enquiry in which they are or were at home and from which
they characteristically derive their particular import."[89] In this case, going
definitions of forgiveness preclude conflict-avoiding forgiveness as not
genuine or inauthentic because they are constructing the necessary and sufficient conditions for what is genuine without considering the historical and
social contexts in which women have learned forgiveness and continued to
practice it. In light of MacIntyre's objection that analytic philosophy suffers
from inattention to context, I am moved to wonder if the problem is with
analytic philosophy per se: that is, is MacIntyre correct that analytic philosophy considers "arguments as objects of investigation in abstraction
from the social and historical contexts"? Greater philosophers than I have
argued that the analytic tradition is not guilty of thinking "historical enquiry is irrelevant."[90] Yet if analytic philosophy at a minimum takes historical context to be relevant to philosophical inquiry, then narratives of
practical experience with forgiveness, and women's narratives in particular,
ought to be at least relevant to definitions of forgiveness, and it is then ille-
gitimate to dismiss such responses as inauthentic and such evidence as irrelevant. I have no interest in denying that women sometimes respond to
sexual betrayal and domestic abuse with lies or intentional disingenuousness. I agree that forgiveness is not the best response to either wrong when
one fails to get properly angry or to pursue one's own safety. Yet to say
these are cases of not really forgiving doesn't seem respectful of moral
agents either. If nothing else, this evaluation falls short of taking seriously
what women convey when they express forgiveness to wrongdoers we'd
rather they resented.

Given the above, I conclude that a masculinist and purportedly neutral bias permeates the philosophical enterprise of theorizing about forgiveness, especially when we look at the predominant Kantian models available. Feminist philosophers have provided good reasons to consider gender more centrally. Gender is a basic metaphysical concept throughout most of our philosophical history. Ignoring gender realities is dangerous since, in the course of ignoring political actualities, one could manage to form prescriptions that may be wildly inapplicable to the lives of those for whom one intended to prescribe. Virginia Held has argued compellingly that ethical theory should be tested against concrete experiences with actual moral problems, and modified as needed in light of contextualized information; this becomes pressing for those of us theorizing about forgiveness if, as said above, men and women in our culture have different experiences with cultural expectations and associations with forgiving.[91] Judith Boss argues importantly that "discussions of forgiveness in our culture . . . cannot be separated from gender politics."[92] That these have been separated, by and large, has resulted in ignoring women's extensive experience with being the group expected to forgive more often, and this is reflected in the construal of paradigmatic forgiving situations as involving disinterested formal relationships between men. Haber notes relatedly that forgiveness "is more likely to be noticed by women in virtue of their historical position of relative inequality."[93]

Taking Notice

Noticing forgiveness for feminist reasons moves us toward the difficult task of evaluating actual occasions of forgiveness. Philosophers of forgiveness, in general, tend to seem far more comfortable with identifying occasions not to forgive, praising its refusal when doing so makes space for victims to recover, seek redress, demand apology. Yet as Robert Enright has demonstrated repeatedly, many of the evils we can identify have been forgiven by particular victims.[94] For this reason, Haber's observation that forgiveness may be a vice for women leaves me with lingering unease. Even granting that some of those who forgive evil may do so hastily or wrongly, I do not wish to write off all difficult counterexamples with arguments that extraordinary forgivers are damaged or deluded. In this section, I begin the task, continued throughout this book, of noticing concrete examples of forgiveness, and evaluating those occasions on which particular victims of evils have achieved varieties of forgiveness.

First, however, I consider those occasions on which feminist philosophers including Robin Schott, Card, Walker, and Govier directly evaluate forgiveness for evils which seem, to many, unforgivable. Walker engages most frankly with "the reticence many of us feel in criticizing the decisions of some victims to give or to withhold forgiveness."[95] Although philosophers' reticence is well-intentioned, I argue that especially from a feminist perspective, the underlying impulse toward respect for victims undercuts our obligations of recognition-respect—that is, our social and moral regard for the relevance of victims' forgiveness of evil to deliberation about forgiveness. Moreover, victims who forgive sometimes facilitate mutual recognition, enabling perpetrators' own acknowledgement and apology, which in turn enables the capacities of others to live better with evils. As Govier says, the basic importance of moral recognition requires more of us than evaluation of victims who forgive as incredible saints. Perhaps attending to those times when unlikely forgiveness occurs may also serve to disrupt the cultural expectation that women forgive more often.

1. Evaluating women's forgiveness

Philosophers are not all equally hesitant to evaluate those who forgive evildoers, although robust evaluations are rare. Schott makes room for negative evaluation of forgiveness of evil, by appealing to factual grounds which include accounts of trauma victims' therapeutic processes. She considers empirical accounts of women's forgiveness for rape, including those provided by Judith Lewis Herman, which Herman characterizes as amounting to "a fantasy of forgiveness," remaining "out of reach for most ordinary humans;" Herman describes survivors' forgiveness as an "attempt to bypass" the "impossibility of getting even."[96] Schott notes that for these victims, their rapists' "genuine contrition is a 'rare miracle.'"[97] Schott adds that "empirical accounts of how victims move on in their lives in fact do not give forgiveness a primary position in the process of recovery."[98]

Schott engages admirably in factual and moral assessment of the decision to forgive, and argues against it. In the accounts Schott considers, those of survivors of rape who will never be entirely safe within rape cultures, the generalization that moving on does not primarily involve forgiveness seems quite right. Social and legal recognition of rape as a wrong is so rare, and hard-won when achieved, that survivors are already hampered in identifying the wrong done, and undoubtedly better off, as Schott says, reconnecting with themselves and trustworthy others, than cultivating compassion or forgiveness for an offender whom prevailing power structures protect all too well, already. In a response to Schott, Card agrees with Schott's negative evaluation of rape victims' hasty, perhaps fantastical forgiveness: "I have never been a fan of forgiveness for survivors of domestic battering."[99] Card does not seem to go so far as to agree with Schott's saying that in the face of the "ungraspable element of atrocity . . . , the proposal that one might either offer or withhold forgiveness may have little relevance."[100] Instead, Card offers a qualified and neutral defense of the possibility that one could forgive perpetrators of atrocity, saying that "elements of forgiveness may be possible and their wisdom debatable."[101]

Indeed, in other contexts of recovery, Schott's wider generalization does not hold; some empirical accounts of victims moving on *do*, according to the victims, prominently feature forgiveness, and although they may reflect something "out of reach for ordinary humans," they also reflect processes of recovery and reflection which amount to more than mere fantasies. Schott notes indirectly the examples of Desmond Tutu's and Nelson Mandela's expressions of forgiveness; Trudy Govier takes up these two examples and evaluates their forgiveness of evil positively. "Whatever the original spiritual source of his ideas," Govier says, "Desmond Tutu was not wrong to believe that South Africans needed forgiveness and to assert that forgiveness is enormously relevant to national reconciliation in his country and to the politics of peace."[102] She argues that Mandela's forgiveness is sensible "in the context of an *ubuntu* philosophy"—that is, a fundamental conception of personhood as only existing through other persons, a deeply relational and interconnected sense of self.[103] Govier argues that forgiveness is "required," at least in principle, because "we should never give up on a human being."[104] "To regard a perpetrator, even a perpetrator of atrocities, as absolutely unforgivable, is to believe in effect that it would be wrong for anyone, ever, under whatever circumstances, to forgive him – to come to see him again as a human being capable of good and deserving of readmission into the human community."[105] In contrast with Schott's observation that most perpetrators do not express guilt or contrition, Govier argues that the absence of remorse makes perpetrators merely "conditionally unforgivable," because future possible repentance changes the circumstances of our response.[106]

If Schott errs in overgeneralizing across cases, Govier may err in the opposite direction, by implying that circumstances never preclude someday seeing a person differently. Card approaches an intermediate ethical recommendation regarding forgiveness, saying, "Perhaps it is not that we cannot forgive extraordinary wrongs, but that often we *ought* not, that forgiveness should be granted only slowly and with caution, depending on what else the perpetrator does . . . , that conditions that make it morally an option are difficult to satisfy, even unlikely."[107] In her most explicitly supportive statements of the usefulness of forgiveness, Card states that forgiveness "can relieve burdens that may not be morally relievable in other ways" and "[can effect] rescue from evil, from deserved punishment or its full measure, and also from the status of irredeemability."[108] Yet these may be taken as statements of bare possibility rather than moral advocacy of forgiving responses. Card tends to err on the side of description, usually avoiding the perils of prescription; as she notes somewhat regretfully, she engages with the logic of forgiveness, occasionally at the expense of other considerations.

2. Perils of prescription

Walker, like Card, comes closer than most philosophers to acknowledging positive value in forgiving evils. Walker is one of the few philosophers to note our presence, and our apprehensions, at work in our own analyses of forgiveness. Observing "Card's resistance to generalization about 'unforgivability,'" Walker appreciates "the reticence many of us feel in criticizing the decisions of some victims to give or to withhold forgiveness, as well as our resistance to holding that forgiveness is obligatory for victims in some circumstances."[109] The role of the moral theorist is constrained, especially in such fledgling fields as forgiveness. In my determined attention to gender as fundamental to identity and relationships, I find it even more difficult to separate my identity from my theorizing. It is not clear on which occasions we're writing as outsiders, which as survivors, complicit witnesses, or perpetrators. The experience of cataloguing victims' sufferings, which can be an affecting and isolated form of witnessing, sometimes adds to the lurking fear that even *looking* too closely at victims' choices increases the victims' burdens. Why add to their pain by visiting choices for forgiveness, which incurs more costs? At the same time, the subject of forgiveness for evils evokes personal testimony and response: Marietta Jaeger recounts her forgiveness of her daughter's murderer; Simon Wiesenthal reflects on his silence in response to the confession and remorse of a Nazi war criminal, a situation Card describes as "a dilemma of forgiveness."[110] Card herself identifies her motivations for writing about responses to evils, which include witnessing atrocities on the world stage and suffering forms of oppression and violence in her personal life.

The multiple reasons for the reticence of philosophers reflect the complexity of different lives. Respect for that which we do not know, and cannot imagine, is mingled, for some of us, with the knowledge of our own experiences, which are likely incomparable to the atrocities we study, and which usually go unspoken even when they might be instructive. Card, indeed, is one of the few philosophers alive to write from her own lived experiences in the course of theorizing about forgiveness and related moral remainders. As I noted above, it is presumptuous to speak for all persons or all women. Humility is even more necessary when deliberating in public and publication about the choices of still-suffering victims. Feminist philosophers have been especially articulate about the moral hubris of speaking for others, in light of the ways privileged men through the history of philosophy have spoken in inappropriately universal terms. Feminists also articulate the urgency of physical safety, which at points in victims' recovery processes entails separation from perpetrators. Awareness of the very privileges allowing some of us to pursue lives in professional philosophy may lend to our deference to the experience of victims; we are loathe to speak about that which we have not suffered.

Assessing the choices of victims of evil who forgive is fraught for all of these reasons: pain at witnessing their suffering, even third-hand; self-consciousness of one's own privilege and ignorance; adherence to philosophical traditions of refraining from self-disclosure; principled opposition to the presumption of understanding or knowing particular victims of oppression; and commitment to victims' physical safety. It is not surprising, therefore, that philosophers approach the fact of forgiveness of evils with wonder, raising questions as often as claims. "Why shouldn't we credit, even admire, the victim's impressive power to forgive?" asks Walker:

> We have seen that people do forgive murderers and torturers and others who have caused terrible ruthless harms. In what sense might they be wrong, rather than exceptionally courageous and resourceful? Who decides the "acceptable" degree or type of repayment that opens the way to morally acceptable forgiveness? Who but the victim can decide what type or magnitude of cost she or he is prepared to absorb?[111]

Noting Jaeger's forgiveness of her daughter's murderer in addition to discussion of many other specific examples of forgiveness, Walker captures the sentiment of many of us when she acknowledges, "It is staggering, sometimes scarcely credible, what individuals are capable of forgiving."[112]

Govier adds a note of caution to such characterizations, arguing against "the view that forgiveness is for saints and moral heroes and is not achievable by the ordinary people who will constitute the majority of group members. (Mandela could forgive, but 'Mandela is a saint' so his capacities for forgiveness are of little general interest)."[113] Govier rightly objects to describing forgiveness for evils as saintly. However, Schott provides a much more intriguing reason to set aside Mandela's and Tutu's forgiveness as incomparable, which bears exploration. Schott quotes a South African woman who astutely observes a possible reason she cannot forgive and Mandela and Tutu can: "They lead vindicated lives."[114] The examples of forgiveness in the next section all have their sources in vindicated lives, by which we mean lives of victims whose wrongs were recognized in social and legal systems as severe, and who were offered forms of moral or retributive responses.

3. Instructive forgiveness

Since 2003, the Forgiveness Project, a London-based "charitable organization which explores forgiveness, reconciliation and conflict resolution through real-life human experience," gathers stories of victims who have considered forgiveness, although not all narratives conclude forgivingly.[115] The father of a victim of the bombing of a government building in Oklahoma City forgave the bomber a year before his execution, saying, "Tim McVeigh and Terry Nichols had been against the US government for what happened in Waco, Texas, in 1993, and seeing what they'd done with their vengeance, I knew I had to send mine in a different direction."[116] Berthe Climbié, the mother of an eight-year-old who was tortured and killed by a relative, forgave because "to be locked into a fixed attitude of retribution is to kill a child twice."[117]

One of the most well-known testimonials is offered by Linda Biehl, whose daughter Amy was a Fulbright scholar working in South Africa against apartheid when she was beaten and stabbed to death. Biehl recounts wanting to meet the men convicted of killing her daughter, because she and her husband "wanted to know what it would take to make things better . . . . I have come to believe passionately in restorative justice. It's what Desmond Tutu calls '*ubuntu*': to choose to forgive rather than demand retribution, a belief that 'my humanity is inextricably caught up in yours.'"[118] Walker observes that reactions to the Biehls' forgiveness are mixed: "Many people find the Biehls' generosity beyond belief; some are awed by it, others see it as puzzling or as a bizarre form of denial of what, it is supposed, they surely must, or ought to, feel."[119]

Interest in the Forgiveness Project surged in the British press after the London bombings of July 7, 2005, even more so after a vicar, and mother of one of the bombing victims, resigned her post, citing her inability to forgive. One reporter noted, "Before encountering [the project] I would have said that some things were unforgivable . . . . But the extraordinary thing is that one can never be sure. People do forgive the apparently unforgivable."[120] The raised awareness of the Forgiveness Project in light of the vicar's resignation prompted an impressive national dialogue about the possibility of forgiveness, and most of those interviewed about their own feelings expressed the mixed resistance, awe and puzzlement that Walker describes. Forgivers were described as saints, observes said they were awestruck at their efforts, and some victims were dismayed at the extraordinary efforts of the few being held up as examples for the many. One man, whose wife died at one of the bomb sites, objects:

> I could never forgive and I think that recently there has been too much pressure put on people to express forgiveness. It's as if we are being asked to apologise for feeling hurt, that society is embarrassed by our anger and would feel better if we would express forgiveness and then disappear. . . . Forgiveness is being offered up as an alternative to justice and that is very dangerous.[121]

The pain of the widower above is palpable, his assessment of the dangers is compelling, and his resistance to looking at forgiveness of evil makes sense in light of his own suffering. Indeed, consider the context in which he said it, in the wake of London's worst terrorist attack, on which 56 people were killed and over 700 injured; the initially conflicting accounts of the events by the government and the press, and the slow release of evidence, fueled speculation and the strong sense that justice was not being done. The government report a year later, concluding that not a single person in the police, security or intelligence services was at fault, rejuvenated calls for a public inquiry, which the government has persistently rejected. In this case, the London victims were recognized as suffering but could be said to not yet lead vindicated lives.

The examples of those who share their narratives of forgiveness bear out research suggesting that recognition promotes the possibility of forgiveness. Not only do the forgivers in these examples receive recognition of their harms, but in addition, the Forgiveness Project publicly displays their photos and tells their stories in a concerted effort to reach others. To be included in the Forgiveness Project is to be listened to, and those interviewed for the project often come to the attention of its founder precisely because they have already received recognition as victims in legal proceedings. All the philosophers cited above note that wrongdoers' repentance and reparative behavior contribute to forgiving; the forgivers' stories point to the necessity of third-party recognition, as well. Some psychologists refer to this as "perceptual validation," by which they mean "social verification that one is correct about one's interpretation of an event."[122] Certainly wrongdoers' own perceptions of their wrong behavior validates victims, as is well established, but "acknowledgement of the transgression by a third party also had a positive effect on forgiveness," and social and political institutions can contribute a great deal in the way of such validation.[123] Because perpetrators of atrocities rarely contribute their own recognition and remorse, witnesses, bystanders, and those in positions of power bear obligations of perceptual validation, because vindicating the lives of victims contributes to the possibilities of forgiveness, even if forgiveness is never achieved. Schott suggests vindicating victims is so important that resulting possibilities of forgiveness may be comparatively uninteresting, even moot; the reverse may be true simultaneously, that rare victims' forgiving allows us to see more clearly the conditions that make it possible. Forgiveness illustrates the importance of vindication of victims, and those who would have victims forgive are therefore required to recognize and support them. As psychologists argue, forgiveness and responsibility are transpersonal and interactional.[124] In other words, forgiveness and responsibility sometimes motivate each other, facilitating mutual recognition between offenders and victims. In the case of the Biehls, above, who wanted to meet the men convicted of killing their daughter, her openness to the possibility of forgiveness actually moved the men convicted to see her and all white people differently:

> Not until I met Linda and Peter Biehl did I understand that white people are human beings too. . . . The first time I saw them on TV I hated them. I thought this was the strategy of the whites, to come to South Africa to call for capital punishment. But they didn't even mention wanting to hang us. I was very confused. . . . I decided to go and tell our story and show remorse. Amnesty wasn't my motivation. I just wanted to ask for forgiveness. I wanted to say in front of Linda and Peter, face to face, "I am sorry, can you forgive me?" I wanted to be free in my mind and body. It must have been so

painful for them to lose their daughter, but by coming to South Africa—not to speak of recrimination, but to speak of the pain of our
struggle—they gave me back my freedom.[125]

4. Responsive recognition

Philosophers who assess forgiveness of evil are in a minority; many of
us who reflect on the nature of forgiveness do not look very long at unusual
forgiveness. We generally agree with those who react with astonishment
and grant that it is beyond most of us. Govier's concern is well taken that to
stress incredibility is morally risky, yet our moral concerns are not the same
as Govier's. Govier argues that accepting pessimistic views of forgiveness
as out of reach for most humans "is to accept that no efforts should be made
to transform or overcome feelings of grievance, bitterness, and resentment,"
a view with which Schott and Card would surely disagree; they argue con-
vincingly for forming safe networks of interpersonal relations, remem-
brance, mourning, reconnection with the world, letting go of hostile feelings, witnessing, and victim support groups, all of which could transform or
overcome bad feelings, while not requiring their annihilation.[126]

Yet presuming forgiveness of evils to be out of reach or inhuman unfortunately commits a different sort of recognition failure. Setting aside
forgiveness of evils as so extraordinary as to be supernatural reduces the
forgiveness of victims of great evils to the irrelevant. Neglecting the
evaluation of victims, who seem saintly or angelic, denies them what
Stephen Darwall calls recognition respect. Darwall distinguishes this from
appraisal respect—that is, respect for something which is to be positively
valued. "Strictly speaking, the object of recognition respect is a fact. And
recognition respect for that fact consists in giving it the proper weight in
deliberation."[127] Moreover, recognition respect implies not just bare awareness of a fact, but regard for some fact or feature as relevant for deliberation, and moral recognition respect is a normative attitude, such that "inappropriate consideration or weighing of that fact or feature would result in
behavior that is morally wrong."[128]

Darwall's argument for recognition respect may be too much to ask of
the London widower, whose own losses occurred in a context of mystery,
secrecy, and rumor, and who felt too much anger to find any appeal in "alternatives to justice." Victims without vindication may not bear the obligation of recognition respect. Witnesses are better positioned to respond with
recognition, at least at the level of including the relevance of extraordinary

forgiveness in decision making, and at the moral level of responding to forgivers. Forgiveness Project director Marina Cantacuzino, a free-lance journalist in England, teamed up with a photographer to collect personal narratives of those who experienced violence, the same year that England joined
the U.S. in invading Iraq. She writes, "The bellicose language of retribution
voiced by our politicians and reflected in the media disturbed me. I needed
to do something different, to give a voice to people who weren't being
heard," and especially at the time, it was the stories of those who chose
peace and forgiveness over anger and revenge which were overlooked.[129] At
one interview, Cantacuzino wept at the story of a woman whose baby son
died after a routine operation, and without her knowledge had his organs
removed by doctors. "When I apologised for being unprofessional, she said,
'No, it's really nice that you've shown emotion. So many journalists don't
show any emotion; they don't seem to care.'"[130] Insofar as Cantacuzino extended, to her interviewees, forms of attention and opportunities to be heard
in wider exhibits of the interviews, she achieved Darwall's moral recognition respect, behaving in morally responsive ways to victims' choices to
forgive, or to resist forgiveness.

Some witnesses and bystanders are not well positioned to attend to forgivers in morally responsive ways; even Cantacuzino, a journalist, started
the project of witnessing in her spare time, with a willing photographer-
friend but no money. Actions of moral recognition respect require effort
and opportunity. Those of us at a distance may be limited to recognition
respect which does the more basic job of attaching relevance to forgiving
acts in our own deliberations about forgiveness. Doing so may still have a
moral valence; Darwall's moral recognition respect seems to center on our
interpersonal treatment of those we recognize, but as Arto Laitinen points
out, recognition is multidimensional, and can take the form of behaviors or
more symbolic forms which send moral messages.[131] Feminist philosophers
are not strangers to the import of scholarly attention as a form of respectful
recognition; principled attention to gender (vs. a 'genderless' universal
view), women's narratives, experiences, and standpoints have importantly
revolutionized philosophy, or at least pulled it in more concrete directions.
Feminists writing about forgiveness of evil have grappled with the pain of
others eloquently. If we have not grappled as directly or skillfully with the
forgiveness of victims of evils, perhaps it is because forgiveness is more
often expected of women.

As a feminist, I appreciate the reluctance to value that which has been
women's disproportionate burden. Seeing it as an ideal incurs obligations
on third parties to bring about the conditions that would make such an ideal

possible. Social and political recognition, including punishment of offenders and provisions for the economic and physical safety of victims, are requisite conditions. The disproportionate cultural expectation that women are more forgiving than men is a reason for women to pursue other methods of recovery, even in the presence of third-party recognition at every level. Philosophers, witnesses, and those in positions to aid victims should regard the forgiveness achieved by victims of evil with respect and attention to the conditions in which it occurs. Doing so recognizes victims' humanity, clarifies the responsibilities of their communities, and even promotes righteous indignation at the lack of conditions that permit forgiveness. It may not be likely that forgiveness is possible. That is to be lamented, and changed. The extraordinary nature of forgiveness of evils is all the more reason to learn from forgivers.

In the next chapter, I consider alternative philosophical models on which to base conceptual analysis of forgiveness, including Aristotelian, Nietzschean and consequentialist models. I conclude that they attend better to our relational nature, the position of power from which we reason about forgiveness, and our everyday experiences with forgiveness, including the ways in which women and men may experience forgiveness differently. I suggest some feminist priorities that are better served by the alternatives, and identify the emerging feminist model that some contemporary theorists have begun constructing.

Notes

Portions of this chapter grew out of my contribution to "The Limits of Forgiveness," co-authored with Jean Rumsey, in *Hypatia*, Vol. 24, no. 1 (Winter 2009); thanks to the editors for their valuable comments and for permission to work with those ideas further, here.

1. Donald Shriver, "Is There Forgiveness in Politics?" in *Exploring Forgiveness*, ed. Robert D. Enright and Joanna North (Madison: University of Wisconsin Press, 1998), 131-149; Margaret Urban Walker, *Moral Repair: Reconstructing Moral Relations after Wrongdoing* (Cambridge and New York: Cambridge University Press, 2006), 27, 151-190.

2. Archbishop Desmond Tutu, *No Future Without Forgiveness* (Los Angeles: Image Publishing, 1999), 260.

3. Hannah Arendt, "Irreversibility and the Power to Forgive," *The Human Condition* (Chicago: University of Illinois Press, 1958/1998), 240.

4. Bishop Joseph Butler, Sermon IX, "Upon Forgiveness of Injuries," *Fifteen Sermons* (Charlottesville, VA: Ibis Publishing, 1987, edition previously published by Robert Carter & Brothers, New York, 1860); Jeffrie Murphy and Jean Hampton, *Forgiveness and Mercy* (Cambridge: Cambridge University Press, 1988), 15, 22; Charles Griswold, *Forgiveness: A Philosophical Exploration* (Cambridge and New York: Cambridge University Press, 2007), 19-37.

5. In philosophy, the two most often-cited monographs on interpersonal forgiveness, over the last few decades, are Murphy and Hampton (1988), and Joram Haber, *Forgiveness* (Savage, MD: Rowman & Littlefield, 1991). Margaret Urban Walker's (2006) more recent book on moral repair, which includes extensive treatment of forgiveness, raises issues including women's forgiveness but not in ways that center gender matters; see also works on political and group forgiveness including Martha Minow, *Between Vengeance and Forgiveness* (Boston: Beacon Press, 1999) and Trudy Govier, *Forgiveness and Revenge* (London and New York: Routledge, 2002). Shriver likewise concentrates on political, theological, and historical issues; see Donald Shriver, *An Ethic for Enemies: Forgiveness in Politics* (Oxford: Oxford University Press, 1995). Griswold (2007) has the most comprehensive recent monograph on forgiveness but seldom mentions gender. In psychology, gender gets much more consideration, yet at the same time Robert Enright, one of the leaders in the field, rarely sorts data along gender lines; with psychologist Sharon Lamb, Murphy edited the anthology *Before Forgiving*, including contributions from feminist psychologists which inform and complement my own arguments; see Sharon Lamb and Jeffrie Murphy, eds., *Before Forgiving* (Oxford: Oxford University Press, 2002).

6. See especially Joram Haber, "Forgiveness and Feminism," in *Norms and Values: Essays on the Work of Virginia Held*, ed. Joram Graf Haber and Mark S. Halfon (Lanham, MD: Rowman and Littlefield, 1998), 141-150; Govier's (2002) consideration of whether groups can forgive, and Cheshire Calhoun, "Changing One's Heart," *Ethics* 103 (1992): 76-96. In "Forgiveness in Counseling: A Philosophical Perspective" (*Before Forgiving*, 2002), Murphy at least mentions the hypothetical battered woman (though who doesn't), 46.

7. Despite psychologist Janice Haaken's (2002) claim that feminists "have been among the more vocal critics of forgiveness rhetoric," they do not seem easily located in philosophy; see Janice Haaken, "The Good, the Bad, and the Ugly: Psychoanalytic and Cultural Perspectives," in *Before Forgiving*, ed. by Lamb and Murphy (Oxford: Oxford University Press, 2002). The growing number of explicitly feminist, if often brief, analyses of forgiveness, include the following: Annette Baier, *Moral prejudices: Essays on Ethics* (Cambridge, Mass: Harvard University Press, 1994); Judith Boss, "Throwing Pearls to the Swine: Women, Forgiveness, and the Unrepentant Abuser," in *Philosophical Perspectives on Power and Domination*, ed. Laura Duhan Kaplan and Lawrence F. Bove (Amsterdam-Atlanta: Rodopi

Press, 1997); Claudia Card, *The Atrocity Paradigm: A Theory of Evil* (Oxford: Oxford University Press, 2002); Robin Dillon, "Self-Forgiveness and Self-Respect," *Ethics* 112 (2001); Larry May and James Bohman, "Sexuality, Masculinity, and Confession," *Hypatia* 12, no.1 (1997), 138-154; Nel Noddings, "Coping with Violence," *Educational Theory* 52, no. 2 (2002): 241-253; Nel Noddings, *Women and Evil* (Berkeley: University of California Press, 1989); Nancy Potter, "Is Refusing to Forgive a Vice?" in *Feminists Doing Ethics*, ed. Joanne Waugh (Lanham, MD: Rowman & Littlefield, 2001), 135-150; Robin May Schott, "The Atrocity Paradigm and the Concept of Forgiveness," *Hypatia* 19, no.4 (2004): 202-209. Alice MacLachlan's emerging work explicitly notes the absence of feminist discourse in forgiveness literature, and she may be the first to use the phrase "dominant discourse" to describe the genderless accounts which prevail; see especially Alice MacLachlan, "Forgiveness, Feminism, and the Diversity of Women's Experiences," online, Society for Women's Advancement in Philosophy 2005 *Conference for Topics of Diversity in Philosophy*, http://conference2005.swapusa.org/papers/maclachlan/ (first presented at the first meeting of the Society for Women's Advancement in Philosophy, Tallahassee, Florida, April 2005).

8. Walker (2006), 162.

9. Margaret Urban Walker, "Diotima's Ghost: The Uncertain Place of Feminist Philosophy in Professional Philosophy," *Hypatia* 20, no.3 (2005): 154,156,158.

10. Walker (2005), 159.

11. Searching *Philosophers' Index* for "forgiv*" yielded 293 entries. Combining this search with citations of "femini*" yielded ten results, not all of which turned out to be relevant.

12. Nick Smith, *I Was Wrong: The Meanings of Apologies* (Cambridge: Cambridge University Press, 2008), 19, 21.

13. Walker (2006), 187, emphasis hers.

14. Alison Jaggar, "Feminist Ethics: Projects, Problems, Prospects," in *Feminist Ethics*, ed. Claudia Card (Lawrence, Kan.: University of Kansas Press, 1991), 86.

15. Karen Warren, "The Power and the Promise of Ecological Feminism," in *The Environmental Ethics and Policy Book*, ed. Donald Van de Veer and Christine Pierce (Belmont, Cal.: Wadsworth Publishing, 1997), 257.

16. Victoria Davion, "How Feminist Is Ecofeminism?" in *The Environmental Ethics and Policy Book*, ed. Van de Veer and Pierce (1997), 278.

17. Jaggar (1991), 96.

18. Jean Grimshaw, *Philosophy and Feminist Thinking* (Minneapolis: University of Minnesota Press, 1986), ch.1.

19. Margaret Urban Walker, *Moral Understandings: A Feminist Study in Ethics* (New York: Routledge, 1998), 28.

20. Davion (1997), 280; Jaggar (1991), 98; bell hooks, *Feminist Theory: From Margin to Center* (Cambridge, Mass.: South End Press; 2nd edition, 2000), ch.1, ch.5.

21. See also Jaggar (1991), 98; Warren (1997), 260; Lorraine Code, "Voice and Voicelessness: A Modest Proposal?" in *Philosophy in a Feminist Voice: Cri-*

tiques and Reconstructions, ed. Janet A. Kourany (Princeton, N.J.: Princeton University Press, 1998), 206; Virginia Held, *Feminist Morality: Transforming Culture, Society and Politics* (Chicago: University of Chicago Press, 1993), 55.

22. Varda Konstam, Miriam Chernoff and Sara Deveney, "Toward Forgiveness: The role of shame, guilt, anger, and empathy," *Counseling and Values* 46, no.1 (2001): 54.

23. Konstam et al (2001), 62.

24. Frederic Luskin, *Forgive for Good* (New York and San Francisco: Harper Collins/Harper San Francisco, 2003), 89.

25. Everett L. Worthington., Jr., Steven J. Sandage and Jack W. Berry, "Group Interventions to Promote Forgiveness," in *Forgiveness: Theory, Research and Practice*, ed. Michael E. McCullough, Kenneth Pargament, and Carl E. Thoresen (New York: The Guilford Press, 2000), 241.

26. Worthington et al (2000), 241.

27. See Konstam et al (2001). See also Ann Macaskill, John Maltby, and Liza Day, "Forgiveness of self and others and emotional empathy," *Journal of Social Psychology* 142, no.5 (2002), 663-665; Todd K. Shackelford, David M. Buss, and Kevin Bennett, "Forgiveness or breakup: Sex differences in responses to a partner's infidelity," *Cognition and Emotion* 16, no.2 (2002), 299-307; Beverlyn Elanda Grace-Odeleye, "An examination of the role of forgiveness in the leadership practices of women leaders in higher education," Dissertation Abstracts International 64 (5-A), (Section A: Humanities and Social Sciences, 2003), 1550; Geoffrey E.W. Scobie, Enid D. Scobie and Alexandros K. Kakavoulis, "A cross-cultural study of the construct of forgiveness: Britain, Greece, and Spain," *Psychology: The Journal of the Hellenic Psychological Society* 9, no.1 (2002), 22-36.

28. Sharon Lamb, "Women, Abuse, and Forgiveness: A Special Case," in *Before Forgiving*, ed. Lamb and Murphy (2002), 165, 163.

29. Haaken (2002), 187.

30. Walker (1998), 132.

31. Walker (1998), 132.

32. Jean-Jacques Rousseau, *Emile*, trans. Allan Bloom (Jackson, Tenn.: Basic Books, 1979; first published 1762), Book V, 479.

33. Alan Schrift, "On the Gynecology of Morals: Nietzsche and Cixous on the Logic of the Gift," in *Nietzsche and the Feminine*, ed. Peter J. Burgard (Charlottesville: University of Virginia Press, 1994), 222.

34. Schrift (1994), 218, 219.

35. Hugh Gusterson, *People of the Bomb* (Minneapolis: University of Minnesota Press, 2004), ch.3, esp. 58-62.

36. Nancy Tuana, *The Less Noble Sex: Scientific, Religious, and Philosophical Conceptions of Woman's Nature* (Bloomington, Ind.: Indiana University Press, 1993), 54-56; Nancy Tuana, *Woman and the History of Philosophy* (New York: Paragon House, 1992), 26.

37. Tuana (1992), 14

38. Rousseau (1762), Immanuel Kant, *Observations on the Feeling of the Beautiful and the Sublime*, trans. John T. Goldthwait (Berkeley: University of California Press, 1960; first published 1764).

39. See Susan Jacoby, *Freethinkers: A History of American Secularism* (New York: Metropolitan Books, 2004), especially Chapter Three, for an especially absorbing analysis of abstract principles in the founding documents that are seemingly inconsistent with the political realities of colonial America but surpassingly consistent in historical context.

40. Haaken (2002), 186; Barbara L. Epstein, *The Politics of Domesticity* (Middletown, CT: Wesleyan University Press, 1981).

41. Haaken (2002), 186.

42. Haaken (2002), 187.

43. Haaken (2002), 186.

44. S. L. Bem, *The lenses of gender: Transforming the debate on sexual inequality* (New Haven, CT: Yale University Press, 1993), 121.

45. Bem (1993), 119.

46. Bem (1993), 154.

47. An excellent overview of critics and evaluation of the BSRI is offered by Rose Marie Hoffman and L. DiAnne Borders, "Twenty-five years after the Bem sex-role inventory: A reassessment and new issues regarding classification variability," *Measurement & Evaluation in Counseling & Development* 34, no.1 (2001): 39-56. The rich literature is almost always informed by the initial criticisms of E. J. Pedhazur and T. J. Tetenbaum, "Bem Sex Role Inventory: A theoretical and methodological critique," *Journal of Personality and Social Psychology* 37 (1979): 996-1016.

48. Alison M. Konrad and Claudia Harris, "Desirability of the Bem Sex-Role Inventory items for women and men: A comparison between African Americans and European Americans," *Sex Roles* 47, no. 5/6 (2002): 259-272; Patricia A. Oswald, "An examination of the current usefulness of the Bem Sex-Role inventory," *Psychological Reports* 94, Part 2, no.3 (2004): 1331-1336.

49. Tuana (1993), ix.

50. Nel Noddings, *Caring: A Feminine Approach to Ethics and Moral Education* (Berkeley: University of California Press, 1984), 40-44.

51. See Held (1993), Eva Feder Kittay, *Love's Labor: Essays on Women, Equality, and Dependency* (New York: Routledge, 1999), and Sara Ruddick, *Maternal Thinking* (New York: Ballantine Books, 1989) for well-known examples of such argumentation.

52. See Haber (1991) for his Kantian position. When I first began looking for the company of feminists in forgiveness study, I was struck by the absence of clearly feminist positions in the literature, and discovery of Haber's (1998) article, "Forgiveness and Feminism," was a welcome surprise; indeed, it remains one of the few written philosophical pieces on forgiveness to herald an explicitly feminist point of view.

53. Haber (1991).

54. Haber (1991), 80.

55. Haber (1998), 142.

56. Haber (1998), 146.

57. Haber (1998), 146-147.

58. Murphy (1988) describes his account as Kantian. Elsewhere Murphy suggests that he "clearly" influenced Haber's account, so the comparison seems apt, although I should note that Haber himself never claims Murphy as an influence, and indeed, Haber's dissertation on forgiveness was well into development before Murphy first published on forgiveness; see Jeffrie G. Murphy, *Getting Even: Forgiveness and Its Limits* (Oxford: Oxford University Press, 2003), 77; Jeffrie G. Murphy, "Forgiveness in Counseling: A Philosophical Perspective," in *Before Forgiving*, ed. Lamb and Murphy (2002), 44.

59. Haber (1998), 146-147.

60. In fairness to my predecessor, he didn't have the advantage I have now of increasingly available empirical data in psychology and related fields; he notes that in presuming women are more likely to forgive for the sake of relationships, "my reasons for thinking this have much to do with my intuitions on the matter and with data gathered in an informal and unscientific survey," which consisted of polling 150 students in his introductory ethics class.

61. Murphy (1988), 21n9.

62. Murphy (1988), 56n16.

63. Haber (1991), 49.

64. Murphy (1988), 16, 20-22.

65. Noddings (1984), 16-20, 70 (for the description of "seeing through another's eyes").

66. Claudia Card, *The Unnatural Lottery: Character and Moral Luck* (Philadelphia: Temple University Press, 1996), 89. For related feminist criticisms of Noddings's feminine care ethic, see the review symposium on care ethics in *Hypatia* 5, no.1 (Spring 1990), including Claudia Card, "Caring and Evil," Sarah Lucia Hoagland, "Some Concerns About Nel Noddings's Caring," and Barbara Houston, "Caring and Exploitation."

67. Govier (2002), 81-83, 92-95.

68. Govier (2002), 95.

69. Govier (2002), 81-83, 96-97.

70. Qtd., Govier (2002), 97, and see also Tutu (1999), 31.

71. In saying this, I do not mean to set Trudy Govier up as in any way opposed to feminist philosophy or excluded from the set of feminist philosophers; on the contrary, her contributions to feminist philosophies are so notable that I was struck by the absence of the connection between feminism and forgiveness in *Forgiveness and Revenge*.

72. Annette Baier, "Cartesian Persons," in *Postures of the Mind: Essays on Mind and Morals* (Minneapolis: University of Minnesota Press, 1985), 85.

73. Carol Gilligan, *In a Different Voice: Psychological Theory and Women's Development* (Cambridge, Mass.: Harvard University Press, 1982); Carol Gilligan, "Joining the Resistance: Psychology, Politics, Girls and Women," *Michigan Quarterly Review* 29 (1990): 501-536; Hekman (1995), p. 30, p. 72-3; Jack (1991), p.21.

74. Susan J. Hekman, *Moral Voices, Moral Selves: Carol Gilligan and Feminist Moral Theory* (University Park, Penn.: Pennsylvania State University Press, 1995), 111.

75. Ann Ferguson, "Feminist Communities and Moral Revolution," in *Feminism and Community*, ed. Penny Weiss and Marilyn Friedman (Philadelphia: Temple University Press, 1995), 379; see also Morwenna Griffiths, *Feminisms and the Self: The Web of Identity* (New York: Routledge, 1995).

76. Examples include Robert D. Enright, Suzanne Freedman, and Julio Rique, "The Psychology of Interpersonal Forgiveness," in *Exploring Forgiveness*, ed. Enright and North (1998), 46-62; Margaret Holmgren, "Forgiveness and Self-Forgiveness in Psychotherapy," in *Before Forgiving*, ed. Lamb and Murphy (2002), 112-135; Berel Lang, "Forgiveness," *American Philosophical Quarterly* 31, no.2 (1994): 105-117. 'Pseudo-forgiveness' is the term used by Enright et al; 'genuine' is the term used by Margaret Holmgren, with many others; 'metaphorical' is Berel Lang's wording. Too many philosophers to enumerate uphold similar models of forgiveness requiring, e.g., resentment, and say that in the absence of resentment one cannot be properly said to forgive at all.

77. For examples of such evidence in psychological studies, see Susan Forward, *Toxic Parents* (New York: Bantam Books, 1989); Dana Becker, *Through the Looking Glass* (Boulder, CO: Westview Press, 1997); Varda Konstam, Fern Marx, Jennifer Schurer, Nancy Emerson Lombardo and Anne K. Harrington, "Forgiveness in Practice," in *Before Forgiving*, ed. by Lamb and Murphy (2002), 54-71.

78. Walker (2006), 152.

79. Smith (2008), 27.

80. Hampton (1988), 39-40.

81. Margaret Holmgren, "Forgiveness and the Intrinsic Value of Persons," *American Philosophical Quarterly* 30, no.4 (1993): 342. Later she qualifies this with the observation that forgiveness is only "appropriate" after one completes this task (343), which suggests a moral recommendation as to when to express forgiveness; like Murphy, she seems to see no difference between the descriptive and prescriptive accounts.

82. Holmgren (2002), 120.

83. Holmgren (2002), 120.

84. Augustine, "On the Liturgical Seasons," in *The Works of Saint Augustine: Sermons, Vol. III*, Book 7, edited by John E. Rotelle and translated by Edmund Hill (New Rochelle, NY: New City Press, 1993), 180.

85. Baier (1994), 95-129; Haber (1998), 141-150.

86. Jean P. Rumsey, "Some Feminist Questions on Forgiveness" (Society of Women in Philosophy conference presentation, Antioch College, Yellow Springs, Ohio, Oct. 2000). She reiterates the importance of moral housekeeping even as she takes a cautionary approach to presuming forgiveness is inherently good, more recently; see Kathryn J. Norlock and Jean Rumsey, "The Limits of Forgiveness," *Hypatia* 24, no.1 (2009). Special Issue: Oppression and Agency: Claudia Card's Feminist Philosophy.

87. Arendt (1958/1998), "Irreversibility and the Power to Forgive," 240.

88. Griswold (2007), 41-42.

89. Alasdair MacIntyre, *After Virtue*, 2nd ed. (Notre Dame, Ind.: University of Notre Dame Press, 1984), 267.

90. Notably William K. Frankena, qtd. in MacIntyre (1984), 264-269.

91. Held (1993), 55.

92. Boss (1997), 235.

93. Haber (1998), 149.

94. Enright (1998); Robert D. Enright, *Forgiveness Is a Choice* (Washington, D.C.: APA LifeTools, 2001). In personal communication (August 2001), Enright put this even more insistently in response to insufficiently reflective use of the term "unforgivable," saying, "Everything you cite has been forgiven by someone! What do you say in light of the fact of these forgivers?" This hard and excellent question has not been considered by many philosophers to date.

95. Walker (2006), 181.

96. Herman (1992), qtd. in Schott (2004), 204.

97. Schott (2004), 204.

98. Schott (2004), 204.

99. Claudia Card, "The Atrocity Paradigm Revisited," *Hypatia* 19, no.4 (2004): 211.

100. Schott (2004), 207.

101. Card (2004), 212.

102. Govier (2002), 145.

103. Govier (2002), 97.

104. Govier (2002), 157, 140.

105. Govier (2002), 118.

106. Govier (2002), 117.

107. Card (2002), 176, emphasis hers.

108. Card (2002), 167, 194-195.

109. Walker (2006), 181.

110. Card (2002), 181.

111. Walker (2006), 181.

112. Walker (2006), 175.

113. Govier (2002), 95.

114. Qtd. in Schott (2004), 207.

115. Description of the Forgiveness Project was copied from the project website by permission of the project director, Marina Cantacuzino, and accessed on Feb. 18, 2008: The Forgiveness Project, "The Project," at http://www.theforgivenessproject.com/project/about/. Established 2004.

116. Bud Welch, "Stories: Bud Welch," from the Forgiveness Project, ed. Marina Cantacuzino (2004).

117. Berthe Climbié, "Stories: Francis & Berthe Climbié," from the Forgiveness Project, ed. Marina Cantacuzino (2004).

118. Linda Biehl, "Stories: Linda Biehl & Easy Nofemela," from the Forgiveness Project, ed. Marina Cantacuzino (2004).

119. Walker (2006), 176.

120. Kate Kellaway, "Could you forgive the unforgivable?" *The Observer* (June 25, 2006), 11.

121. Anonymous interview, qtd. in Allison Morris, "How could you ever forgive the evil killers? As grieving vicar quits, we ask other victims' relatives," *The Mirror* (March 13, 2006), 13.

122. Judy Eaton, Laurier Wilfrid, C. Ward Struthers, and Alexander G. Santelli, "The Mediating Role of Perceptual Validation in the Repentance-Forgiveness Process," *Personality and Social Psychology Bulletin* 32, no.10 (2006): 1389.

123. Eaton et al (2006), 1400.

124. Kerrie James, "The interactional process of forgiveness and responsibility: A critical assessment of the family therapy literature," in *Hope and despair in narrative and family therapy: Adversity, forgiveness and reconciliation*, ed. Carmel Flaskas, Imelda McCarthy, and Jim Sheehan (New York: Routledge/Taylor & Francis Group, 2007), 127-138; Janet L. Lewis, "Forgiveness and psychotherapy: The prepersonal, the personal, and the transpersonal," *Journal of Transpersonal Psychology* 37, no.2 (2005): 1-24.

125. Easy Nofemela, "Stories: Linda Biehl & Easy Nofemela," from the Forgiveness Project, ed. Marina Cantacuzino (2004).

126. Schott (2004), 205; Card (2004), 211-212.

127. Stephen Darwall, "Two Kinds of Respect," *Ethics* 88, no.1 (1977): 39.

128. Darwall (1977), 40.

129. Marina Cantacuzino, "The Forgiveness Project: A journalist's storytelling experiment," from The Storyteller and the Listener online: Essays on the role of story and narrative in peacemaking, bridge building, healing and reconciliation, at http://storyteller-and-listener.blog-city.com/marina_cantacuzino.htm, accessed February 19, 2008, first published 2007.

130. Marina Cantacuzino, "Stories of Forgiveness," from Dart Center for Journalism and Trauma: Personal Stories, at http://www.dartcenter.org/articles/personal_stories/cantacuzino_marina.html. Accessed February 19, 2008.

131. Arto Laitinen, "Interpersonal Recognition: A Response to Value or a Precondition of Personhood?" *Inquiry* 45, no.4 [Symposium on Axel Honneth and Recognition] (2002): 465.

Chapter Two

Relational Selves and Related Meanings

In the last chapter I argued that a Kantian model of forgiveness predominates in philosophical discourse, and noted that some of the philosophers who espouse it refer to it as the paradigm view.[1] In this chapter, I examine alternative philosophical models in an attempt to find a more promising approach. To do so, I must first return to the argument that we are selves-in-relation, to show how this conception of individuals yields a different paradigm case. I evaluate non-Kantian approaches in light of the self-in-relation, and I find that all of them turn out to be preferable to a Kantian approach. Despite their advantages, I conclude that, given the drawbacks of the usual alternatives generated by considering Aristotelian, Nietzschean and consequentialist insights, a distinctively feminist ethic is required to theorize about forgiveness.

Relational Forgivers

Almost everyone who writes on forgiveness attends to the presence of more than one person in the moral event.[2] Philosophers such as Jean Rumsey rightly lament the agonistic dyad which prevails in philosophical treatments of forgiveness, but even a dyad is at least interpersonal.[3] Forgiveness unavoidably involves relationships. Indeed, between the feminine associations identified in the previous chapter, and the inherently relational aspect of forgiveness, it is no wonder that until recently, forgiveness was a neglected topic in traditional Euro-American analytic philosophy, of which concern for feminine and relational topics are not hallmarks! Advocates of dyadic paradigms are usually minimally attentive to social contexts, as well. Murphy, for example, observes that we're all in great part products of socialization, including cultural habits and enforced emotions, and therefore it is socially, politically, and philosophically important to "deal with the question of the degree to which, if at all, these passions or emotions should be reinforced, channeled in certain directions, or even eliminated."[4] This is a rare occasion on which Murphy uses feminist arguments and nonhypothetical women as illustrative examples; he cites Mill's *Subjection of Women*, and Fay Weldon's poem in which she decries the excessive learned passivity of the good daughter.[5] Murphy acknowledges,

> It is a limitation of the liberal tradition to think that social and political matters are restricted to concerns with how we act—how we treat others and what we get to do . . . a concern with just rules of conduct. . . . [In] focusing exclusively on this concern, the liberal tradition leaves out something of great social and political importance . . . a concern with what kind of people will grow up and flourish. Will [they be virtuous], or will they be stunted and limited and alienated?[6]

Yet the attention here is to inward virtue; it seems that it is bad to be alienated for the individual, rather than that relations are inherently valuable.

An account of the self more suitable to our understanding forgiveness construes persons as both distinct and constituted by their chosen and unchosen relationships. As stated in the previous chapter, varieties of this account have been articulated by both feminists and non-feminists, and called conceptions of the social self, relational self, the self-in-community, and embodied accounts; in environmental philosophies, similar accounts debate the nature of holistic entities. Since I take gender to be central to understanding and recommending forgiveness, I rely on feminist accounts which prioritize the experiences of women in the course of their conceptual analyses. With many feminists, I refer to this idea as the relational self, and I argue that it can provide a more accurate account of individuals as both distinct and bounded; one's boundaries include one's relations of identification and what Ann Ferguson calls relations of disidentification with those to whom one's psychological connection is one of opposition.[7]

Although feminists do not have a monopoly on the insight that selves are relational and embodied, a feminist perspective on forgiveness motivates attention to the ways our relationality is central to seeing whom we can forgive, and why. Centering attention on gender reminds us that all relationships are gendered; relations are the connections between embodied individuals whose gendered experiences and positions of power inform our understanding and our conduct. This may seem so self-evident to some that it doesn't require explication, but in a field in which much has been written on relationships of forgiveness while avoiding gender matters, I gather that it bears stating.

At a minimum, the self-in-relation includes the idea that "relationships to others are intrinsic to identity," as Marilyn Friedman notes; "indeed, the social conception of the self tends to blur the distinction between self and other."[8] The blurring of one's boundaries is a site of discomfort for theorists who prefer to see individuals as independent and sharply distinct from each other, in keeping with modern liberalism. As a result, at times it becomes difficult to disentangle philosophers' ontological and moral commitments, as moral positions which value independence and noninterference lend themselves to descriptions of human beings as ontologically separable and opposed. The commitment to dyadic paradigms of forgiveness in much literature on forgiveness and justice demonstrates this sometimes puzzling equivocation, especially when philosophers refer to direct victims of clearly identifiable wrongdoers. On such occasions, the interest so many of us share in being able to write easily about clear cases of offense and recompense seems to dictate both an overvaluing of the moral independence of the agents involved, and a presumption of their ontological boundedness. This calls to mind Claudia Card's insight that philosophy is often written from the perspective of an administrator: "Paradigmatic ethical problems for most of modern ethical theory have been the problems created by distributions of power, not those presented by affiliation and attachment."[9] When conceptual analysis of forgiveness begins behind a judge's bench, the temptation to reduce paradigms of forgiveness to claimants and defendants can be great.

When feminist perspectives take caregivers rather than legislators as their paradigmatic agents, the value of carework directs attention to a more relational ontology. As Martha Fineman puts it most bluntly, in arguing that traditional liberalism presumes a family that provides caregiving for the individual, she suggests that autonomy and independence are myths.[10] Eva Kittay likewise asserts, "Independence, except in some particular actions and functions, is a fiction."[11] Kittay and Ellen Feder jointly argue, "We must take account of the fact of dependency in our very conceptions of the self."[12] To the extent that liberalism holds up independence and an inviolate, bounded self as ideals, liberal accounts redescribe these ideals as real attributes of selfhood. Jennifer Nedelsky describes this as a "pathological conception . . . of boundaries against others," in which "the most perfectly autonomous man is thus the most perfectly isolated."[13] In what follows I suggest that boundaries are not necessarily undesirable, as long as they are reconceived.

Yet care-centered paradigms may likewise overdescribe agents as lacking boundaries, in the course of valuing their relations. Noting this, Val

Plumwood recognizes the resistance to seeing oneself as all-too-constituted by one's relations, as a concern for both individualists and feminists. She criticizes the extreme holism of some environmental theorists as guilty of "indistinguishability," and argues against views such as that of Warwick Fox, who says, "The world simply is not divided up into independently existing subjects and objects. . . . To the extent we perceive boundaries, we fall short of a deep ecological consciousness."[14] She draws a parallel between extreme holism and the "traditional feminine-merger accounts" of the individual caring woman as one who disappears into her relations.[15] As I argued in Chapter One, the egoistic individualism of Murphy's and Haber's accounts result in the same indistinguishability; only "direct" victims can forgive, so in the case of intimate relationships, the hypothetical mother is described as having identical injuries and interests to her son's. (She is "really forgiving" her own injuries.)

We are neither identical to those with whom we stand in relationships, nor are we discontinuous, since our relations contribute to our very identities. The sensible alternative is to see individuals as selves in relation, who are distinct without being discontinuous, and embedded in webs of relationships which have intrinsic value. Our chosen and unchosen relationships are, in effect, our boundaries, insofar as they define us. Explicating the idea that relations could be boundaries as they define one's identity, Ferguson says, "All self-defining social practices involve . . . connections with others, that is, emotional identification or bonding with those considered like oneself. . . . Such practices often also involve disidentification with those defined as different or in oppositional roles."[16] This implies unchosen relations of inclusion, like one's relation to one's parents, serve as rather more fuzzy boundaries, which seems intuitively correct. Although most of us, to varying degrees, consider our family background a part of who we are, we do not settle for having these relationships and none others. Instead we go looking for friends, lovers, and intellectual communities with which to identify, in part to intentionally separate from our family and discover our distinctiveness. That family boundaries are fuzzy implies they are more permeable; several non-blood relations can come to be part of what we consider family, but not just anyone can wend their way into my relations of chosen inclusion. Who I consider my partner, or a part of my circle of friends, is a far less permeable boundary, in part because altering that boundary radically changes the person I consider myself to be. And yet it is a further strength of the relational account that it explains how our conceptions of our selves do change as our relations change. Figuratively (and sometimes literally) speaking, we change shape as we include some people and exclude others. Thinking of past relations we have altered or severed, we may find ourselves thinking, "I do not resemble the person I was then."

Warwick Fox was wrong, then, to say that perceiving boundaries falls short of being a wider and relational self. Perceiving our boundaries does not fall short of consciousness of interconnection. Instead, our relations are our boundaries, and perception or awareness of them is awareness of our own self-identification. These relations of identification can include that between the mother and son in Murphy's and Haber's example, making sense of the idea that she shares in his pain, resents his wrongdoer on his behalf, and does so in a way that affirms her agency rather than misplaces it. In this example, the mother identifies with her son because their relation of identification is presumed to be the product of an intense emotional bond, but other relations of identification in every person's life can include less intimate ties to those like oneself. In *The Sunflower*, Simon Wiesenthal says of fellow Jews he'd never met but were told had been burned alive, "I could have been one of the Jews carrying the petrol cans into the house."[17]

At the same time, if Ferguson is right that disidentification is a self-defining practice, then relations of disidentification could serve as those boundaries that make sense of wrongdoing, in the absence of the language of egoism and individualism. Insofar as we are defined by our relations of disidentification, this adds a revealing element to the story of a victim resenting a wrong done to her. Kantian philosophers refer to the victim's reaction to wrongdoing as a process of defending her self-worth, or reasserting her self-respect. Recast to include the idea that one's relations are one's boundaries, we see that asserting oneself can include changing one's relation to one's wrongdoer; in moving from a relation of identification to a relation of disidentification, the victim limits the wrongdoer's access to her in order to reclaim her own agency. Claudia Card says similarly of lesbian separatism, as a "retreat from affective to formal relationships with men, from intimacy to something more distant," that "we can withdraw from some without withdrawing from all connections," because "formality does not preclude communication but structures it. Putting our relationships with men on a formal, rather than affective, basis puts us in a better position to . . . appeal to rights."[18] In other words, separation is not necessarily a severing of a relationship. To separate closely joined relata changes their locations; indeed, *to separate* only makes sense if we understand their distance relative to each other.

With a relational account we can better understand the difficulties for a child, perhaps, who does not yet have the sense of disidentification with his wrongdoer; in childhood development, when one is still seeking out one's own identity, one may identify with one's wrongdoer all the more when child and wrongdoer have emotional bonds, or a common family. Let's add to Murphy's and Haber's examples that the son's wrongdoer was his own father. Let's also add that the son does not perceive a wrong was done to him; in identifying with his father, he may believe that he deserved what

turns out to be disproportionate punishment. In this case, he does not have
the requisite integrity to disidentify with his father, to do anything but agree
with his own treatment. His mother's resentment on his behalf changes that
relation. Seen this way, it is clearer that the mother doesn't resent the
wrong done to her. She is asserting the son's worth, and not her own. In
doing so, the agents involved remain distinct; it is the relations between
each that shift. The son can move from identifying to disidentifying with
his wrongdoer, while the mother exhibits agency that shows her to be
distinct even as it increases her identification of relationship with and to her
son.

The exercise involved in re-viewing moral problems as inherently
involving selves in relation allows us to more sensibly discuss the behaviors
of agents in intimate relationships. It is notable for my purposes that the
intimate relationship, in the much-discussed mother-son example, is a
relationship between agents of unequal power and capacities. It is striking
that such an unequal relationship would be a bandied-about exception to
paradigms of interpersonal forgiveness, since our intimate relationships are
so often unequal, especially in the family relations which one would think
provide so many occasions for forgiveness. Indeed, the paradigm of roughly
equal, educated, and highly employable coworkers who can apparently take
or leave their relationships, which appears in numerous discussions of
forgiveness, would seem to be one of the last relationships in which
forgiveness is required, or fraught with as much difficulty. Relationships
between family members or members of the same domicile, between
caregivers and the recipients of care, and between the men and women who
report sharing the sense of the unequal expectation that women will forgive,
would seem much more typical or likely sites of forgiveness. Prioritizing
the view of the self as relational makes this much more apparent, and
important, in working out conceptual analyses of forgiveness.

A relational account also draws attention to the ways in which
wrongdoing rarely affects one clearly identifiable victim in a select time-
slice. Trudy Govier argues that acts of wrongdoing can involve many
victims, and I would add that those victims are often not neatly separated,
making restitution to each difficult, perhaps at times impossible.[19] The
argument for a relational paradigm is an argument for correctly seeing
forgiveness as messy, and not an attractively neat arrangement between
contractually minded coworkers. In saying this, I am influenced by Robin
May Schott's critique of paradigm views as unreflective of actual
practices.[20]

So far, I have referred to paradigm views in ways which turn out to
serve several functions. Appealing to a paradigm may perform the entirely
neutral job of identifying a pattern in contemporary theorizing, without
endorsing it as correct or even as very widely shared; rather, a paradigm

view is a dominant, organizing account which tends to affect the way discourse proceeds, and I suggested in Chapter One that the Kantian account preferred by Murphy and Haber tends to do just that. Alice MacLachlan has noted similarly that even as forgiveness theorists proceed in our often critical fashion, the predominance of the Murphy-Haber model "has severely limited the emerging debate."[21] In the neutral sense, then, the paradigm is just the ruling model of forgiveness.

We also often appeal to a paradigm to indicate an area of general agreement among theorists, a point of convergence, as when we say that paradigm forgiveness does not condone or excuse the wrong, a common feature among otherwise disparate accounts of forgiveness. This second sense of 'paradigm' is often used to connote an ideal, and is not merely a neutral report of a pattern. It identifies desirable definitional elements. Claudia Card suggests that the ideal need not be ethical, saying, "My paradigm (or ideal) case of forgiveness is not an ethical ideal but only a conceptually unproblematic case . . . , one with all the central features of a clear case of forgiveness."[22] This is demonstrated by Charles Griswold's comment that most parties to the discussion of forgiveness take the dyadic model as the paradigm, as does he. Griswold argues against perfectionist views of human nature and idealizing moral theories, but argues for a paradigm of forgiveness, "the model case" of "forgiveness at its best," which does not have the "special problems" that arise from what he considers legitimate, morally important, yet nonparadigmatic examples of forgiveness, such as self-forgiveness or third-party forgiveness.[23] Clear cases and central features are appealing, allowing us to feel we have arrived at some consensus about the nature of forgiveness. Yet Schott's criticism of this approach correlates with my argument in the preceding chapter; "The risk of this strategy . . . is that the conceptual analysis of forgiveness becomes a lens that directs the lines of inquiry, instead of creating an opening for other moral lenses."[24] This should give anyone in pursuit of a paradigm pause.

Third, we occasionally argue for new paradigms, by which we mean models which many may not share, but which serve as more accurate and reflective examples of occasions for moral behavior, and promote certain priorities. Consider, for example, Virginia Held's suggestion that the mother-child relationship serve as a new paradigm of moral relations, rather than the contractual relation between adults in the liberal tradition; she argues the point is "an exercise of the imagination," desirable because "it might sometimes be more suitable to imagine how we would wish to be treated" in an unequal, intimate relationship, "rather than to imagine what we and others would choose from the even more remote and inappropriate position of the fully independent, self-sufficient, and equal rational agent."[25] She criticizes "the liberal image of the individual citizen" for "taking the ideal circumstances of an adult, independent head of a household as paradigmatic" and overlooking social relations while promoting self-interest over care.[26] In psychology, recent work suggests taking layperson understandings of forgiveness into account in developing new paradigms, which "will require abandoning notions of what is 'true' forgiveness and what forgiveness is not," notions which scholars advance yet which do not cohere with nonscholarly subjective experiences.[27] In his feminist critique of his own model of forgiveness, Haber describes himself as guilty of "taking injuries to solitary moral agents in an impersonal setting as paradigmatic and moving from there to personal and caring relationships"; he asks, "Why not move from a personal and caring relationship . . . to an individualistic relationship?"[28] Haber and Held suggest the intimate and unequal relation may be more typical, or more indicative, or provide what Schott may consider the opening for other moral lenses.

In this chapter I employ the third sense of a paradigm. I suggest that seen through other moral lenses, such as alternative ethical theories and ontologies of identity, forgiveness admits of multiple definitions, appropriately problematic cases, and varieties of relationships and values which better attend to women's experiences. Seeing forgiveness through theories with a view of agents as having relational natures and gendered bodies, without ignoring differences in identity, experience, and context, without assuming that feminist attentiveness to relational selves presumes a 'care-based' (feminine) approach, taking experiences of women into account in formulating conceptions instead of theorizing about it in abstraction, deprioritizing a Kantian duty-hierarchy of self-respect over relations, and shifting attention away from the robustly reflective, autonomous, Kantian agent with all the integrity of one with "true internal resolution," yields a rich conception of forgiveness which is more reflective of actual practices.

In the remainder of this chapter, I consider non-Kantian models of forgiveness including (1) an Aristotelian virtue ethics model, (2) a Nietzschian model, and (3) modern consequentialist models, and explore their potential contributions to a feminist and relational paradigm. Each model is the source of important insight into forgiveness, yet inadequately consider those aspects which I find fundamentally important to such a discussion: (1) that forgiveness inevitably involves the negotiation of one's relationship with another, and (2) that the disparate experience of women and men with forgiveness must be taken into account in analyzing the role of forgiveness in those often unequal relations. Although Aristotle is most explicitly appreciative of the importance of our relations, his account of friendship includes self-interested and individualistic elements which I wish to resist. Certainly we need friendships, yet we don't seem constituted by them on his account, and our friends appear to be somewhat interchangeable. Nietzsche comes closest to attending to the power relation between wrongdoer and victim as centrally important, but as Hannah Arendt's work indicates, he misconstrues what kind of relationship forgiveness establishes. And consequentialism may justify benefiting those whose power, relative to their victims, confers all too many benefits, already. Insights from all these perspectives inform my conclusion that a feminist approach is necessary to a discussion of forgiveness.

Aristotle and virtue ethics

As Charles Griswold and Joram Haber observe, the ancients address concepts importantly related to forgiveness; Haber mentions the works of Plutarch and Seneca, whose writings specifically argue that there are times when one's anger is inappropriate or out of proportion to the wrong done.[29] Griswold carefully considers "the range of meanings of *sungnômê* – from sympathize, to forbear, forgive or pardon, excuse or make allowance for," at work in Aristotle's ethics, and also considers Aristotle's discussion of the mean with respect to anger.[30] Aristotle is most often quoted by forgiveness theorists for making room for appropriate anger, suggesting that its deficiency is a vice correspondent with its excess. "For those who are not angry at the things they should be are thought to be fools, and so are those who are not angry in the right way, at the right time, or with the right persons."[31] It is less often noted in forgiveness literature that, when discussing the mean between the two extremes of angry behavior, Aristotle notes the virtuous person "seems to err more in the direction of deficiency, since the mild [virtuous] person is ready to pardon, not eager to exact a penalty."[32] Although pardon is only a related concept to forgiveness and, as I will show later, there are good reasons to see these as distinct, it is worth considering Aristotle's insight for the purpose of establishing the value of forgiveness. We do tend to praise those people who have what one might call forgiving characters, even if they're forgiving at times when their anger would otherwise be justified. We can say sensibly of someone that she's too kind for her own good, but such a criticism is often lovingly given, and usually carries its hint of praise. Given Aristotle's account of virtuous behavior, erring on the side of deficiency in anger need not entail that one fails to get angry enough at times, so much as it implies that one doesn't live long with one's anger over time. If having a virtue with respect to anger entails that one is a less enduringly angry person, overall, this seems to recommend that we take the appropriate steps to overcoming it, and so practicing forgiveness seems built into having this virtue.[33]

It is intriguing for my purposes, as a feminist seeking alternatives to Kantian forgiveness models, that Aristotle is so attentive to relations, and that he would have us be kinder to some individuals than to others; his account of what true friends do for each other differs from his account of what we owe to people to whom we are not so intimately connected. When one's virtuous friend has fallen into vice or done something unjust, Aristotle considers what our response ought to be; should we discontinue our relationship?

> Then should the friendship be dissolved at once? Surely not with everyone, but only with an incurably vicious person. If someone can be set right, we should try harder to rescue his character than his property, in so far as character is both better and more proper to friendship. . . . But if the one remains a better person than the other, they can no longer be friends.[34]

For Aristotle, it is possible for a virtuous person to act badly without thereby becoming incurably vicious. For instance, "it is possible to do injustice without thereby being unjust."[35] Since the curable friend is not obviously irredeemable, a true friend who loves this individual for his character will stay in the relationship and try to help his friend improve himself. Aristotle's account of how to live virtuously, although it doesn't mention forgiveness, would seem to require practicing it on occasion if we are to stay in relationships with those whose friendship we value.

Although one could suggest that the above commits him to nothing regarding forgiveness, consider also that for Aristotle true and complete friendship "is most necessary for our life. . . . For no one would choose to live without friends even if he had all the other goods."[36] Aristotle wisely argued that men do not, indeed cannot, live in isolation, an insight the importance of which is mirrored in the priority current feminist theory gives to our essential relatedness to other individuals. Other philosophers including Joanna North, Donald Shriver and Margaret Urban Walker have separately argued that an important function of forgiveness, in particular, is to repair these interpersonal relationships. North has argued correctly that relatedness is neglected in moral philosophy in general and in the study of forgiveness in particular; Shriver notes that without forgiveness our relations with others cannot thrive.[37] Walker says most boldly that forgiveness is indispensable to human relationships, a position with which I gently disagree in later chapters.[38] Despite my unease with seeing forgiveness as indispensable in all human relationships, if one is to heed Aristotle's recommendation that we stick around for our friend and help him out of his currently vicious state, then forgiveness may be necessary to our own friendship-retaining purposes; it would be difficult to improve the life or character of a friend whose vice I don't forgive. Many philosophers have noted that friendship gives rise to special obligations. North has argued more specifically that forgiveness in such relationships amounts to a duty, given "the internal demands and imperatives of relationships."[39]

Last, Aristotle's idea that someone may be so far beyond hope that the friendship should be dissolved suggests that someone could exhibit enough vice that we consider them unforgivably bad, or irredeemable. This is not to say that in this situation we harbor angry feelings; instead, dissolving the friendship seems to require neither pardoning nor begrudging the other. Psychologist Robert Enright refers to this as the writing off of one's offender.[40] Martha Minow suggests that there are possible responses to unforgivable persons that involve neither vengeance nor forgiveness.[41] Dissolving relationships in a way that writes off the offensive person may accomplish just this. All three seem to appreciate the loss involved in this, however, even as they recognize that it may be the best option available.

The renewed philosophical interest in virtue ethics in general and attention to the ethics of relationships in particular suggests that many of us find something worth keeping in Aristotle's account of the importance of maintaining such relationships. A robust account of forgiveness should include the valuable role of forgiveness in our relationships with others, indeed in our having intimate relationships at all. In addition, his idea that we are better off dissolving some relationships is intriguing, and potentially liberating to women who are traditionally expected to maintain even damaging relationships. On the other hand, Aristotle doesn't seem deeply invested in arguing that we retain one good friend in particular as opposed to another; it is a matter of some debate in Aristotelian scholarship whether virtuous friends are interchangeable. Although Aristotle provides some account of the ethics of our unchosen relationships, his attention is devoted mainly to relations men are free to pursue or cut off at will. While friendship is the greatest external good to a virtuous man, Aristotle never says that only one particular friend can fulfill this function. Griswold offers the valuable reminder that Aristotle's is a "perfectionist ethical scheme, for it is one that seeks to articulate and recommend the character of the man— and it is a man—of complete virtue," a self-sufficient and magnanimous man in a hierarchy of superior and inferior.[42] This reflects, to some extent, the masculine bias in Aristotle's philosophy, a bias further revealed by his arguments that women can neither be as virtuous as men nor have the sorts of true and complete friendships that men have.[43] In light of this, it is instructive to reconsider the rest of the quote cited earlier, in which he said those who do not get angry are thought to be fools: "for such a man is thought not to feel things nor to be pained by them, and, since he does not get angry, he is thought unlikely to defend himself; and to endure being insulted and to put up with insults to one's friends is slavish."[44]

Philosopher Jerome Neu takes the above to suggest that "feeling anger . . . when appropriate may be a condition of self-respect," and he is in company with most philosophers of forgiveness.[45] Yet taking Nancy Tuana's advice to read philosophy as a woman, I draw different inferences from Aristotle's characterization.[46] Aristotle's related descriptions of bravery are quite literally associated with being a man, or being manly; on his view, it seems a man unlikely to defend himself and endure insult is hardly a man at all.[47] Where are women in the above characterization of anger? It is not built into Aristotle's notion of woman to be brave, to be stirred to battle, to draw one's sword to defend oneself or others. The usual response to such absences in philosophy is to simply 'read women into' the above, as Neu seems to do, and infer that anger could be required for self-respect for everyone. Yet this succeeds in retaining the priorities of masculinity in a particular world-view while purportedly advancing a gender-neutral concept of self-respect and appropriate forgiveness. Recall the example from Chapter One of the wife who forgives a boorish visiting father-in-law; on universalizing conceptions of anger, self-respect and bravery, she is slavish and failing in duties to herself. From a relational and caregiving paradigm which retains the fact of her gendered relationships, however, she may be exerting herself to exhibit competing virtues. Feminist theory is instructive in cautioning against extensions of Aristotle's gendered theory to 'nongendered' universal moral agents, extensions which erase the essential role that gender plays in Aristotle's own conceptual work.

Nietzsche's perverse model

Feminist philosophers would then find an odd sort of ally in Nietzsche, who explicitly connects being slavish with being womanly (as, I suggest, does Aristotle). A digression is here in order, since it's worth noting that much excellent work has been done on the uses of Nietzsche in feminist scholarship; I am certainly not the first to find him an odd ally, given his debatable misogyny. And interpreting Nietzsche for any purpose is notoriously fraught with difficulty. Nietzsche himself cautions the reader not to take him literally, not to read him selectively, and not to follow him blindly. For this very reason, those theorists who argue that what Nietzsche describes isn't *really* forgiveness are both right and wrong, right because Nietzsche's view is hardly comprehensive, and wrong because such an argument takes Nietzsche on terms to which he deliberately does not conform.

Having said that, Nietzsche comes closer than does any pre-twentieth century philosopher to associating forgiving with femininity. In suggesting this, I am influenced by Lynne Tirrell's observation that Nietzsche's list of slavish virtues "promotes values that ease the lot of the sufferer, and the list looks like a short list of womanly virtues: pity, humility, kindness, altruism and the like."[48] For Nietzsche the noble virtues exhibit power, in the senses of activity and creativity, while the actions of the slavish are fundamentally passive reactions, dictated by others instead of creative; many philosophers have observed that Nietzsche associates the slavish with the feminine, for instance, in the passage of the *Gay Science* in which he describes the instinct for deceptive acting, borne of necessity.[49] Those in "deep dependency" like slaves and women must "cut their coats according to the cloth, always adapting themselves again to new circumstances," and in taking on the values of others rather than values of their own, such people "always had to change their mein and posture, until they learned gradually to turn their coat with every wind and thus virtually to become a coat"; Nietzsche adds that when we "reflect on the whole history of women," they "have to be first of all, and above all else, actresses."[50] Barbara Helm notes that Nietzsche describes women as "beasts of prey," as opposed to noble predators, and "[described] women as bearers of 'slave values' and resentment."[51] Learning to excel at servility makes slaves cunning and clever, and at this, Nietzsche finds, women are cleverer than men. The successful slave revolt in morals achieves the cleverest manipulation of all; in his *Genealogy of Morals*, Nietzsche argues that forgiveness was a creation of spiritual revenge, born of the submerged hatred, impotence and vengefulness—the *ressentiment*—of the weak to gain power over their strong injurers.[52] Forgiveness, like other such "slavish" virtues, is not only not a virtue; it is a vice of the worst kind, giving rise to "the guilty feeling of indebtedness to the divinity."[53] And relatedly, he suggests elsewhere that women who suffer at the hands of more powerful men exert a reactive power of their own by making men feel guilty and then forgiving them. Last, Tirrell argues that Nietzsche "captures the constraining normativity of the definition of woman as slave when he says, 'A man who loves like a woman becomes a slave; while a woman who loves like a woman becomes a more perfect woman.' . . . It sounds as if calling her a slave would be redundant."[54]

I do not intend these selections to serve as evidence that women really are slavish and manipulative. My point is not that women are accurately described in the above, or that Christianity is "malice spiritualized," as Nietzsche says.[55] And it is not clear that Nietzsche himself always intends to portray slave values, Christianity or women as unchangeable and uncomplicatedly negative. Scholars have debated the extent of his essentialism, at times arguing that Nietzsche himself sees all these categories as socially constructed, mutable and worthy of different kinds of respect. Even at those times when women, slavish and Christian folks are described as patient ruminants, cows and camels, one gets the sense that they have strength and capabilities that are virtuous, or at least worthy of some admiration; as beasts of burden, cows and camels can bear a great deal. At the same time, I do not wish to downplay Nietzsche's misogyny; his worst evaluations of women are well documented by other feminists. Rather, I'm struck that Nietzsche is perhaps the first philosopher to strongly associate forgiveness with negative value, and to associate forgiveness with aspects of femininity that many feminists today find detrimental to women's well-being. In some ways he is to date the only philosopher to be so unequivocal, although Jeffrie Murphy has gone to great length to argue against "trendy forgiveness boosterism" and give "two cheers for vindictiveness."[56] As I argued in Chapter One, culturally coded associations are indicative in ways that are often unaddressed in philosophy, but that point to the role gender plays as an organizing category in conceptual analysis. How do the associations of forgiveness with femininity in Nietzsche's work function as a critique, and is there any truth to the story that forgiveness is the virtue of the slavish? At the least, Nietzsche provides a rare cautionary note, and allows the inference that to the extent forgiveness is gendered in contexts of oppression, it is suspect as a moral good.

Nietzsche further suggests that forgiveness can be used to manipulate another, and that women are manipulators par excellence, by necessity. When he describes Christian virtues like forgiveness as sneaking, hateful, and vengeful, he brings to light the way in which forgiveness can be an expression of one's power over another, if a sort of passive (aggressive) power. Psychologist Robert Enright refers to forgiveness that abuses this power as pseudo-forgiveness, because it manipulates the person it purports to let off the moral hook. "If we 'forgive' so that we will make the other perpetually indebted to us, we...misunderstand true forgiveness. . . . Genuine forgiveness, in contrast, is centered in a courageous act of giving."[57] The argument that Nietzsche does not describe forgiveness in the best sense is noteworthy, yet Enright's addition seems to reinforce the association of forgiveness with femininity rather than steer away from it. We are presented with the choice of seeing forgiveness as either the manipulation of the less powerful or a courageous form of self-sacrifice and giving, another behavior with which women are traditionally associated, especially in the mothering role. Alan Schrift argues relatedly that Nietzsche frequently uses the feminine as a defamatory qualifier, yet associates sacrifice and giving with femininity; "woman gives herself away."[58]

Here we collide again with the ambiguities of interpreting Nietzsche. In his critical portrayal of *ressentiment* as including grudge-holding and slavishly remembering every wrong, Nietzsche describes the strong man, in contrast, as one who generously forgets. Healthy reactions to injury, including anger, are sudden and quickly over; a truly strong person can then shrug off injuries done to him. "To be incapable of taking injuries and enemies seriously for very long" is virtuous; a noble creature has the power "to recuperate and forget."[59] Only a weak and vicious person remembers the wrongs done him so well, and seizes power through condemnation. The strong man, in short, is giving, if not self-sacrificing. Nietzsche's description of giving from a position of strength is at least evocative of a sister concept, that of mercy.

The associations of giving, in Nietzsche's works, with the feminine and with the strong, noble man seem conflicting, and perhaps we're well advised not to try reconciling Nietzsche's ambiguities. Yet the differences between his depictions of the giving of slavish women and the merciful giving of noble men are intriguing for the present purposes. The strong give because it's easy, because they hardly notice the negligible cost of doing so, because their mercy is the mercy of the giant to the fly, brushing off that which hardly seems like a harm. As women are characterized, in contrast, they give because they can manage to remain standing under crushing burdens, because they bear the high costs of self-sacrifice well, because, indeed, they seem to want to give until it hurts. (One can imagine Nietzsche shrugging and saying, "Whatever makes you happy.")

Enright may be correct that forgiveness is centered in an act of giving, and I am not inclined to argue against giving per se. However, Nietzsche's critique calls to mind John Mill's arguments against sacrifice for its own sake. In light of the distinction between easy mercy and painful sacrifice, I am moved to consider, not whether women are expected to forgive more often, but why. Forgiveness may be more often expected of those presumed to be inclined to, even desirous of, self-sacrifice. The ideal of femininity described in the previous chapter includes that of being a domestic harmonizer, and women striving to conform to such an ideal may strive to be self-sacrificing, as Virginia Woolf described the "angel in the house:"

> She was intensely sympathetic. She was immensely charming. She was utterly unselfish. She excelled in the difficult arts of family life. She sacrificed herself daily. If there was chicken, she took the leg; if there was a draught, she sat in it - in short she was so constituted that she never had a mind or a wish of her own, but preferred to sympathize always with the minds and wishes of others. Above all—I need not say it—she was pure. . . . Thus, whenever I felt the shadow of her wing or the radiance of her halo upon my page, I took up the ink pot and flung it at her. She died hard. Her fictitious nature was of great assistance to her. It is far

harder to kill a phantom than a reality. She was always creeping back when I thought I had dispatched her. [60]

Murphy similarly quotes Fay Weldon's bleak view of forgiveness, always ending with the image of the mother teaching her daughter "a miserable, crawling, sniveling way to go, the worn-out slippers placed neatly beneath the bed, careful not to give offense."[61] Yet miserable or no, such utter self-sacrifice and deference can require great personal wherewithal, a variety of strength of its own. This suggests that to center forgiveness in a courageous act of giving is not yet to free it from the danger of being slavish. Nietzsche's insights point to the consideration that slaves can be courageous, slaves can be giving, even in admirable ways, but not from the sort of strength that liberates them from a slave's lot. In other words, the power relation between the forgiving person and the object of her forgiveness is critical to evaluating whether or not courageous giving is the wise thing to do.

On this account, one's position of power relative to one's wrongdoer may even dictate different reasons for forgiving. The less powerful, the woman or slave, is not in a position to forgive because it's easy, or because one can afford to. Given the ways in which I have argued forgiveness is feminized, a moral agent in this position may forgive because doing something so difficult is praiseworthy, because it is the act of a good woman, because it is expected, encouraged, or rewarded. Nietzsche argued that acts which are justified by raising one's moral status, earning oneself a place in heaven while simultaneously bringing another low, are manipulative and false; Enright sidesteps the Nietzschean critique with the argument that to the extent one uses the language of forgiveness in order to manipulate, one isn't really forgiving at all, hence the moniker "pseudo-forgiveness." However, Nietzsche provides us with reason to see the slavish agent as doing something more complex than lying or maliciously manipulating. As I have characterized Nietzsche's slavish woman, Woolf's angel, and Weldon's miserable mother, they could be described as exerting themselves to do different sorts of giving than that of the privileged noble man. In other words, Enright may be correct to characterize forgiveness as courageous giving; rather than exclude the acts of those who forgive with unusual, suspect or servile motives as non-genuine, however, perhaps we should see such giving as genuine, active, yet personally costly to those who can least afford it, on some occasions morally outstanding, akin to giving away one's last penny, on other occasions even morally wrong, the final deep cut that completes someone's loss. As Pamela Hieronymi and Margaret Walker observe, in forgiving someone, "the one wronged absorbs the cost," and instead of being absolved or washed away, the wrongdoing is digested or absorbed.[62]

Hannah Arendt, too, suggests, in ways contrary to and compatible with Nietzsche, that forgiveness is not merely passively aggressive, rather a powerful form of human labor. For Arendt, forgiveness is essentially creative; it is vengeance which is reactive, because it "incloses both doer and sufferer in the relentless automatism of the action process," and forgiveness is its "exact opposite" because it is active and creative.[63] "Forgiving . . . does not merely re-act but acts anew and unexpectedly," and establishes a new relationship, making it "an eminently personal . . . affair in which what was done is forgiven for the sake of who did it."[64] Arendt does not argue that forgiveness amounts to a duty; like Nietzsche, she prizes that which is active and creative. Both refer with distaste to that which is calculable. For Nietzsche, the idea of duty itself reduces the agent to a calculable debt; for Arendt, revenge is predictable and reduces one to a passive receptor of natural urges.

The combined insights of Nietzsche and Arendt reveal the importance of evaluating the value of forgiveness itself before we enter into recommending it, if only to ask ourselves whether establishing new relationships with our wrongdoers is desirable and done for the right reasons. For those who have long been in the position of always forgiving, extending it again may not break the cycles of injury that ideally forgiveness ought to end. Instead of distinguishing between genuine forgiveness and pseudo-forgiveness, as Enright does, it may be more instructive for our purposes to ask what relationship forgiving will create in the context in which we give it. For some givers, forgiveness may be predictable in ways which leave them "confined to one single deed from which [they] could never recover," an uncreative cog undesirable to both Nietzsche and Arendt.[65]

Potentially helpful, despite its errors, is Nietzsche's insight that those who exhibit nobility have the power to recuperate quickly, whereas those who need to forgive wrongdoers are weak, at least insofar as they must have held their grudge longer, and perceive much more to forgive than one might expect. On his account, only a weak and vicious person remembers the wrongs done him so well, and seizes power through condemnation. Griswold remarks that in his way, Nietzsche, like Aristotle, operates from an ideal conception of a strong and self-sufficient agent for whom holding grudges is not necessary, for he cannot be harmed; Griswold instead emphasizes the importance of taking as a paradigm a more accurate view of humans as imperfect, interdependent, and vulnerable to each other.[66] Yet in light of the fact of our interdependence, Nietzsche's description of recuperation is intriguing; bearing in mind the examples in Chapter One of victims who lead vindicated lives, I suggest that witnesses and communities are in positions to foster recuperation, or prevent it through lack of acknowledgement. Victims denied resources of vindication and strength remember their grudges in the absence of anyone else noticing that which they've suffered, and if grudge-holding is associated with weakness, that is, if grudge-holding saps strength, then selves in relation have the power to lift the sole burden of memory from the unacknowledged victim.

Indeed, Nietzsche's observations apparently resonate with the conditions that contemporary philosophers often attach to ethical recommendations regarding forgiveness. First, it is difficult to forgive when one still suffers from the wrongdoing, or is too vulnerable to the wrongdoer. A victim in a position of vulnerability to the wrongdoer will need to recuperate to a point where he or she feels strong enough to move on from the wrong. Second, when the injury doesn't "take," when it glances off in such a way that we don't really suffer from it, forgiveness is inappropriate. Third, and painful to translate into ethical recommendation, some grudge-holding itself seems morally blameworthy. For Nietzsche, apparently, all grudges are out of proportion to the wrongs they take as their objects. Without holding this, we can all think of examples of grudges that are excessive relative to their objects.

For all that we mustn't manipulate others with (pseudo-) forgiveness, Nietzsche doesn't seem to have much trouble with casting off wrongdoers, either. In referring to injurers as mere flies to be brushed off, Nietzsche rejects them as less than equal. As Griswold observes, this is less useful to those of us who center the experience of victims and take imperfect and vulnerable agents as paradigmatic. The most vulnerable and powerless often have the fewest options with respect to whether or not it is possible to separate oneself from one's wrongdoers; casting aside those who have hurt us seems the privilege of those with the muscle and the space to do so. However, Nietzsche provides a rare note of self-preservation in the literature on forgiveness, attractive from a feminist perspective which includes awareness of the disproportionate expectation upon women to maintain relationships of any quality. He at least moves one to consider the question whether one has a relationship worth saving, whether one has a relationship at all. Granted that we are all interconnected, would we say that we stand in relationships with all other humans? Do all these relations require forgiveness? These are questions for later chapters, but it is enough to note, for now, that in his way he joins the company of those philosophers who argue that some evildoers either can, or should, be written off, rather than forgiven.

Consequentialism and its critics

Many philosophers who write about forgiveness usually come to the subject through their work on retributive justice, so perhaps it is not surprising that few philosophers even offer a consequentialist analysis of forgiveness. Consequentialist arguments are more often reflected in the attention of psychologists to beneficial outcomes of forgiveness processes, which get wide circulation in journalism and popular culture; it is worth considering these arguments to understand why so many philosophers find non-consequentialist accounts superior.[67] Conveniently, psychologist Robert Enright mentions three consequentialist justifications of forgiveness in what turns out to be descending order of their frequency of citation; "Forgiving . . . may be positively transforming for self, the injurer, and our communities."[68] Enright himself does not lay claim to being a consequentialist, and explicitly rejects those justifications of forgiveness that appeal solely to its benefits to the forgiver, arguing, "Forgiving is more than making ourselves as forgivers feel good."[69] Nevertheless, arguments that forgiveness is important for its consequences most often appeal to its benefits for the victim of injury.

Well-known, and popularly read, authors of such accounts include clinical social worker Beverly Flanigan and psychiatrist Richard Fitzgibbons. Flanigan considers forgiveness "a tool of peacemaking" and argues that clinicians who help deeply hurt clients forgive "contribute to the possibility of peace."[70] Fitzgibbons identifies forgiveness as "a powerful therapeutic intervention which frees people from their anger."[71] Flanigan reports that forgivers go through a process in therapy which enables them to re-establish their basic beliefs about the world and about themselves which had been shaken by serious harm; these victims "created new assumptive sets in which the world again appears to be orderly and the self of inherent worth."[72] Fitzgibbons argues for the use of forgiveness in psychiatry because its "healing power" for the victims of wrongdoing "resolves hostile feelings and vengeful thinking"; forgiveness-supportive processes "result in a significant diminishment in the . . . suffering in our clients and . . . contribute to successful reconciliations in a variety of relationships."[73] Both Flanigan and Fitzgibbons report that although many clients feel more positive about themselves and their wrongdoers as a result of forgiveness, for some the best they can feel about their wrongdoers is "neutral," and thus forgiveness can best be said to admit of degrees.[74]

More recently, Enright's own process model of forgiveness has offered some evidence that his model of forgiveness processes in clinical practice succeed in securing measurable improvement in clients' mental and physical well-being.[75] Psychologists including Michael McCullough and Everett Worthington have offered empirical measurements of their own, demonstrating positive association between forgiveness or forgiving dispositions and adjustment, relationship closeness, and reducing the stress and negative emotions which result from perceiving injustice.[76] It bears repeating that McCullough and Worthington do not necessarily advocate forgiveness or advance consequentialist arguments for its role in therapy. Studies in the social sciences often seek to measure outcomes and their effects on life functions, and sometimes describe life-assisting outcomes as goals to be desired and achieved, although the extent of actual advocacy of forgiveness varies greatly between social scientists. Beneficial outcomes for physical health are less often replicated in the literature, but beneficial outcomes for mental health and resilience are repeatedly demonstrated, as are improvements in personal relationships with others and personal growth.[77]

Joram Haber argues forcefully against accounts of outcomes like the above as instructive of the moral appropriateness of forgiveness, saying the beneficial results to forgivers "are largely irrelevant from a moral point of view."[78] Rather than argue that these results do not occur (although he suggests that they sometimes don't), Haber objects that "consequentialist reasons . . . are essentially practical, rather than moral."[79] Like Murphy's aforementioned rejection of forgiveness boosterism, Haber appeals to the priorities of justice as cautionary brakes on the question of whether to forgive at all. For Haber, what makes forgiveness morally permissible rests on the repentance of the wrongdoer; therapeutic concerns which don't address the repentance of the wrongdoer are then morally uninteresting and such "consequentialist reasons ought not to be countenanced."[80]

There is a fairly intractable sense of "moral permissibility" which, if it is the one Haber uses, means it is pointless to argue with Haber; it may be that only our treatment of others is morally relevant, while our treatment of ourselves is not subject to moral evaluation. In this case, going through therapy which benefits me greatly, or refusing to seek treatment for something very damaging to me inwardly, can be said to be good or bad for me but neither right nor wrong to do. If this is the case, then Haber is correct that consequentialist justifications of forgiveness are completely irrelevant to moral philosophy. However, given that Haber places a great deal of importance upon acting in a manner consistent with self-respect, I don't think this is his view; I interpret Haber's Kantian position to be that we can do right or wrong by our selves, and I believe his position is correct. If I am right, then it seems Haber ought to take evidence of the above benefits, including feeling renewed self-worth, into account in deciding whether the repentance of my wrongdoer always trumps the duties I may have to myself. This seems especially important, for instance, when the wrongdoer has died—a dilemma Haber resolves by suggesting that forgiveness of the dead is morally permissible if there is evidence that the wrongdoer "*would have repented*" if he had lived.[81] I suggest we needn't engage in the counterfactual approach in the case of forgiving the dead, that instead this can be an occasion wherein, given the possible enhancement of one's self-respect through forgiveness, the duty to heal oneself can appropriately trump the duty to forgive only repentant wrongdoers.

Duties to oneself are therefore compatible with at least acknowledging the evidence of beneficial outcomes of forgiveness. More importantly for the purposes of this chapter, however, a relational and feminist perspective directs more careful attention to the potential value of outcomes that include improved relationships. Recall, too, the evidence previously stated that women are far more likely to participate in forgiveness research, evince interest in helping such studies, and contribute disproportionately to the outcomes so described. Taking the experience of women seriously, then, it is mistaken to consider the benefits of therapeutic outcomes as irrelevant to moral philosophy. Clearly, therapeutic considerations are not nearly so irrelevant to the women so integrally involved in generating the data. Men *and* women who exhibit interest in such outcomes as a thriving life, improved close relationships, and improved adjustment to changed circumstances pursue goals which a relational view may better account for as morally significant. This is not to say that good consequences of forgiveness for relationships entail that forgiveness is to be recommended. Measurable outcomes are useful evidence to weigh in moral decision-making between options, which may also include securing other personal and social goods, including the physical safety that at times only distance can secure, or the motivation to act on one's own behalf or others', which righteous anger may better inform. Yet surely such evidence is morally relevant.

Therapeutic accounts of interpersonal forgiveness primarily refer to the benefits to the forgiver, and secondarily to the benefits to the wrongdoer whose relationship with the forgiver is sometimes repaired and even improved. Research in this area is so preliminary that it seems the one thing all social scientists agree on is the need for more study, but early data suggests that forgiveness facilitates repentance and deters future offenses Despite the fairly peripheral attention to recipients of forgiveness in psychology, it is still far more attention than wrongdoers typically receive in philosophical treatments of forgiveness, where the benefits which wrongdoers receive from forgiveness are generally held to be either uninteresting or by definition undeserved and implicitly regrettable. Again, the tradition of proceeding from questions of justice plays a large role in the philosophical tendency to regard benefitting wrongdoers distastefully. Further, the dominant discourse tends to focus on Murphy's change of heart, or as McCullough says, the intraindividual process, which entails the existence of an offender but scarcely considers the interactional aspect of forgiveness at all.[82]

Social scientists who study the role of forgiveness in restorative justice at the political level offer evidence for a consequential justification of forgiveness as it benefits the community or wider society. In philosophy, Bishop Joseph Butler provides parallel arguments; Butler was not a consequentialist, but what he says about forgiveness can inform an account that takes this to be important. Butler defends the necessity of our resentment at wrongs done as a natural response without which we wouldn't pursue justice—"The end of resentment is to prevent or remedy injury"—but worries that overly gratifying resentment produces more misery in the world, "contradicting the end of resentment." Therefore, we must forgive "to prevent excess of resentment, to avoid malice or revenge." Forgiving our trespassers reduces to "no more than that we should not indulge a passion which, if generally indulged, would propagate itself so as almost to lay waste the world." It is instructive for our discussion of consequentialism that Henry Sidgwick notes some philosophers "think that a deliberate and sustained desire to punish wrong-doers is required in the interests of society. . . . Butler recognizes that [moral] resentment 'has in fact a good influence upon the affairs of the world'; though 'it were much to be wished that men would act from a better principle.'"[83]

Butler doesn't rely on the good influence of resentment and forgiveness to justify their moral permissibility, but what he says prompts us to consider the effects of forgiveness or its absence on those not directly involved in the original injury. Recent history provides us with plentiful examples of responses to wrongdoing that, in their way, lay waste to the world around them into successive generations—the intermittent and ongoing conflicts in Darfur, in Somalia, between Israel and Palestine, and hate crimes here in the U.S. which are sometimes the product of perceived past harms.[84] Forgiveness as the foreswearing of revenge, in these cases, may benefit not just the forgiver and the forgiven, but succeeding generations who would otherwise take part in indefinitely continuing cycles of vengeance.

Yet even these benefits to the wider world may come at too high a price, at times. Minow and Susan Jacoby both caution against forgiving for the sake of others when one is not yet strong enough oneself. Jacoby suggests that the same consequentialist concerns that rule out vengeance may mistakenly rule out specific and justified acts of retaliation, further devaluing victims already devalued by the original wrong.[85] And although precluding further misery is one reason to forgive, it isn't the only or, for Minow, even the most important reason to forgive; forgiving for the sake of the community is an act that "raises questions about whether the victim has enough self-respect or strength to view the injury as a violation."[86] In short, such objections stem from considerations of power, in light of which, I wish to add another consideration—that of the relationship the forgiver has to someone who benefits from their forgiveness. Not only must we consider the self-respect of the victim, although this is critical, but we are as constrained to consider whether we are about to benefit someone who already stands in a greatly advantageous position to us and to the community; if the wrongdoer who would benefit from forgiveness shares in a grossly unequal share of social benefits already, it may be a mistake to confer more on him without first seeing all those affected by our forgiveness in a more just distribution of social goods.

I am not talking here about a case like that in Simon Wiesenthal's memoir, *The Sunflower*, wherein he was asked forgiveness from a dying Nazi soldier in a position of material disadvantage himself. However, in the case, for instance, of two remaining members of the Pol Pot regime, they were welcomed back into their society by the justice system "with flowers and not with handcuffs," and retained the monetary wealth they amassed from oppressing others; they apologized in press interviews and asked for society's forgiveness, but the consequentialist argument that forgiveness might benefit them seems a reason to withhold it rather than grant it.[87] It seems a mistake to consider benefiting another good in itself, without considering whether the relationship of forgiver to beneficiary is one of powerless to powerful. For attention to this aspect of what makes forgiveness appropriate, we are best served by turning our attention to contemporary feminist analyses of forgiveness, related emotions, and narrative accounts, which I do in the next chapter.

The philosophical treatments above certainly offer some worthwhile insights into the value, and at times the disvalue, of forgiveness as it pertains to the well-being of the one forgiving, and less often the well-being of the society which relies on our practicing forgiveness. However, the ethical recommendations we can derive from these models are necessarily limited since they usually do not take into account the nature and value of the power relation between the forgiver and the forgiven. I suggest that the weight of these considerations, when taken together, amounts to an argument for the need for feminist theory in the study of forgiveness, especially since feminist analyses, to date, are few and far between. I argue for a feminist and multidimensional account of forgiveness that takes seriously everyday experience with forgiving, and the nature of the power relationship in which forgiver and forgiven stand. This requires avoiding the more often traveled route of identifying those necessary and sufficient conditions for what is alternately called 'genuine,' 'real' or 'true' forgiveness, and then inspecting ordinary uses of the term to see if they conform to said conditions. Instead, I draw on our experiences and ordinary language uses of forgiveness in order to construct a model of forgiveness which accounts for those occasions. In the next chapter, I identify the emerging feminist model that some contemporary theorists have begun constructing based on the insights of these earlier models. I argue that feminist accounts are preferable because they rightly take into account the actual experience of women in a way that the five early models of forgiveness largely fail to do, and the best accounts avoid adopting a feminine paradigm of moral agents as opposed to a feminist paradigm. I construct my own account of forgiveness based on the feminist framework I identify; I suggest that forgiveness is best construed on a multi-dimensional model including both an attitude and a speech act, and that in some circumstances forgiveness amounts to a duty, specifically when the injured stands in a position of power over vulnerable wrongdoers who do not threaten one's self-respect.

Notes

1. Joram Haber and Alice MacLachlan are the two to most explicitly identify the Kantian model, influentially articulated by Murphy, as the paradigm view; see Joram Haber, "Forgiveness and Feminism," in *Norms and Values: Essays on the Work of Virginia Held*, ed. Joram Graf Haber and Mark S. Halfon (Lanham, MD: Rowman and Littlefield, 1998, 141-150; Alice MacLachlan, "Forgiveness, Feminism, and the Diversity of Women's Experiences," online, Society for Women's Advancement in Philosophy 2005 *Conference for Topics of Diversity in Philosophy*, http://conference2005.swapusa.org/papers/maclachlan/ (first presented at the first meeting of the Society for Women's Advancement in Philosophy, Tallahassee, Florida, April 2005). Margaret Urban Walker provides an overview and critique of Murphy's and others' closely related accounts; see Margaret Urban Walker, *Moral Repair: Reconstructing Moral Relations after Wrongdoing* (Cambridge and New York: Cambridge University Press, 2006), especially 153-158.

2. That is, interpersonal forgiveness, since there is to date so little philosophical literature on self-forgiveness, and a lot of those who write on the interpersonal don't, or only fleetingly, address self-forgiveness. The notable exception to this rule is Robin Dillon's excellent article, "Self-Forgiveness," cited by Charles Griswold, who at least addresses self-forgiveness, yet includes self-forgiveness in a set of non-paradigmatic and less-than-uncomplicated varieties of forgiveness; see Robin Dillon, "Self-Forgiveness and Self-Respect," *Ethics* 112 (2001): 53-83; Charles Griswold, *Forgiveness: A Philosophical Exploration* (Cambridge and New York: Cambridge University Press, 2007), 122-29. This is a glaring contrast with psychological literature, which includes a plethora of scholarly studies and popular self-help books on forgiving oneself, satisfying a need among general readers which once again points up a possible way in which philosophy does not attend to practical experience with what people mean by, or want from, forgiveness.

3. Jean P. Rumsey, "Some Feminist Questions on Forgiveness" (Society of Women in Philosophy conference presentation, Antioch College, Yellow Springs, Ohio, Oct. 2000); Kathryn J. Norlock and Jean Rumsey, "The Limits of

Forgiveness," *Hypatia* 24, no.1 (2009), Special Issue: Oppression and Agency: Claudia Card's Feminist Philosophy.

4. Jeffrie Murphy and Jean Hampton, *Forgiveness and Mercy* (Cambridge: Cambridge University Press, 1988), 9.

5. Murphy and Hampton (1988), 14.

6. Murphy and Hampton (1988), 14.

7. Ann Ferguson, "Feminist Communities and Moral Revolution," in *Feminism and Community*, ed. Penny Weiss and Marilyn Friedman (Philadelphia: Temple University Press, 1995), 379; see also Morwenna Griffiths, *Feminisms and the Self: The Web of Identity* (New York: Routledge, 1995).

8. Marilyn Friedman, "The Social Self and the Partiality Debates," in *Feminist Ethics*, ed. Claudia Card (Lawrence, Kan.: University of Kansas Press, 1991), 165.

9. Claudia Card, *The Unnatural Lottery: Character and Moral Luck* (Philadelphia: Temple University Press, 1996), 66.

10. Martha Fineman, "Masking Dependency: The Political Role of Family Rhetoric," in *The Subject of Care: Feminist Perspectives on Dependency* (Lanham, MD: Rowman & Littlefield, 2002), 215.

11. Eva Feder Kittay, "When Caring is Just and Justice is Caring: Justice and Mental Retardation," in *The Subject of Care: Feminist Perspectives on Dependency*, ed. Ellen K. Feder and Eva Feder Kittay (Lanham, MD: Rowman & Littlefield, 2002), 268.

12. Ellen K. Feder and Eva Feder Kittay, "Introduction," in *The Subject of Care*, ed. Ellen K. Feder and Eva Feder Kittay (2002), 10.

13. Jennifer Nedelsky, "Reconceiving Autonomy," *Yale Journal of Law and Feminism* 1, no.1 (1989): 12.

14. Val Plumwood, *Feminism and the Mastery of Nature* (London and New York: Routledge, 1993), 256-258; Warwick Fox, qtd. in Michael J. Zimmerman, "Rethinking the Heidegger - Deep Ecology Relationship," *Environmental Ethics: An Interdisciplinary Journal Dedicated to the Philosophical Aspects of Environmental Problems* 15, no. 3 (Fall 1993): 195-224.

15. Plumwood (1993), 262.

16. Ferguson (1995), 379.

17. Simon Wiesenthal, *The Sunflower* (New York: Schocken Books, 1969), 15.

18. Claudia Card, "Pluralist Lesbian Separatism," in *Lesbian Philosophies and Cultures*, ed. Jeffner Allen (Albany: State University of New York Press, 1990), 128.

19. Trudy Govier, *Forgiveness and Revenge* (London and New York: Routledge, 2002), Chapter 5, especially 92-95.

20. Robin May Schott, "The Atrocity Paradigm and the Concept of Forgiveness," *Hypatia* 19, no.4 (2004): 205-206.

21. MacLachlan (2005).

22. Claudia Card, "The Atrocity Paradigm Revisited," *Hypatia* 19, no.4 (2004): 210-211.

23. Griswold (2007), xvi, 38.

24. Schott (2004), 206.

25. Virginia Held, *Feminist Morality: Transforming Culture, Society and Politics* (Chicago: University of Chicago Press, 1993), 77.

26. Held (1993), 81.

27. Nancy DeCourville, Kathryn Belicki and Michelle M. Green, "Subjective Experiences of Forgiveness in a Community Sample: Implications for Understanding Forgiveness and Its Consequences," in *Women's Reflections on the Complexities of Forgiveness*, ed. Wanda Malcolm, Nancy DeCourville, and Kathryn Belicki (New York and London: Routledge, 2008), 17.

28. Haber (1998), 54.

29. Joram Haber, *Forgiveness* (Savage, MD: Rowman & Littlefield, 1991), 3.

30. Griswold (2007), 3, 6-12.

31. Aristotle, *Nicomachean Ethics* (EN), translated by Terence Irwin (Indianapolis, Ind.: Hackett Publishing, 1985), Book IV, Chapter 5, 1126a4-5.

32. Aristotle, *EN*, Book IV, Chapter 5, 1126a1. See also Nancy Potter, "Is Refusing to Forgive a Vice?" in *Feminists Doing Ethics*, ed. Joanne Waugh (Lanham, MD: Rowman & Littlefield, 2001), 135-150; Potter is one of the few philosophers of forgiveness to attend to this (147).

33. I should add that Aristotle himself does not call the virtue of being angry in the right way, time, etc. the 'virtue of anger,' per se. He refers to it as one of the virtues with no name. Thanks to Paula Gottlieb for this valuable reminder.

34. Aristotle, *EN*, Bk. IX, ch. 3, 1165b, 10-38.

35. Aristotle, *EN*, Bk. V, 7, 1134a17.

36. Aristotle, *EN*, Bk. VI, ch. 1, 1155a1-7.

37. Joanna North, "The 'Ideal' of Forgiveness: A Philosopher's Exploration," in *Exploring Forgiveness*, ed. Robert D. Enright and Joanna North (Madison, WI: University of Wisconsin Press, 1998), 15-34. Donald Shriver, "Is There Forgiveness in Politics?" in *Exploring Forgiveness*, ed. Enright and North (1998), 131-149.

38. Walker (2006), 27.

39. Joanna North, "An Obligation to Forgive?" *The World of Forgiveness: An International Forgiveness Institute Periodical* 4, no.2, Issue 14 (2001): 31; she cites David B. Annis, "The Meaning, Value, and Duties of Friendship," *American Philosophical Quarterly* 24, no. 4 (1987): 352.

40. Robert D. Enright, Suzanne Freedman, and Julio Rique, "The Psychology of Interpersonal Forgiveness," in *Exploring Forgiveness*, ed. Enright and North (1998), 48.

41. Martha Minow, *Between Vengeance and Forgiveness* (Boston: Beacon Press, 1999), chapter 1.

42. Griswold (2007), 8-9.

43. Nancy Tuana, among others, points out that on Aristotle's account, whether free or slave, a woman must be ruled by a man, and her excellences are those of industry; she will not have the leisure the "higher" excellences required, or be the true, that is, the equal, friend, to a man to whom she is necessarily subject and mentally inferior. Nancy Tuana, *Woman and the History of Philosophy* (New York: Paragon House, 1992), 28-30.

44. Aristotle, *EN*, Book IV, Chapter 5, 1125bff.

45. Jerome Neu, "To Understand All Is to Forgive All – Or Is It?" in *Before Forgiving*, Sharon Lamb and Jeffrie Murphy, eds., (Oxford: Oxford University Press, 2002), 22.

46. Tuana (1992), Chapter One.

47. Aristotle, *EN*, Bk. II, ch. 7.

48. Lynne Tirrell, "Sexual Dualism and Women's Self-Creation: On the Advantages and Disadvantages of Reading Nietzsche for Feminists," in *Nietzsche and the Feminine*, ed. Peter J. Burgard (Charlottesville: University Press of Virginia, 1994), 212.

49. Friedrich Nietzsche, *The Gay Science* (GS), translated and edited by Walter Kaufmann (New York: Vintage, 1974), GS, Book 5, §363.

50. Nietzsche (1974), GS, Book 5, §361.

51. Barbara Helm, "Combating Misogyny? Responses to Nietzsche by Turn-of-the-Century German Feminists," *Journal of Nietzsche Studies* 27 (2004): 67.

52. Friedrich Nietzsche, *On the Genealogy of Morality* (GM), first published 1887, trans. M. Clark and A. J. Swensen (Indianapolis, IN: Hackett, 1998), Essay 1, §7.

53. Nietzsche (1998), GM, Essay 2, §20.

54. Tirrell (1994), 212.

55. Friedrich Nietzsche, "Beyond Good and Evil" (BGE), in *Basic Writings of Nietzsche*, translated and edited by Walter Kaufmann (New York: The Modern Library, 1992), Part Seven, #219.

56. See Jeffrie Murphy, "Preface," in *Before Forgiving*, ed. by Lamb and Murphy (2002), x, and Jeffrie Murphy, *Getting Even: Forgiveness and its Limits* (Oxford: Oxford University Press, 2003), 17.

57. Enright et al (1998), 49.

58. Alan Schrift, "On the Gynecology of Morals: Nietzsche and Cixous on the Logic of the Gift," in *Nietzsche and the Feminine*, ed. Peter J. Burgard (Charlottesville: University of Virginia Press, 1994), 211, 217.

59. Nietzsche (1998), GM, 475.

60. Virginia Woolf, "Professions for Women," *Collected Essays* (London: Hogarth Press, 1966), 168, 170.

61. Fay Weldon, *Female Friends* (London: Heinemann, 1975), qtd. in Murphy and Hampton (1988), Murphy (2003).

62. Walker (2006), 181; Pamela Hieronymi, "Articulating an Uncompromising Forgiveness," *Philosophy and Phenomenological Research* 62, no.3 (2001): 551n39.

63. Hannah Arendt, "Irreversibility and the Power to Forgive," *The Human Condition* (Chicago: University of Illinois Press, 1958/1998), 240.

64. Arendt (1958/1998), 241.

65. Arendt (1958/1998), 237.

66. Griswold (2007), 14-15.

67. Haber (1991, 107) also notices that psychologists often focus on the consequential benefits of forgiveness; Murphy notes the celebration in popular culture of forgiveness, especially self-forgiveness; see Jeffrie Murphy, "Jean Hampton on Immorality, Self-Hatred, and Self-Forgiveness," *Philosophical Studies* 89 (1998): 216, n.3.

68. Enright (1998), 47.

69. Enright (1998), 48.

70. Beverly Flanigan, "Forgivers and the Unforgivable," in *Exploring Forgiveness*, ed. Enright and North (1998), 104.

71. Richard Fitzgibbons, "The Cognitive and Emotive Uses of Forgiveness in the Treatment of Anger," *Psychotherapy* 23 (1986): 630.

72. Flanigan (1998), 102.

73. Fitzgibbons (1998), 63.

74. Fitzgibbons (1998, 67) discusses this, and Flanigan (1998) addresses this throughout; both argue that forgiveness is, all things considered, good for clients whether it results in absence of pain or presence of love and compassion for wrongdoers.

75. Gayle L. Reed and Robert D. Enright, "The Effects of Forgiveness Therapy on Depression, Anxiety, and Posttraumatic Stress for Women After Spousal Emotional Abuse," *Journal of Consulting and Clinical Psychology* 74, no.5 (October 2006), Special issue: Benefit-Finding, 920-929. Participants in the interdisciplinary conference *Forgiveness: Probing the Boundaries* (Salzburg, Austria: March 7-9, 2008; forthcoming conference proceedings in 2009) discussed the extent to which Enright's EFI is reliable, vs. the extent to which forgiveness interventions in therapeutic contexts have the desired beneficial outcomes, but indeed, the conclusion was that both seem true, and while discussion of EFI reliability and aimed-for outcomes can blur, evidence for both is mounting. For a more skeptical discussion of the relation between forgiveness and women's health, see Kathleen Lawler-Row and Kimberly A. Reed, "Forgiveness and Health in Women," in *Women's Reflections on the Complexities of Forgiveness*, ed. Wanda Malcolm, Nancy DeCourville, and Kathryn Belicki (New York and London: Routledge, 2008). See also Kristina Coop Gordon, Shacunda Burton, and Laura Porter, "Predicting the Intentions of Women in Domestic Violence Shelters to Return to Partners: Does Forgiveness Play a Role?" *Journal of Family Psychology* 18, no.2 (2004): 331–338; the answer to the titular question is, sadly, that indeed forgiveness is a strong predictor of returning to abusive spouses.

76. McCollough (2000), Worthington and Scherer (2004).

77. Lawler-Row and Piferi (2006).

78. Haber (1991), p.108.

79. Ibid.

80. Ibid.

81. Emphasis his. Ibid., p.114n.

82. Michael E. McCullough, Kenneth Pargament, and Carl E. Thoresen, ed., *Forgiveness: Theory, Research and Practice* (New York: The Guilford Press, 2000); Kerrie James, "The interactional process of forgiveness and responsibility: A critical assessment of the family therapy literature," in *Hope and despair in narrative and family therapy: Adversity, forgiveness and reconciliation*, ed. Carmel Flaskas, Imelda McCarthy, and Jim Sheehan (New York: Routledge/Taylor & Francis Group, 2007), 127-138.

83. Bishop Joseph Butler, Sermon IX, "Upon Forgiveness of Injuries," *Fifteen Sermons* (Charlottesville, VA: Ibis Publishing, 1987, edition previously published by Robert Carter & Brothers, New York, 1860; Henry Sidgwick, *The Methods of Ethics*, 7th edition, Forward by John Rawls (Indianapolis, Cambridge: Hackett Publishing Co., first published 1907, 1981), 323.

84. Minow (1999, 11) provides the observation that those one may think of as aggressors in conflicts like Bosnia and Rwanda see themselves as victims of "perceived past harms," sometimes real, sometimes propaganda-induced, sometimes a complicated mix of the actual and perceived. This insight can be extended to include conflicts here at home. Consider the justification Timothy McVeigh offered for detonating a building and killing innocent people; he

identified with the victims of the FBI attack on cult leader David Koresh's compound in Waco, Texas; see Brian Cox, "Television: The Face of Evil," *Guardian* (London), May 21, 2001: Features, 16.

85. Susan Jacoby, *Wild Justice: The Evolution of Revenge* (New York: Harper & Row, 1983), 352.

86. Minow (1999), 17-18.

87. Ker Munthit, "Khmer Rouge leaders say they're sorry about deaths," *Chicago Sun-Times*, Wed., Dec. 30, 1998, News, 26.

Chapter Three

Feminist Ethics and Differences

At the end of "Forgiveness and Feminism," Joram Haber laments that "feminist ethics . . . is not action-guiding in the sense many of us demand of an adequate ethic. Specifically, even if we grant that considerations of care, particularity, affection, and relationships have the priority that feminists insist upon, we are still left wondering when we should and should not forgive."[1] To remove some of that wonder, I attend to what philosophers of feminism have said about forgiveness and related moral responses in relationships, in the interests of establishing what might guide victims' actions. An adequate ethic must do more than guide action, however. Many clearly action-guiding moral theories are inadequate in other ways, especially insofar as they seem disconnected from practical moral experience. Of more interest to me is the nature of forgiveness as a moral act—that is, what happens, and what ought to happen, when we extend forgiveness to another.

In what follows, I argue that feminist articulations of relational ontology accomplish at least four different tasks at which traditional models of forgiveness often fail. My last chapter included arguments for a relational ontology of the self, in order to advance the argument that (1) feminist frameworks challenge the atomism present in the dominant discourse, arguing that we are *constituted* by our relations, and some feminists do so in a way that still manages to avoid the problem of women seemingly disappearing into their relations. In this chapter, I add that (2) in addition to calling attention to our relatedness, those feminist theorists who evaluate the relations themselves in order to make ethical recommendations add a missing, but essential, element to accounts of forgiveness that consider the well-being of the one forgiving separately from the nature of her relations. (3) In doing (2), we discover that feminist research on women's anger is enlightening for what it tells us about women's well-being in relations; to the extent that women are likely to maldevelop with respect to proper anger, we are inclined to identify with our wrongdoers to our detriment. (4) Feminist theories that are otherwise disparate share in common an attentiveness to the experience of women and to self-defining narratives, which philosophy overall often lacks. In light of these four critical, though neglected, aspects of forgiveness, a model of forgiveness accommodating of complexity should be explicitly feminist and multi-dimensional.

Relations Constitute Identities

A look at the highly influential work of Nel Noddings is in order, since she famously articulates what Haber calls a care-based theory, and argues our relations to others are essentially constitutive of persons. In *Caring: A Feminine Approach to Ethics and Moral Education*, Noddings cites the work of feminist psychologists such as Carol Gilligan who argued in the late 1970s and early 1980s that the moral development of some females differs from the moral development of some males.[2] As a result, men typically value autonomy, rights, disconnection from others, and independence, while seeing other persons and intimate relationships as dangers, obstacles to pursuing those values. Some women's moral concerns, in contrast, involve valuing intimacy, responsibility, relationships, and caring for others, while seeing autonomy as "the illusory and dangerous quest," in tension with the values of attachment.[3] Noddings appeals to the neglected importance of the values of attachment to argue that the relation between a person in a position of being the one-caring and the person cared-for should be the focus of how we think about right and wrong. She argues against using generalized moral principles to decide what we should do on the grounds that they ignore the particular relationship in question. Forgiveness, like caring or patience, "is not in itself a virtue," on her account, but "must be assessed in the context of caring situations. . . . The fulfillment of virtue is both in me and in the other."[4]

Regarding instances of forgiveness in particular, she says that what makes forgiveness appropriate depends on the relation between two individuals, and any appeal to *a priori* precepts that one ought to forgive or ought not ritualizes forgiveness in a way that allows us to see it as somehow existing separately from the person we would forgive. To illustrate this she refers to the predicament described by Simon Wiesenthal in *The Sunflower*, a memoir in which he received the account of a dying Nazi soldier's war crimes against Jews, while Simon himself was a concentration camp prisoner. Noddings suggests that Wiesenthal reduced his dilemma to one involving a "right to pity" and a "right to forgive."[5] Noddings argues that in seeing his dilemma this way, Wiesenthal fails to respond in a morally adequate way, by reducing the other to a symbol with rights, rather than entering into a relation with him as an individual in pain.

"Thus we can see that ritual forgiveness involves the evil of separa-tion," she concludes.[6] If Haber is right that theories like Noddings's are not action guiding, he may be missing the point of such a theory of care; on Noddings's view it is a strength, not a weakness, that an ethic of care does not instruct one as to how to act prior to knowing the particulars of the rela-tion involved. In addition, Noddings's theory succeeds where Haber finds his own theory fails, in that it takes personal and intimate relations to be paradigmatic occasions of forgiveness; indeed, Noddings argues that for-giveness is not appropriate until one enters into such a personal relation. To the extent that Wiesenthal still saw the dying Karl as a symbol, a Nazi, or a mystery, he failed to enter into the sort of truly interpersonal encounter that Noddings requires for moral action. Although most forgiveness theorists, including me, would disagree that Wiesenthal didn't enter into an interper-sonal moral relationship with the soldier, she has in common with many theorists the position that forgiveness is inherently interpersonal, requiring face to face encounter, a position I do not necessarily share, but which highlights the importance of relationship.

Given Noddings's prioritization of the particular relationships between individuals who have encountered each other, her discussion of interper-sonal altruism turns out to be helpful in filling out her brief remarks on for-giveness, and clarifying how relations constitute identities. Noddings sug-gests that the life narrative of a nurse and midwife who loves helping others and cares what they think of her is an example of "beautiful altruism," call-ing it "a testimony to goodness far beyond the ordinary call of duty."[7] Key to understanding this concept of altruism and caring is the element of joy in one's affirmed connection to others. It is not the expectation that one will accomplish an altruistic act which brings the joy she describes. It is the ac-tual observation of one's efforts on others, the realization that she is con-nected to the world, which makes the altruist joyful. This is not the same as saying she "gets something out of it," as the colloquial egoist might say. On Noddings's account, the altruist is not expecting to get back a reward; rather, the altruist is joyful because she is reminded that she is not alone, she is acknowledged, and she is fulfilled.

More recently, Noddings has argued that the agent's fulfillment of connection, through giving acts like forgiveness and altruism, is compatible with taking care of oneself, rather than giving until it hurts, if only because no one could be a very effective altruist if she is exploited to the point of uselessness.[8] Caring involves the fulfillment of the giver and the other, whereas altruism is often described as having an absolute cost to the giver, who receives no benefit from her actions. Yet feminist theories have long argued that to the extent we're constituted by our relationships and identifi-cations with others, actions that prioritize those do not reduce to benefiting either the self or the other; our identities are bound up in others. Noddings's insights suggest that altruism is not just a moral or social good; it may be fundamental to the identities of women who identify altruistic motivations for forgiveness, and whose happiness is uniquely fulfilled by relation-affirming activity. Indeed, an implication of her later work is that for some, altruism is not only a motivation and an aspect of identity, but in addition, seeing its realization in the world and in others is what makes life worth living.

Noddings's language calls to mind the related arguments by Margaret Walker that forgiveness is indispensable to human relationships, and Claudia Card's argument for seeing evils as basic deprivations of that which is necessary to make a life decent. Although altruism may not make life worth living for everyone, the broader point that acknowledgement within relationships make life worth living is intuitively appealing. Most philosophers would agree that a life without any relationships is difficult to imagine, and their prevention or deprivation by culpable others would be a serious wrong, even evil. To the extent that a minimally good life is one with relationships at all, Walker's argument for seeing forgiveness as indispensable makes sense as a way to retain these necessary relationships. Recall Aristotle's argument that friendship is the greatest external good; it is hard to imagine a friendship of any duration with an utter absence of forgiveness. Considered this way, a relational paradigm yields clear value for forgiveness in one's life as a tool which functions to maintain minimally intimate relationships.

Yet on Walker's account, moral relationships are ubiquitous, and seem to be more diffuse than Noddings's interpersonal relationships entailing encounter; we stand in moral relationships with those we trust, those who trust us, those subject to our power and those to whom we are subject. It may be that all human beings therefore stand in moral relationships to all other human beings. Walker acknowledges that people in disparate power positions may refuse to recognize moral relationships, deny or distort them, but this is a moral failure within the relationship, and not a successful way to escape them. Walker's arguments for seeing us as enmeshed in webs of relations is convincing, so convincing that her argument for forgiveness as indispensable becomes less compelling. These are not all the sorts of intimate or friend relationships described by Noddings and Aristotle, and yet they are also the sorts of relationships that are inextricable from a life, or a good life. If I understand her correctly, then I stand in moral relationships with those who have political power over me, and those over whom I enjoy power, those who deliver my mail, and those who drive to work on the same highway I drive, those moneyed interests whom my legislators serve at my expense, and those unlike me who lose out at times when politicians pander to me with "middle-class tax cuts." In a globalized economy, my consumption patterns affect individuals across the world whom I will never meet, yet whose lives are affected by my choices as a citizen of the U.S., which consumes more resources than any other single country. What are we to say of our pervasive relationships? Which ones do we need, which constitute identities, and which require acknowledgement, which forgiveness?

In light of such questions, relationships may come to seem so innumerable they are uninteresting, or lack moral valence. Although I intend to portray them as indefinite, I do not wish to imply that relationships are therefore morally unimportant. Relationships, so conceived, are the preconditions of our existence, the moral universe in which we operate, and both acknowledged and unacknowledged relations constitute identities; indeed, what it means to say that I am a citizen of the country which consumes more of the world's resources than any other country is only sensible when taking into account relationships between all the world's countries and citizens. The relations that constitute identities include chosen and unchosen relations, those cared-for and recklessly abused, those with which we locate ourselves, and those with which others locate us.

To say we need relationships is to say something about only a subset of all our relations. It is impossible to be born into this world and not stand in relationship to its members; the relationships we *need* are those necessary to live, or as many philosophers emphasize, to live decently. Feminist philosophers have argued eloquently for the importance of our first relationships of dependency, including relations to parenting figures, care-laborers and educators. Philosophers who call attention to the social self further point to the necessity of political relationships; as authors from Hannah Arendt to Robin May Schott point out, dispossession of rights and government protection permits the exclusion of people from political and therefore human communities.[9] Affectional relationships with friends and family can preserve and foster our emotional lives, even acting, as Claudia Card says, as one's first line of defense, "a bulwark against a hostile world."[10] And as I argue in later chapters, relationships with oneself, or rather, with the multiplicity of one's fragmented selves, may be necessary to continuing to live, a truth more readily apparent to those who struggle to live with themselves.

It is easy to confuse those relationships we need with those relationships we want, a distinction which becomes important when talking about forgiveness. Erring on the side of discussing the interpersonal, we tend to focus on chosen relationships or unchosen family relations to which we thoughtfully commit ourselves. Yet the relationships we need are often neither interpersonal nor even desirable. Victims of sectarian or regional conflict who attempt forms of repair and reconciliation find that they need to find a way to live together, proceed into the future, whether they care for each other or wish the other's nonexistence, whether or not the members of different groups will even meet each other. Some sociopolitical relationships are those of reliance, and if members of safer and more privileged

groups do not find it intuitively correct that they need their impersonal political relationships, it may be because they believe that they have the
wealth and resources which permit them an independence from their own
geopolitical setting which most human beings don't enjoy.

Evaluating the Relations Themselves

It is worthwhile to note that we are social beings who need relationships.
Further, we must attend to what kinds of relationships are being maintained,
or to whether forgiveness is necessary to maintain or reestablish those
worth rebuilding. The ethics of forgiveness may differ depending on
whether we are talking about intimate relationships or formal relationships,
between adults, between children, or an adult and a child, between those
with roughly equal personal or political power or between individuals with
notable differences in social privilege. The responsibility to maintain a relationship may also depend on whether the relationship is chosen or unchosen; most of us do not feel as free to sever relations with family as with
friends or coworkers.

Given the following feminist criticisms of Noddings's theory, Haber
perhaps overstates the case when he says that care-based considerations
typify a feminist approach to morality, if he means that theories like Noddings's embody the essential characteristics of feminist ethics. Noddings's
own subtitle indicates that hers is "a feminine approach," and critics within
feminist theory question this commitment to valuing the traditionally feminine role of care-giver; at times we are better off evaluating the relationships themselves than presuming we ought to enter into and maintain these
relations.

Claudia Card, for example, criticizes Noddings's care ethic for "valor-
izing relationships better dissolved. . . . Issues of justice often involve
wrongful boundary crossing rather than failures of connection."[11] Marilyn
Friedman rejects the notion of separation as evil, and notes that "it is important to distinguish between individualistic behaviors and traits that harm
other persons from those that do not."[12] Elsewhere she has said of forgiveness in particular that "the pressures on a woman to forgive and forget her
injuries, to kiss and make up, for example, in those wife-battering cases that
manage to reach family court, are infamous."[13]

Sarah Hoagland, in observing that altruism is a feminine virtue, says,
"As one might suspect, altruism accrues to those with lesser power."[14] Despite Noddings's arguments for taking care of oneself in order to continue
maintaining relationships, my sense that the altruistic woman is in danger
of being used remains; in the individualistic and self-interested culture I
described previously, the egoist stands to benefit greatly from someone

with the other-directed "habit of the heart." As Sarah Hoagland argues, "the feminine is not an antidote to the masculine. Rather, it is a supporter and nurturer of the masculine. . . . [In] a patriarchal world we need something far more radical;" Hoagland concludes that among other things, an ethic of care "must have a vision of, if not a program for, change."[15]

It's possible, despite the fact that we ought to evaluate the relevant relationship, that the project of evaluating relationships is itself a source of unease to women who have traditionally accepted feminine roles like that of forgiver. Psychologists note that women are more likely to be researchers of forgiveness, and more likely to volunteer for forgiveness research, but the interest in debating the worth of the relationships in need of repair is comparatively low. In contexts of physical violence, especially, the need for such reflection is not matched by the quantity of available data; in contrast to studies arguing that forgiveness repairs relationships and may even be necessary for lifelong commitments, "only a few scholars have countered that forgiveness may be maladaptive because the offended individual may be placed at risk of repeated harm."[16] Not coincidentally, psychologists who call attention to the relationship within which one forgives also note that scholars' definitions do not match well at all with the understanding of lay-people who express interest in forgiveness, a note repeated in multiple recent studies. For example, subjects of studies asked, "Is reconciliation a necessary part of forgiveness?" more often answer maybe or yes than no. "This tendency to blur forgiveness and reconciliation is not just observed in questionnaire responses," as authors arguing the dangers of empathy say, noting that in one study, "forgiveness was the strongest predictor of an intention to return to an abusive partner in women living in a domestic violence shelter."[17]

Because feminists are well aware that we are accustomed to being caregivers, including what Haber called "a proclivity in women to forgive" which works to our detriment, relevant feminist work often centers on when to refuse forgiveness; the answer has much to do with the relationship of power between the agent in the position to forgive and her wrongdoer. Judith Boss argues, for instance, that recommending women's forgiveness of their unrepentant male abusers legitimizes, or at least fails to challenge, the patriarchal structure that gives men power over women.[18] Martha Minow extends this worry in her discussion of forgiveness in political contexts, in which she argues that forgiveness should not be presumed good if it "forecloses the communal response, the acknowledgment of harm, that vengeance, and indeed justice, demand. . . . Forgiveness is a power held by the victimized, not a right to be claimed."[19]

If moral recommendations regarding forgiveness can only be made when we first evaluate the relation in question, this suggests that forgiveness itself is not prima facie good. That persons need intimate relations, and that forgiveness is essential to maintaining these relations, entails nothing with respect to when and whether we ought to forgive. I argue that forgiveness is only as valuable as is the relation it maintains or repairs. This coheres with the spirit if not the letter of Noddings's point when she suggests, as said above, that forgiveness is not in itself a virtue. She argued that forgiveness cannot be discussed as a virtue separately from seeing it as essentially involving a relationship; I am adding to this that forgiveness cannot be discussed as a good separately from evaluating the quality of the relation involved.

What makes forgiveness appropriate, then, depends on the nature and the quality of the relation between the forgiver and the forgiven. This is arguably compatible with the positions of those theorists who say forgiveness is good when consistent with self-respect, but I suggest occasions to forgive where one's self-respect is present are not always occasions wherein the relation between the two parties merits forgiveness. Summarizing the documentary *Long Night's Journey into Day*, journalist Kevin Thomas observes, "Widows of two anti-apartheid activists do understand why Eric Taylor, a white former security forces officer who participated in the murders of [their husbands] would seek forgiveness. The women want to hear what he has to say in his confession, but they forthrightly state that they see no reason they should be moved to forgive him for the pain and loss he caused."[20] The women's own separate senses of self-respect do not seem threatened. If anything, their refusals to forgive him indicate the opposite, that their self-respect is intact and buttresses their belief that they are right to refuse him. Therefore, although theorists like Haber, Jeffrie Murphy, and Margaret Holmgren seem intuitively correct that forgiveness in the absence of self-respect is dangerous, or even sometimes morally wrong, the presence of self-respect does not yet indicate to us that forgiveness is the right thing to do. The decisions of the two widows to refuse forgiveness seem correct when we consider their position in society relative to the white police officer, and not their self-respect. These are two members of a minority group whose oppression cannot be said to be yet over, especially in light of the unease many feel about the amnesty granted to many confessors at the Truth and Reconciliation Commission meetings.

Those injured parties in a position of power relative to their wrongdoers, on the other hand, may have more of an obligation to extend forgiveness. As children and adolescents, for instance, we need to believe that our parents won't eternally resent us for our culpable wrongdoing, especially as we are vulnerable to them in part because our relationship with our parents is unchosen; our inability to leave the relationship is part of the power our parents have over our well-being. In a society which feminists have rightly pointed out expects heterosexuality and marriage, and fails to defend women in battering relationships, a woman's relation to her battering husband is arguably unchosen in many ways as well. On my analysis, this mitigates her responsibility to forgive her abuser even after she recovers her self-respect.

A new direction to take evaluation of these relations is reflected in Simon Wiesenthal's comment on his own experience with being asked forgiveness by a dying Nazi soldier, even as Wiesenthal himself was a prisoner of Nazi Germany. At the critical moment in his narrative, he reflects, "Two men who had never known each other had been brought together. . . . One asks the other for help. But the other was himself helpless and able to do nothing for him."[21] These two met in circumstances, severely constrained as they were, in which neither of them were clearly in a position of power over the other. It seems that in one sense, the soldier was not a threat to him, and if so Wiesenthal might be in a position to extend forgiveness. Yet Wiesenthal implies otherwise, that if the relation in which two stand is one of powerlessness to powerlessness, this is an obstacle to forgiveness which bars anyone from morally requiring it of the victim.

This has serious repercussions for a discussion of political forgiveness between groups of people. Setting aside for now whether groups can forgive, we can think of peoples during and after terrible conflicts who stood in that powerless-to-powerless relation that Wiesenthal and the soldier exhibit, further complicated when neither side is unambiguously innocent. As noted in Chapter One, these are occasions in which both sides can also seem themselves as the victims of wrongdoing. If Wiesenthal is correct, then still-suffering, rebuilding groups always have an out for saying no one can expect them to forgive, and cycles of resentment and retaliation can continue indefinitely. In these cases, perhaps individuals and groups in this relation must first commit to seeing each other restored to positions of safety and empowerment, in which neither is the other's subordinate. Taking steps to see justice done may aid in the change in that relation.

Yet this may not be possible without these persons or groups separating from each other in some ways in the meantime. Minow argues that "refusing relationships [is] especially justifiable after mass violence."[22] Although I find the language of refusing relationships to be too close to refusal of bare recognition, I agree that in situations where individuals and groups are fairly equally powerless, they may be best served by putting their relations on a more formal footing until they separately recover their sense of identity and agency. As noted above in the first section, this need not entail throwing up a wall between the parties and having no relationship; Card describes separatism as not precluding communication, but structuring it. In examples like South Africa's Truth and Reconciliation Committee, formal dialogue between individuals who previously lived in the same community actually facilitated communication.[23] If Carol Gilligan and Susan Hekman are right that our relations, our psychological, identity-building connections to each other, are the product of dialogue, then formal discourses may be necessarily prior to either reconciliation or forgiveness, which do not entail each other. We must have relationships, to be able to repair or maintain them. And I would further add that we must see to it we have the capacity or the potential capacity to be able to contribute to repair, before we enter into negotiations of relationships. However, this is not to say we must completely recover or even feel much better; on the contrary, in what follows, I argue for the compatibility of relationship-repair with the presence of anger.

Recovering Anger

Feminist theory contributes greatly to the necessary paradigm shift in moral theory from talking about atomistic selves to talking about relational selves, but feminist philosophers have not played the most prominent role in the study of forgiveness as a tool of relation-maintaining. However, the presence of feminist theorists in analyses of anger is more notable, at least in comparison, as they comprise almost a quarter of the monographs and articles on anger in the last fifty years. The latter fact suggests a possible reason for the absence of feminism in forgiveness, which has to do with the necessary conditions for forgiveness even in those relations we find worth maintaining.

In many of the traditional models of forgiveness I considered in the preceding chapters, to be able to forgive wrongs we must first recognize that we have been wronged, and identify ourselves as wronged parties. I showed that in the influential works of Murphy, Haber and Holmgren, this process includes having the appropriate emotional response, such as anger, consistent with what self-respect requires. I also suggested that for Aristotle forgiveness may be an aspect of showing appropriate anger, and Butler's account included the necessity of resentment in pursuing justice. However, the available evidence shows that women have been, and are still, socialized to suppress righteous anger. As early as the age of 5, girls are already socialized to suppress their anger, or at the least to give less expression to it; a group that learns anger is not acceptable is more likely to engage in overcoming it through forgiveness as well as other methods.[24]

Moreover, learning to recognize and express anger at a young age is an important source of self-identity and autonomy; it is the "alarm system" to even young children that they are bumping up against something in the outside world which hurts them and which they have to defend themselves against.[25] In other words, it is through practice with anger that we develop a sense of our own boundaries, of where we stop and others begin. Yet girls are not encouraged to recognize or express their own anger to the extent

that boys are, and the level of anger expression tolerated of young and adolescent boys is significantly higher than the level tolerated of young and
adolescent girls.[26] As a result, the very sense of self necessary to satisfying
the criteria for proper forgiveness, including the criterion that we recognize
a wrong has been done to us, is inhibited in even adult women. Most
women learn to place more emphasis on the feelings of others than on their
own, and in their efforts to avoid conflict blur the boundaries between
themselves and others.[27]

These observations at least bear out a reason that feminist theorists
have not rushed to discuss forgiveness in the past. If girls are socialized to
suppress or not express anger, and anger is necessary for developing a sense
of identity, then the work of building a sense of self must be necessarily
prior to overcoming one's feeling that one has been wronged. Clearly much
work needs to be done if women are to recover a sense of righteous anger,
rather than turning their anger inward and finding fault most often in themselves.[28] Gilligan thus identifies anger as "the political emotion par excellence – the bellwether of oppression, injustice, bad treatment, the clue that
something is wrong in the relational surround."[29]

The complexity of this difficulty for models of forgiveness is further
deepened when we consider the evidence that girls who don't express or
even recognize their own anger become women who suppress and internal-
ize anger until it becomes, for some, an ongoing stress fed by day-to-day
injustices.[30] As a result, the ultimate expression of one's anger outwardly
reflects "a long, slow accumulation of responses to everyday occur-
rences."[31] Given this, we need to reconsider the suggestion of those philosophers who say that forgiveness is called for when one's anger is "unreasonable," "excessive," or "out of proportion" to the wrong done. These
descriptions generally refer to a time-slice in which one's anger is seen as
the result of a particular event, and has a specific object. But this standard
ignores the context in which object-specific anger occurs. In other words, it
may be mistaken to identify anger at a particular event unreasonable, when
the same person has suppressed her anger at similar events, by society or by
the same person, over years or even over a lifetime. This hearkens back to
our discussion of women's experience with bitterness, and brings to light a
fairly unconsidered aspect of wrongdoing in forgiveness literature, which is
that bitterness or newly expressed anger can have as its object more than an
individual occasion. In light of Murphy's argument that forgiveness is appropriate "when our anger has become unreasonable," consider Susan Griffin's image of the woman as Volcano, losing containment of her anger at
past harms.

That she made them feel guilty. That guilt kept them from moving.
She was bringing them to tears, they said. . . . Be Fair: "You are

unreasonable," they told her. But she answered them, "You have called me unreasonable before.". . . She was certain she would explode. Yes, she said, she had grown unreasonable.[32]

Without denying Murphy's point that anger can be unreasonable, Griffin's image prompts us to question how we define unreasonableness. Models of forgiveness usually describe our forgiving individual acts in a time-slice which starts with a particular wrongful act and ends with the victim's response. Yet the suggestion borne of women's experience is that our anger can be the result of more than a single, particular wrongful act; bitterness can have as its object series of acts or even relationships themselves.

This may be good news, however, if the off-putting nature of the subject of forgiveness, for feminist theorists in particular, is that it requires us to let go of our anger. In light of the possibility that anger is not discreet and limited to individual acts, perhaps we need not think of forgiveness as requiring us to let go of anger. Indeed, I wish to suggest in the next chapter that the speech act, "I forgive you," is an instance of forgiving that is compatible with still experiencing angry feelings. If anything, we may need to achieve greater awareness of our ongoing anger in order to be able to simultaneously forgive particular wrongful acts. Susan Brison notes that her own experience of articulating her first-person experience with a group-based trauma, sexual violence, involves continually identifying with different groups depending on which parts of her narratives, and which parts of herself, she is attempting to narrate.[33] She describes our social construction as occurring through group-based narratives, arguing, "To the extent that we say anything about ourselves, we are using language to categorize ourselves as members of groups."[34] She concludes that if our identities are constructed through group-based narratives, then "the self is not a single, unified, coherent entity."[35] Our multidimensional and fragmented selves, I add, can accommodate anger and forgiveness at the same time, and allow us to tell stories which would add richness to going accounts of forgiveness.

My emphasis so far has been on women gaining greater facility with identifying and expressing anger, but of course, anger is interpersonal as well as intrapersonal, and acknowledgement of anger from within is not always adequate to the task of rectifying harm. Feminist philosophers have been articulate, as well, about the necessity for our anger to receive recognition from our offenders and from witnesses. As Marilyn Frye argues, anger requires "uptake," which further recognizes that one has the right, the standing, and good reasons to be angry.[36] Feminists know this conundrum well, especially in a culture in which the phrase, "angry feminist," is seen as redundant, another way to deny that anger is appropriate, by implying that it is so thoroughgoing it cannot be justified. From the point of view which centers the standard of a reasonable man, the burden of justification is on the angry woman to show good reason for her anger, and uptake is anterior to the presentation of evidence. Centering a feminist perspective, however, would require a rather different direction of attention; if women's experiences and women's narrative were a starting point of reasoning about anger, then uptake would be a required precondition.

Narrative: Attending to Women's Experience

I presume most philosophers would agree that narrative is not central to the analytic tradition; since that tradition dominates the philosophical literature on forgiveness, I claim further that narrative is not central to most conceptual analyses of forgiveness. In saying this, I do not mean to claim that narratives are entirely absent. On the contrary, in Chapter One I identified three often-repeated examples: a mother forgiving injuries to her son, a sexually betrayed wife forgiving her wayward husband, and the abused wife forgiving her abuser (that they are married seems a requisite feature). These three examples of questionably valuable forgiveness may constitute what Hilde Lindemann Nelson calls master narratives, "the stories found lying about in our culture that serve as summaries of socially shared understandings."[37] Although the three standard examples above are usually posed as thought-experiments rather than stories, clichés rarely fleshed out with comparison to cases of lived experience, I suggest that philosophers use them so often because they are both socially shared in the wider culture, and reinforcing of common understandings in philosophical subculture. Master narratives are not necessarily lived accounts of actual moral experience. As Lindemann describes them, "master narratives are often archetypal, consisting of stock plots and readily identifiable character types. . . . As the repository of common norms," master narratives can include "foundation myths, . . . fairy tales, landmark court cases," and even "movie classics."[38] Because master narratives inform, and, I would add, limit, our moral imaginations, they can enable "dismissive forces and preservative forces," contributing to oppression, though not all master narratives do this.[39]

This is not to suggest that the many philosophers who employ the standard examples are bent on oppressing others. As I have argued, they may employ the dominant discourse (typically Kantian and occasionally consequentialist) and the three examples in the interests of offering a genderless account, though not, I find, successfully. Yet whether intentionally employed or not, such standard examples do seem to have dismissive and preservative effects; the heteronormative habit of referring to married heterosexual couples, for example, seems guilty of reverting to "the stories found lying about," and simultaneously limits our moral imaginations even as the authors seemingly forswear the centrality of gender in the same accounts. Such narrative habits are also dismissive of reports to the contrary, or in Lindemann's terms, counterstories; many accounts of forgiveness that identify necessary conditions for the term argue that common uses of the expression which do not meet their conditions are instances of pseudo-forgiveness, disingenuous, non-genuine even when sincerely given, or forgiveness only in a metaphorical sense.

Yet many stories, especially women's stories, of forgiveness regularly transgress the necessary and sufficient conditions for forgiveness in prevailing accounts. I'm not suggesting we commit the fallacy of appealing to the masses, but if we can, we should avoid developing analyses of moral expressions that reflect so many people's experiences so badly. I argue that theorists have put the cart before the horse; that is to say, the disconnect between philosophy and experience, at least in the study of forgiveness, stems in part from constructing conditions for conveying forgiveness in the utter absence of narratives, or indeed any consideration of the socio-historical context in which forgiveness occurs, and then construing those narratives as mistaken or not genuine instances of the moral expression. If we attend to the social and historical context in which forgiveness comes to have its meaning(s), then women's narratives make more sense as the result of learning to forgive as women in Euro-American and predominantly Christian culture. Women's narratives can shed light on the current moral climate in which we say, "I forgive you," and their narratives can contribute to constructing a better account of what it means to convey forgiveness. Working up analytic accounts of forgiveness, or any moral practice, in the absence of narratives which may helpfully reflect the historical roots of the term, results in a problematic disjunct between the philosophical definition and the meaning the word actually has for many of the individuals who do the moral acts in question. Better accounts of the meanings of moral expressions like, "I forgive you," can include analyses of the narratives of moral agents, and provide insight into the function of such moral expressions

On those occasions when women appear in thought-experiments in forgiveness literature—in those three standard, belabored examples—we find not first-person narrative, but usually arguments that in cases like these forgiving is either the morally wrong thing to do, or is disingenuous and so not really forgiveness. The latter can mean either that the woman involved is lying in order to protect herself, telling her wrongdoer what he wants to hear in order to restore the peace, or that this example of "forgiveness" fails analytically; if forgiveness is the emotional transformation that follows appropriate resentment once one's self-worth is recovered, then betrayed or abused wives who "forgive" without seemingly exhibiting resentment or full self-worth are by definition not really forgiving.

It is entirely possible that some women respond to sexual betrayal or domestic abuse with lies or unintentional disingenuousness. Further, I agree that forgiveness is not the best response to either wrong when one fails to get properly angry or to recover one's own sense of self-worth. Yet to assume these are all cases of not really forgiving doesn't seem respectful of women's agency. If nothing else, this evaluation falls short of taking seriously what women convey when they express forgiveness to wrongdoers we'd rather they resented.

Consider, for instance, the following story in light of the argument by Thomas Hill that a hypothetical "deferential wife" who waives her rights in order to devote herself to her husband is morally wrong to do such things as forgive every injury with no thought for her own welfare. A (non-hypothetical) woman who was insulted by the man she was seeing decided that for once, instead of forgiving or apologizing for provoking him, she would insult him in kind "in a spontaneous reversal tactic."[40] His response included "something about ramming his fist down my throat." It brought home to her that she usually forgave unrepentant wrongdoers because "almost always getting along with men involves not reacting to their sexism. One can survive by being submissive and live knowing one's own cowardice, or fight back each instance as it occurs, with the inevitable inconvenience, psychological battering and loss of connection."[41] Nevertheless, she did not conclude that her past forgiving wasn't really forgiving, nor is it obvious that forgiving in these cases wasn't best for her own welfare.

Consider the woman from Bosnia who gave up hating her torturers because "hatred is exhausting," and found comfort in the realization, "I am not like them."[42] Consider too the story of the mother of an abducted girl who received a call from the still-at-large kidnapper, during which she forgave him, asked what she could do to help him, and caused him to break down and weep. "As desperate as I was for Susie's return, I realized I also wanted to reach and help this man," she says.[43] Listening to what women say who forgive when it seems unwarranted may not reveal universally satisfying justifications for their actions, but can point to alternative reasons for forgiving which the usual conceptions of forgiveness do not know how to accommodate. Yet account for it we should, even if we argue they ought not to do it; as Martha Minow observes, "Restoring dignity to victims . . . should at minimum involve respecting their own responses."[44] Forgiving one's adulterous partner, or one's abuser, cannot be morally evaluated unless we agree that it is an action worthy of the respectful response due agents, if damaged agents. To cast these women as simply mistaken about what they did is to trivialize what little agency is left to them.

I have argued that the cultural expectation persists today that women do most of the emotional work of maintaining relationships and promoting family unity. Consideration of this social and historical context prompts Dana Jack's observation that women's "legacy of thought, and the long history of gendered patterns of interaction, profoundly shapes women's self-perceptions," and leads to traditionally feminine virtues of "self-denial, self-sacrifice, self-effacement, self-restraint."[45] I want to take her insight a step further and argue that the legacy of thought she describes has the effect of shaping women's conceptions of virtues such as forgiveness. Women learn for generations that, for example, a good wife doesn't let the sun go down on her anger, the right thing to do is accept and forgive the wayward husband, and in more modern terms to do less is "quitting" too easily on marriage. I add that many women then learn meanings of moral expressions which may differ from the meanings learned by relevantly similar men, so that what it means to forgive sensibly includes, for someone operating in this context, the justification that one forbears to be angry to maintain harmony or sacrifice one's justified feelings for the good of the other, or for the good of both persons or the relationship itself.

In the absence of consideration of such cultural legacies, we should question whether analytic accounts of forgiveness can identify necessary and sufficient conditions in an informed way. I suggest they cannot, and we would do better to attend to narratives as a source of information on men's and women's differing conceptions of forgiveness. Rather than excluding the experience of so many forgivers from the category of genuine or true forgiveness in influential accounts with the definitional stop, we would do better to take narratives into account as evidence of alternative moral reasons to forgive. The moral reasons in the narratives that follow may point to conflict avoidance, which is problematic for theorists who would argue that avoidance is morally suspect to the extent that it is incompatible with robust senses of self-respect. Nevertheless, the moral merit of one's reasons shouldn't lead to the conclusion that one does not forgive after all, especially if we take seriously the learned meaning of one's expressions.

I have in mind accounts in popular psychology, magazine articles and news reports of women who forgive in interpersonal relationships. Consider the case of a woman in her thirties who resented her father for years of emotional distance and "benign neglect." When she was moved to forgive him, she cited as her primary reason, "The anger was eating me alive." During a later conflict with him, "she let him know she was hurt" as an alternative to "stewing in her anger," and forgave him when he apologized.[46] In the past philosophers and psychologists have typically referred to such narratives as revealing an "inauthentic" self who is, in short, lying about her "true" feelings. This results in the frustrations identified by more recent theorists with correctly interpreting women's narratives as something other than neurotic inauthenticity. It was after Carol Gilligan gathered narrative accounts of moral reasoning from girls and women that she suggested different genders may develop different perspectives on moral priorities. Such insights led counselors like Jack to conclude that rather than listen to depressed clients "through a filter of theories," we would do better to "return and listen carefully to depressed women in order to formulate new insights and concepts" with "a new standpoint from which to hear their narratives."[47] In other words, narratives themselves move us to develop new standpoints in theory, which in turn enable us to better understand the narratives and make sense of the way their accounts diverge from previous versions of moral concepts and expressions.

Such narratives then allow us to gather new evidence of the moral reasoning behind previously 'ungenuine' forms of forgiveness, including forgiveness to promote peace or avoid conflict. In the story of a woman who forgave her father for his alcoholism and resultant mistreatment, she said, "The first thing I had to do was ask, 'What does hanging on to all this anger do for me?'" The therapists who counseled her to forgive describe her forgiveness as "compassionate."[48] I am not here proposing that the moral reason in question is justified, merely that it is a sensible and genuine instance of forgiving. There is certainly room for criticism of the justification; one psychologist was prompted to caustically call such reasoning the "transformative Barbie belief in the power of abiding love," as in the story of the woman who broke up with, then returned to O.J. Simpson when he was accused of the murder of his wife and her boyfriend. Her justification for her forgiveness and reconciliation was that she heard pain in his voice, so she responded, "If you need me, I'll be there."[49] Just as model Yael Abecassis is famous for saying, "I'm the forgiving type—love conquers all," the sense that one should forgive to indicate compassion or love is reflected in narratives that tie compassionate gestures to forgiveness. A middle-aged woman recounted the story of heavily tipping a hairdresser who did a terrible job on her hair. "It was obvious he had no skill at his job," she said. "I usually find that when it's necessary to forgive someone it goes hand in hand with feeling sorry for the person. I gave him the tip as a way of saying, 'I forgive you.'"[50]

In such narratives, there seem to be many and related moral reasons for the extension of forgiveness. The reasons often stem from a view of one's duties and obligations that runs somewhat counter to Kantian notions of what constitutes self-respect. While I hesitate to say that all such narratives reflect an ethic of care rather than justice, I argue that we can at least conclude the following: A justice-based account of forgiveness misconstrues the moral reasons that make many instances of forgiveness sensible and genuine, especially those that proceed from a care perspective. Such care-based narratives reveal the need for new conceptions of the meaning and function of moral expressions of forgiveness. At the least, they indicate the need for better defense of the influential Kantian accounts of "genuine" forgiveness that do not reflect the experience of so many. If so, then philosophers would do well to observe the efforts of psychologists who work so often with narrative, and who find that narratives not only prompt us to develop new theory but make better sense in light of our changed theoretical approach.

Having said that, it is still the case that psychologists find their own discipline has a great deal of work to do in letting lay characterizations of forgiveness drive theory, rather than the other way around. As in philosophy, part of the methodological problem is scholars' quests for definition of forgiveness prior to considering testimony of the study volunteers interested in discussing forgiveness, regarding their subjective experiences, relational needs or moral and religious contexts. A resistance to multidimensional accounts of forgiveness, or even just sufficiently complicated definition, is usually part of the quest for a definition, "a tendency for both researchers and laypersons to assume a common understanding of the term 'forgiveness.'"[51] The evidence from many psychologists points to wide variation in how scholars, religious leaders, and laypeople define and practice forgiveness. Centering the administrative point of view, the variation in definition and practice may be seen to be wrong, failing to conform to an orderly rule. Centering the practices and definitions of forgivers, however, especially those of women expected to forgive, requires us to attend to their stories as evidence that forgiveness is multidimensional, complicated, and admits of multiple meanings and manifestations.

Women's stories of forgiveness offer one kind of experience worth considering. Women's experience with refusing to forgive is enlightening, as well. In the case of the two South African women, for example, whose husbands' murderer asked for their forgiveness, Thomas refrains from evaluating their actions, but he notes approvingly later that the more forgiving actions of other women allow the movie to conclude "on a note of hope," and describes scenes including the widows' above as depicting "unrelenting bitterness."[52]

Bitterness is here implied to be a bad thing, of course; while no one believes we really are made of sugar and spice, it is unexpected when women's behavior is the opposite of sweet. But some feminists have argued forcefully that bitterness itself is liberating. Lynne McFall, while acknowledging that bitterness can be, and generally is, harmful to oneself, argues that there are circumstances in which "active bitterness is not always bad for its host."[53] Bitterness may be rational and justified, according to McFall, and in its active form includes "intense animosity or virulence of feeling"; these are appropriate as a response to the culpable harms inflicted by human agents from whom one had legitimate hopes of better treatment (for example, because of a former promise).[54] Similar to unforgiving anger, bitterness exceeds merely being unforgiving by being vindictive, but McFall suggests this is a justified response when one must actively "move away from self-deception" toward such responses as "truth-telling and bearing witness;" in some cases, one ought to want vindication.[55]

Although one could object that the South African women in the above example had no reason to expect better than murderous behavior from the white police officer, McFall counters that this perspective sinks into cynicism, which is not preferable to bitterness. Cynicism involves seeing one's hopes for better treatment as false; the adage that "life is unfair" is McFall's example of the cynical position.[56] Extending her argument to the case of the widows' bitterness, it seems correct that they ought to do more than accept the unfairness of life; indeed, to see their bitterness as the product of false hope would be to let the confessing police officer off the moral hook. We cannot hope to build a better nation if it is one in which we cannot expect better of a policeman than murder. Seen this way, bitterness may hold out more hope for the future, since in its active form it could include constructing a better society that does not forget what happened to the two murdered husbands.

South African Justice Minister Dullah Omar argues that "bitterness can only exacerbate tensions in society."[57] But to Churchill Mxenge, brother of an antiapartheid lawyer killed under apartheid orders, calls for reconciliation and forgiveness amount to a betrayal, objecting, "Unless justice is done it's difficult for any person to think of forgiving."[58] Put this way, bitterness may be the most reasonable response to systematic injustice when one stands in a position of powerlessness. In South Africa, the extension of amnesty to many who testify to the TRC engenders more bitterness for some witnesses than healing, when it seems to maintain the relationship of unequal power rather than reform it. This provides evidence that the task to which first-person narratives contribute is that of evaluating the relations we find ourselves in.

As Walker argues eloquently, bearing witness is an optimistic act, entailing the belief that one is or will be in a position to be heard.[59] Brison adds that those of us who are recipients of narratives may have a collective responsibility to listen to victims.[60] If so, then perhaps, whether or not people tend to listen or want to, the moral argument is that they ought to. Eric Katz argues that one task of the moral philosopher is to articulate and examine expressions of values in actual moral experience and public policy.[61] Given these combined insights, philosophers should not just incorporate the narratives of victims of wrongdoing into accounts of forgiveness; we are morally required to seek them out if we intend to offer useful definitions. One unfortunate upshot of this is that philosophers may feel doomed to fail in our duties to listen. Yet Brison's argument is not just that we each have millions of individual responsibilities. She proposes collective responsibility on the part of groups and societies. How do we make sense of listening as a collective responsibility? How might philosophers, as groups which assemble in organizations, review each others' works, and teach to future generations, to go about listening to victims? One route worth taking is to discuss together and self-consciously how we go about our tasks of articulating and examining values; if a value is gendered, then our cooperative projects must center the experience of gender.

I have not addressed the difficult question as to the epistemological risks involved in taking narratives as evidence of the different functions of forgiveness. Such a project is a book in itself, and indeed others have written excellent and lengthy treatments of the epistemology of narrative already. Further, women's narratives are so profoundly marginalized in the dominant discourse on forgiveness that I find I am entirely justified in pleading for their importance first, and leaving the task of interpretation to later works. My argument is really quite conservative; it is the minimal suggestion that narratives of those who have expressed and refused forgiveness offer insights into the function such an expression is intended to perform. Moreover, philosophers ought to seek out those narratives that contrast with going definitions precisely in order to gather information on alternate views of its function, the better to argue against or incorporate these alternate positions. I continue to resist taking unproblematic cases as paradigms. The evidence is in that forgiveness is inherently complicated and problematic. This is clearer when practical narratives are at the center of engaged theorizing.

Conclusion

Arguments that on balance we ought to forgive, or try to forgive, often notice our relatedness to others at least in passing. Philosophers including R.S. Downie and H.J.N. Horsbrugh note the importance of relatedness in arguing for the positive value of forgiveness. Downie argues that we should always try to forgive repentant wrongdoers, because refusing to ever forgive a wrongdoer indicates that they can never resume membership in the moral community, which is disrespectful of the person the wrongdoer can become.[62] Horsbrugh argues similarly that being open to forgiving wrongdoers in the future recognizes the desirability of their eventual acceptance in the moral community, so we should make an effort to forgive wrongdoers, "seek reconciliation and a renewed relationship."[63] And Trudy Govier argues that by and large we ought to forgive each other for "small matters" because without doing so "life would be difficult and intimate relationships impossible," not just between the two parties typically involved but for many whose lives connect with theirs, "because relationships have an effect on more than two people."[64]

A feminist paradigm of forgiveness involves a more complex view of the individual and her relations than philosophers have commonly entertained. At a minimum, a feminist model of forgiveness that improves on past ones must see persons as at least partly constituted by their relations in a way that allows us to say coherently what we do when we resent or forgive wrongs done to intimate others. I have also suggested that a feminist model must do more than simply celebrate the fact that we are related; forgiveness is not, on this account, prima facie good when it repairs relations, because the relations themselves may be those we ought to change or dissolve. To see forgiveness as a mechanism for relationship maintenance also makes better sense of those occasions in our actual experience in which someone forgives whose self-respect is threatened, and in which someone with intact self-respect refuses to grant it. Last, the more robust literature on women's experience with anger suggests difficulties for those models that both require the ability to perceive a wrong has been done and that we let go of unreasonable anger. If forgiveness requires having this robust sense of self, women may have good reasons to refuse forgiveness on many occasions; at the same time, the relational model of forgiveness I am describing may account for our ability to forgive even in the presence of what has formerly been called unreasonable anger. To do the latter may involve sometimes giving the speech act involved in forgiveness before one has all the concomitant emotions. That forgiveness is a speech act, among other things, and that it may even be morally required before one feels forgiving, is an argument I defend in the next chapter.

Notes

1. Joram Haber, "Forgiveness and Feminism," in *Norms and Values: Essays on the Work of Virginia Held*, ed. Joram Graf Haber and Mark S. Halfon (Lanham, MD: Rowman and Littlefield, 1998), 146-47.

2. In this passage I believe I avoid representing Noddings's controversial *interpretation* of Gilligan, but I should note that what she believes Gilligan's findings entail is subject to some dispute. See Donald Vandenberg, "Caring: Feminine Ethics or Maternalistic Misandry?" *Journal of Philosophy of Education* 30, no.2(1996): 253-69.

3. Carol Gilligan, *In a Different Voice: Psychological Theory and Women's Development* (Cambridge, Mass.: Harvard University Press, 1982), 48.

4. Nel Noddings, *Caring: A Feminine Approach to Ethics and Moral Education* (Berkeley: University of California Press, 1984), 96-97.

5. Nel Noddings, *Women and Evil* (Berkeley: University of California Press, 1989), 212.

6. Noddings (1989), 212.

7. Noddings (1989), 172.

8. Jean Grimshaw (*Philosophy and Feminist Thinking*, Minneapolis: University of Minnesota Press, 1986, 255), citing Noddings (1984, 105) makes a similar point.

9. Robin May Schott, "War Rape and the Political Concept of Evil," forthcoming; Hannah Arendt, *The Origins of Totalitarianism* (New York: Harcourt Brace Jovanovich, 1951/1973).

10. Claudia Card, *The Atrocity Paradigm: A Theory of Evil* (Oxford: Oxford University Press, 2002), 148.

11. Claudia Card, *The Unnatural Lottery: Character and Moral Luck* (Philadelphia: Temple University Press, 1996), 85-86.

12. Marilyn Friedman, "Autonomy and Social Relationships: Rethinking the Feminist Critique," in *Feminists Rethink the Self*, ed. Diana T. Meyers (Boulder, CO: Westview, 1997), 54.

13. Marilyn Friedman, *What Are Friends For?* (Ithaca, N.Y.: Cornell University Press, 1993), 239.

14. Sarah Hoagland, "Some Concerns About Nel Noddings' 'Caring,'" *Hypatia* 5, no.1 (1990): 247.

15. Hoagland (1990), 256, 261.

16. Nancy DeCourville, Kathryn Belicki and Michelle M. Green, "Subjective Experiences of Forgiveness in a Community Sample: Implications for Understanding Forgiveness and Its Consequences," in *Women's Reflections on the Complexities of Forgiveness*, ed. Wanda Malcolm, Nancy DeCourville, and Kathryn Belicki (New York and London: Routledge, 2008), 2.

17. Kathryn Belicki, Jessica Rourke, and Megan McCarthy, "Potential Dangers of Empathy and Related Conundrums," in *Women's Reflections on the Complexities of Forgiveness*, ed. Wanda Malcolm, Nancy DeCourville, and Kathryn Belicki (New York and London: Routledge, 2008), 179.

18. Judith Boss, "Throwing Pearls to the Swine: Women, Forgiveness, and the Unrepentant Abuser," in *Philosophical Perspectives on Power and Domination*, ed. Laura Duhan Kaplan and Lawrence F. Bove (Amsterdam-Atlanta: Rodopi Press, 1997), 235.

19. Martha Minow, *Between Vengeance and Forgiveness* (Boston: Beacon Press, 1999), 17.

20. Kevin Thomas, "'Journey into Day' Tells of Apartheid Horror," *Los Angeles Times Newspaper*, Home Edition; Part F, Friday, March 9, 2001, 8.

21. Simon Wiesenthal, *The Sunflower* (New York: Schocken Books, 1969), 37.

22. Minow (1999), 18.

23. Minow (1999), 72-76.

24. Deborah L. Cox, Sally D. Stabb and Karin H. Bruckner, *Women's Anger: Clinical and Developmental Perspectives* (Philadelphia: Brunner-Routledge, 1999), 71-80.

25. Cox, Stabb and Bruckner (1999), 63.

26. Cox, Stabb and Bruckner (1999), 72.

27. Cox, Stabb and Bruckner (1999), 71.

28. Cox, Stabb and Bruckner (1999), 103-106.

29. Carol Gilligan, "Joining the Resistance: Psychology, Politics, Girls and Women," *Michigan Quarterly Review* 29 (1990): 527.

30. Cox, Stabb and Bruckner (1999), 104-105.

31. Cox, Stabb and Bruckner (1999), 208.

32. Susan Griffin, *Woman and Nature: The Roaring Inside Her* (New York: Harper & Row, 1978), 184.

33. Susan J. Brison, *Aftermath: Violence and the Remaking of a Self* (Princeton, N.J.: Princeton University Press, 2002), 94-95.

34. Brison (2002), 145n17.

35. Brison (2002), 95.

36. Marilyn Frye, *The Politics of Reality: Essays in Feminist Theory* (Freedom, CA: Crossing Press, 1983), 84-94.

37. Hilde Lindemann Nelson, *Damaged Identities, Narrative Repair* (Ithaca, N.Y.: Cornell University Press, 2001), 6.

38. Nelson (2001), 7.

39. Nelson (2001), 117.

40. Anonymous, "Experiments in Hostility," *off our backs* 3, no.5 (February 28, 1973): 10.

41. Anonymous, "Experiments in Hostility," *off our backs* 3, no.5 (1973): 10.

42. Quoted in Minow (1999), p. 8.

43. Marietta Jaeger, "The Power and Reality of Forgiveness: Forgiving the Murderer of One's Child," in *Exploring Forgiveness*, ed. Robert D. Enright and Joanna North (Madison: University of Wisconsin Press, 1998), 13.

44. Minow (1999), 135.

45. Dana Jack, *Silencing the Self: Depression and Women* (Cambridge, Mass.: Harvard University Press, 1991), 85, 87.

46. Susan Reimer, "Forgiveness: Healing the heart and mind," *Baltimore Sun*, City Section, August 3, 1996, 4.

47. Jack (1991), 3.

48. Barbara Mathias-Riegel, "Discovering the Bliss of Forgiveness," *Washington Post*, July 14, 1997, C5.

49. Paula Barbieri, *The Other Woman* (New York: Little, Brown & Co., 1997), 204.

50. Megan Rosenfeld and Brooke A. Masters, "The Ultimate Team Player," *Washington Post*, September 26, 1997, Section C, Page 1.

51. DeCourville, Belicki and Green (2008), 2.

52. Thomas (2001), 8.

53. Lynne McFall, "What's Wrong with Bitterness?" in *Feminist Ethics*, ed. Claudia Card (Lawrence, Kan.: University Press of Kansas, 1991), 152.

54. McFall (1991), 147.

55. McFall (1991), 154,155.

56. McFall (1991), 147.

57. Minow (1999), 78.

58. Minow (1999), 81.

59. Brison (2002), 52.

60. Brison (2002), 56-57.

61. Eric Katz, *Nature as Subject: Human Obligation and Natural Community* (Lanham, MD: Rowman & Littlefield, 1996), 165.

62. R.S. Downie, "Forgiveness," Philosophical Quarterly 15 (1965): 133-34.

63. H.J.N. Horsburgh, "Forgiveness," *Canadian Journal of Philosophy* 4 (1974): 281-82.

64. Trudy Govier, *Dilemmas of Trust* (Montreal and Kingston: McGill-Queen's University Press, 1998), 186, 189.

Chapter Four

Forgiveness as a Performative Utterance

Experiences of forgiveness admit of variation, and those variations include its expressive aspect. Some may go their whole lives without ever saying the phrase, "I forgive you," especially in a culture that discourages such statements. Yet surely it would be a mistake to conclude that those who can avoid the expression never forgive; likely they forgive, but either express it differently or do not express it at all. In part because the illocution isn't required, some theorists would argue that the illocution is therefore not a sensible instance of forgiveness at all. However, this conclusion errs in the opposite direction, negating the experiences of some because of the contrary experiences of others. Philosophers seeking a univocal, exclusory definition of forgiveness, or as Nick Smith describes it, a binary definition (of X vs. ~X), seek to determine whether expressing it in so many words is either necessary or sufficient for forgiveness to take place, and upon finding it is neither, relegate it to the "not forgiveness" category.[1] I reject the quest for a univocal definition, against which all would-be forgivers must be tested, although I sympathize with philosophers who find it difficult to imagine definitions that lack conditions.

The evidence that forgiveness may take many forms compels us to consider that forgiveness is multidimensional. Recall that in Chapter One, I described forgiveness as a moral (and therefore at least partially deliberative) action or set of actions, functioning as a remedy in responding to blame or condemnation, releasing offenders from the fullness of their blameworthiness, in relational contexts which therefore require considerations of power between relata. Seeing forgiveness as multidimensional allows for multiple methods of releasing offenders from their blameworthiness, including our ordinary-language uses of forgiveness, specifically those times one gives something aloud to one's wrongdoer that conveys forgiveness, perhaps even before one has completely overcome negative feelings about the wrong done. I argue in this chapter that the statement, "I forgive you," can be, itself, an instance of forgiveness; more than reporting, truly or falsely, how one feels, saying "I forgive you" may also perform an act that sets something new in motion, and changes the relation between wrongdoer and victim. I argue against philosophers for whom, as I said in Chapter One, forgiveness is only 'genuine' when one has overcome these feelings, and for whom expressions of forgiveness merely report this overcoming.

It is important to note that the view of forgiveness as a speech act is not a popular one among contemporary philosophers, although Joram Haber, arguably the first to write a comprehensive work on forgiveness, argues that it has a performative dimension.[2] Peter Digeser extended Haber's arguments to distinguish between the different types of illocutionary acts involved in political forgiveness as well as interpersonal forgiveness.[3] Trudy Govier approaches a similar position in arguing forcefully about group forgiveness, that "groups can act."[4] However, she seems more committed to a view of forgiveness as a change of attitude, and focuses her arguments on group responsibilities and sharing attitudes. More recently, Glen Pettigrove offers an account more helpful to my own, in which he identifies a "composite" account of locutions of forgiveness that may accomplish reports of inward states, release from debts, or commitments to future attitudes.[5] The array of philosophers opposed to viewing forgiveness as a speech act is much more well populated, and in what follows, I consider and reject specific arguments against the view that forgiveness can take the form of a speech act. Interestingly, feminist theorists (at least in the scant literature available on feminist views of forgiveness) don't take a position on illocutionary forgiveness one way or the other, but in this chapter I hope to show that a view of forgiveness as a speech act is in keeping with feminist attention to putting theories to the test of practical experience.

I first appeal to J.L. Austin's conception of speech acts to show that forgiveness can be, at times, what he calls a performative utterance. Although my interest is in developing a feminist model that accounts for such uses of "I forgive you," I rely primarily on the non-feminist models by Haber and Pettigrove, who do similar work defending the idea that forgiveness is a speech act. While I agree with both philosophers that forgiveness is not always performatory and that the speech act is just one dimension of forgiveness, I argue that Linda Ross Meyer's account of performative forgiveness is preferable to explicate the content of what we express with the statement, "I forgive you."[6] I consider and reject arguments from philosophers including R.S. Downie and Jeffrie Murphy that forgiveness does not have a performative dimension. I find more multidimensional accounts of forgiveness to have greater potential for incorporating the possibility that forgiveness is a speech act, and for feminist reasons, I argue against univocal definitions that seem to issue from administrative points of view.

I argue that forgiveness is a moral act or set of acts with at least two dimensions, namely (1) the choice to take seriously a new attitude toward one's wrongdoer, which functions as a remedy in responding to blame or condemnation, releasing offenders from the fullness of their blameworthiness, and (2) the performative utterance to the wrongdoer of one's accomplishment of, or commitment to, the choices and actions that releasing them requires. I consider and reject the position that the two dimensions together may constitute 'full forgiveness,' and suggest that (1) and (2) are distinct, that either can coherently be considered manifestations of forgiveness and, depending on the circumstances, exercising one of these is not inherently inferior to exercising both of these. In some cases the choice to commit to an attitudinal change toward offenders ought to occur without the speech act, and in some cases the speech act ought to occur even prior to the opportunity to meaningfully commit to a new attitude. I argue against those philosophers who seem to recommend or idealize "complete" or "full" forgiveness characterized by both a completed attitude shift and expression of the new attitude, by victims and by their communities. I do not argue that an ideal forgiveness involves both (1) and (2); in some cases this may not be possible, for instance when the wrongdoer has died, and in some cases this may not be morally preferable, if the wrongdoer is unrepentant or still a danger to others.

Austin's Conception of Performative Speech Acts

Philosopher Linda Ross Meyer observes, "I can imagine someone saying, 'I am still angry, but I forgive you anyway.' I have said so myself, to my children."[7] Such expressions are what J. L. Austin calls performative speech acts. Performative utterances do not, in the appropriate circumstances, merely describe what one is doing; to say the performative utterance is to do it.[8] Because utterances like these are not merely reportive—that is, they are not a simple report of our inward state—Austin argues that these performatives are neither true nor false.[9] In the above instance, Meyer is in part reporting her inward state—"I am still angry"—but doing something more when she says "I forgive you." Austin's examples of performative utterances include "I bet," "I take this woman," and "I christen this ship."[10] Austin never cites "I forgive" as an example of a performative utterance, although he suggests such close relatives as "I accept your apology," "I pardon" and "I absolve."[11]

Although performatives do not have a truth value—in the above example, Meyer's being angry is verifiable in a way her forgiving is not—it is possible for them to be, as Austin puts it, infelicitous. Austin identifies a variety of ways that a performative can be uttered infelicitously.[12] First, he says of a performative that it misfires if the formula is executed incorrectly, by the wrong persons, or the circumstances are inappropriate. When delivering "the utterance when one or another of its concomitants is absent . . . [in] no way do we say that the utterance was false but rather that the utterance . . . was void, or given in bad faith, or not implemented, or the like."[13] In the case of saying a performative and not inwardly meaning it, he refers to it as abused when the speaker has thoughts or feelings contrary to the performative, or completely fails to act in accordance with the performative.[14] Austin's example is that of the false promise, which despite the valuing term "false" doesn't mean one didn't really promise. "For he does promise: the promise here is not even void, though it is given in bad faith."[15] Although Austin does not go into detail on this point, he seems here to be distinguishing between the intrapersonal and interpersonal aspects of speech acts.

It is not enough, as Austin implies, to consider only the internal state of the speaker in moral assessments, as so many investigations of forgiveness do, deliberating as to whether a speaker *really* meant it, an inquiry doomed to epistemological impossibilities which only purely hypothetical examples could escape. In addition to examining inward sincerity and personal predictability, interpersonal analyses must also take into account the relational nature of speech, how it is received by listeners—who may include witnesses as well as intended objects—and how it functions in the relationship in which it is expressed. It is a fascinating aspect of speech acts that they are, in this respect, unpredictable and risky—further reason, if we needed it, for a multidimensional and sufficiently complex account of forgiveness.

In identifying statements as speech acts, it is important to note that these utterances, such as "I bet" and "I forgive you," are not exhaustive of the classes of betting or forgiving. As Austin points out, his argument that illocutions such as betting are speech acts does not limit us to saying that these are the only instances of what they perform. He notes, "In very many cases it is possible to perform an act of exactly the same kind not by uttering words . . . but in some other way."[16] We might under common law marry someone simply by cohabitating with them long enough. Ahab's wife may inwardly promise her absent husband to walk the widow's walk of their house every day looking for his ship in the harbor. Betting can be done coherently by putting a quarter in a slot machine. These performatives aren't necessary conditions of marrying, promising and betting *simpliciter*.[17] They are, however, sensibly referred to as instances of these acts. Therefore, the objection that some individuals rarely say, "I forgive you," is not an objection to forgiveness having a performative dimension.

The Performance of "I Forgive You"

Similarly, I suggest that saying "I forgive you" can also be, itself, an act, even if not a necessary condition of forgiving; therefore, objections that we can forgive in the absence of verbalizing anything do not, on this Austinian account, prove that forgiveness does not have a performative dimension. Forgiving the dead, for example, can be accomplished without the forgiver saying anything aloud. Interestingly, Meyer argues that not only does one's forgiveness of the dead fail to disprove the performative dimension, in some cases expressing forgiveness of the dead to others is a performative as well. Arguing against Murphy's position that forgiveness is essentially an emotional transformation, Meyer suggests that public reception of and agreement with our forgiveness of the dead involves such moral actions as "communal remembering."[18] She adds, "The public rehabilitation of the deceased's memory, or a 'clearing of her name,' may mean something much more . . . than forgiveness as emotional transformation."[19]

Meyer and Haber offer different defenses of forgiveness as a performative; they disagree with, but credit, William Neblett and R.J. O'Shaughnessy with being the first defenders of this idea. Neblett and O'Shaughnessy separately argue that the utterance, "I forgive you," can succeed in achieving several different purposes, including forgiving a debt, conveying an emotional transformation, and in O'Shaughnessy's most controversial example, Prospero's calling off the demons with which he has been tormenting his wrongdoer.[20] Neblett argues a Wittgensteinian position that forgiveness has no absolute definition, rather a number of uses with a family resemblance between them.[21] Importantly for our purposes, both argue that we know what "I forgive you" means when we know what function the speaker intends it to perform.

Haber's analysis of Neblett and O'Shaughnessy, tellingly included in the section of his book called, "What Forgiveness Is Not," rejects their position that forgiveness can refer to many things; I include Haber among those philosophers who seek a univocal definition of forgiveness. However, Haber retains the idea that forgiveness can be a performative utterance. Responding to O'Shaughnessy's more controversial examples in particular, Haber notes that evidence of someone using "I forgive you" idiosyncratically proves all the more that such uses are diverging from a paradigm, that we ordinarily think "I forgive you" has a non-idiosyncratic use. On the paradigm he identifies, "I forgive you" is typically taken to mean the speaker (S) is "inviting the listener to believe he is forgiven," where forgiven means "S is willing to/has overcome his resentment for X's doing A."[22]

As Haber characterizes it, the performance of "I forgive you" seems most like the utterance of a promise. As evidence of this, consider his example of John and Mary; Mary sincerely said to John regarding a past injury, "I forgive you," but when John later finds himself needing her help, she says, resentfully, "Why should I help you after what you did to me?" John's response, "But you already forgave me for that," could be answered by Mary with either "I guess I really didn't" or "Yes, you're right." In this example, Haber depicts John as having a claim of sorts against Mary on the strength of what she said in the past, or in Haber's terms, what she invited him to believe was true, namely, that she's overcome or plans to overcome her resentment.[23]

It is a strength of Haber's Austinian account that giving this statement does not necessarily turn out to be infelicitous just because Mary has angry feelings when thinking about John's wrong act at later dates. The speech act only misfires if Mary said it while resentment "was festering in her," on Haber's account.[24] His insight is valuable; seeing forgiveness as a performative speech act explains, without dismissing, our forgiving at an earlier time even if we feel anger when reflecting on the harm done at a later date. Glen Pettigrove wisely observes that in examples like this, forgiveness is in the class of commissive illocutions—in other words, a commitment both related to and distinct from promising, as "not all commitments bind as firmly as promises."[25] It is further appealing that, using Haber's analysis, we may avoid the job other theorists do, badly at times, of differentiating between partial and full forgiveness, between genuine forgiveness and whatever its opposite may be, between intending to forgive and really forgiving; drawing these distinctions occasionally borders on seeming to sell short the acts of agents, connoting inferiority where these speech acts may instead be the most appropriate responses to wrongdoing. Even on those occasions when it is not appropriate, where it seems instead blameworthy or exhibiting a lack of self-respect, to characterize these as acts of something other than forgiveness denies the agency of those who grant it, failing to respect the choices, if bad ones, of the forgivers. Most often, though, opposition to the idea of expressing hasty forgiveness seems to turn on its simply being a bad idea, but the fact that an act is highly undesirable does not make it logically impossible.

Haber's account provides us with grounds to see forgiveness as multidimensional, consisting in speech acts as well as in emotional transformations. Yet as I have argued before, Haber's characterization of the content of the speech act may be too limited; overcoming resentment at injury to oneself is only one reason to extend forgiveness. I agree with Haber that the speech act expresses an attitude, but the attitude itself is more fluid than perhaps Haber allows. Meyer's analysis of "I forgive you" allows for a more open-ended interpretation; she argues that the utterance of forgiveness expresses (1) a commitment to deal with offenders and (2) a commitment to make sense of their actions.[26] Sense-making is here intended to imply better understanding the action, and not excusing it. Making sense of the injury is necessary to forgiving because it allows us to see the wrongdoer as an agent we can properly forgive instead of a monster, predator, or barbarian.[27] Pettigrove adds to commissive accounts that depending on the context, expressing forgiveness can be reportive or executive instead, so the commissive account is not intended to supplant all other possibilities. I agree with Pettigrove's composite account of expressed forgiveness, but emphasize the primacy of commissive forgiveness in my own account because the epistemic problem with knowing whether future selves will agree with past reports or pardons concerns me more than most theorists. Feminist theorists are persuasive that we are not unified egos, that we lack full control, and in the contexts of wrongdoing in which forgiveness becomes an issue, memories of harm or trauma are especially unpredictable.[28] Of this, more in the last chapter; it is enough to note for now that on my account, forgiveness is always in part commissive to our future selves even if it comes across as reportive or executive to our intended objects.

On Meyer's account, forgiveness sounds somewhat like Haber's promise, but it is often more like an agreement to enter negotiation than it is a contract or promise. This is indicated by her saying of the performative, "The battered wife need not welcome her abuser back into the home. [Forgiveness] merely places the victim at the table, ready to begin the perhaps painful process of working on a rapprochement."[29] Meyer herself doesn't characterize the performative as a negotiation, per se, and its implication was intended metaphorically. Still, to see forgiveness as, at times, a negotiation rather than a unilateral promise captures something intuitively important which others have noticed before about the emotions involved in forgiving—that forgiveness is a process, and a difficult one to boot. As Charles Griswold says, memory is intrinsic to forgiveness, and I add that it is morally important to bear in mind the ways memories are often uncontrollable. As Laurence Thomas so eloquently says, "Surely feelings of resentment over wrongdoing can come and go, wax and wane"; he argues rather that forgiveness enables "us to navigate occasional bouts of psychological turbulence."[30] Because we are both temporal and atemporal, I suggest that forgiveness, in light of our own intrusive memories, often involves continual recommitment, in the same way that promises often involve continual recommitment. For some, such commitments are easily chosen, and easily kept, but I suspect that for most of us, it is not always possible to predict what future selves will decide.

That forgiveness is difficult, however, does not by itself weigh against the arguments of those who hold that forgiveness ought to be a unilateral promise. Joanna North argues that forgiveness is unconditional by definition, and that its difficulty comes with the territory, saying, "If I am to forgive, I must risk extending my trust and affection, with no guarantee they will not be flung back in my face, or forfeited in the future."[31] For North, forgiveness just is "an unconditional response to the wrongdoer, for there is something unforgiving in the demand for guarantees."[32] However, her characterization of forgiveness presents a false dilemma between unconditional forgiveness and forgiveness predicated on what North calls guarantees. In entering the kinds of negotiation I described above, we may not be asking for guarantees; many of us have had the experience of saying, even as we forgive, "Don't do it again." We are not obviously requesting a guarantee so much as we are looking for an expression of some sense of the other's commitment to repair the relationship and take seriously the feelings of the one forgiving. When my less punctual friend apologizes to me, saying, "I promise, I'll never be late again," and she has done so many times, it is more important to me that she thus recognizes the importance of the commitment itself, than that she live up to what I'm sure is an unrealistic guarantee. I suggest that we add to "I forgive you" such conditions as, "Don't do it again," precisely because we trust that the request falls on fertile ground, and not because we condition our forgiveness on guarantees.[33]

In other words, the presence of reasonable grounds for minimal trust is necessary to being able to enter negotiation with one's wrongdoer, to ask for such conditions as not repeating the harm, as Govier points out in articulating an ethical objection to the unconditional view. On her view, North rightly observes that asking for guarantees would suggest we have too much doubt and too little trust to forgive, but as Govier argues, "Forgiveness turns out to presuppose some *basis* for trust."[34] Against North's position that one ought to trust the person one is about to forgive, Govier argues that it is unwise to "ignore risk and such things as the notorious battered woman syndrome. People may be exposed to terrible risks in some contexts where they feel they 'should' trust and forgive; they may feel compelled to try to be reconciled in contexts where they remain vulnerable to harm from the very people they trust and forgive."[35] Granted, some of us trust the wrong people. If trusting the right people requires having good grounds for one's trust, some of us could be faulted for placing our trust in those who've given us every reason to do the opposite.

Unconditional forgiveness is one version of what Meyer calls a "commitment to deal," but this variety of the commitment may be one we ought not to give very often. Although I do not deny that forgiveness can be extended unconditionally, I suggest that in some cases, morally appropriate forgiveness is best seen as a negotiation, or a commitment to enter into negotiation, because forgiveness is a moral act that can accomplish many things other than unconditional trust and relationship renewal.

The literature is littered with examples of those who try but fail to forgive. Perhaps Meyer's description of the speech act points to a reason we sometimes fail. Although it's possible to extend unconditional forgiveness, for many of us forgiveness is not unconditional; it relies on such things as our ability to trust that the other won't wrong us again, our ability to feel better about ourselves, and so forth. If "I forgive you" were identical to a promise, such as "I promise to hold a new attitude toward you," we'd live up to it regardless of many factors, but it does, often, seem more like negotiation: "If you commit to X," where X can mean not doing it again, going to couples' counseling with me, treating my private space with more respect, and so on, "then I commit to Y," where Y means taking up a new attitude toward one's offender. And we are not predictable; memory is not predictable, nor is one's own person. As said above, forgiveness for some things may require continual recommitment—and who is to say we failed at every turn, if we decide not to recommit to forgiveness at a later time?

In Chapter Three, I argued for attention to the relation involved in forgiving. Now Govier's and Meyer's insights taken together provide us a reason for thinking that forgiveness is a negotiation of the relationship itself. It does not necessarily renew it, as so many have suggested, although it can do that as well. But it does have the power to change how the relationship will or must go in the future if I am to "release you from the consequences of your act," as Arendt puts it. More, this provides us with another way to look at the forgiveness of those who give it too hastily; where we wish they negotiated, they may have capitulated, or at the least didn't ask for the kinds of commitments they agreed to live up to themselves.

The Unpopularity of Performative Forgiveness

As Haber notes correctly, the position that forgiveness has a performative dimension goes against the mainstream of philosophical thought. Since my account differs from the standard view of forgiveness, it is worth considering the arguments for the position that forgiveness does not have a speech act dimension. The earliest objections from this position, by R.S. Downie (and, more briefly, P.F. Strawson), portray the utterance of forgiveness as merely reportive of the feelings or behaviors that forgiveness involves, and argue that what I call a performative is neither necessary nor sufficient for forgiveness to occur.

Downie, the first philosopher to consider the possible speech act of forgiveness, argues that "A cannot be said to have forgiven B unless he acts towards B in a certain manner," and such behavior is a necessary condition for something to be forgiveness.[36] For this reason, Downie concludes, "It is not satisfactory to say that the mere uttering of the words 'I forgive you' constitutes forgiveness. The uttering of these words or their equivalent, is certainly not sufficient to constitute forgiveness. . . . In this respect forgiving differs from promising."[37] Downie acknowledges that a similar expression, pardoning, is a performative speech act, but suggests that a "crucial difference . . . between pardoning and forgiving is that we pardon as officials in social roles but forgive as persons." He concludes that an official in his capacity "sets in motion the normative machinery" just by uttering a pardon, but "to say 'I forgive you' . . . is not in a similar way to set anything in motion. The forgiver is merely signaling that he has the appropriate attitude and that the person being forgiven can expect the appropriate behavior."[38]

A few objections to Downie's conception of what makes expressed forgiveness non-performative are in order. First, as noted above, that the mere utterance of performative forgiveness is not always necessary to constitute forgiveness does not prove that forgiveness does not have a performative dimension, as Austin himself noted. Although betting can be done coherently by putting a quarter in a slot machine, we wouldn't then say that "I bet you" is never performative. I suspect that the intuitive force of Downie's argument turns on a couple of factors, not the least of which is the rarity with which people, especially in American culture, perform the illocution of forgiveness. Pettigrove describes those of us uncomfortable on the moral high ground as "foraging for another expression. . . . We find ourselves running through our mental thesaurus precisely because the locution 'I forgive you' thematizes the wrongness of the act being forgiven."[39] For a variety of social and personal reasons, many of us find it difficult to say, "I forgive you," even when it's asked for, and clearly called for. Certainly we wouldn't then say that we've never forgiven anyone! Although an argument like this is appealing, and I suspect underpins Downie's own account, it doesn't create a problem for a performative account; some illocutions make some of us sweat more than others, and where I have trouble delivering forgiveness, others may have trouble making promises or bets. In addition, that Downie refers to the appropriate attitude at the end implies that the bare utterance of the words in the absence of the attitude therefore fails as a moral act. Yet it's difficult to see how this wouldn't be an objection to apology or promising, the performative status of which Downie doesn't dispute. Many of us with siblings have had the experience of being ordered to apologize, and if we did it, we likely did so in the utter absence of the appropriate attitude. Yet our parents, correctly or not, presumed that the bare utterance of the words was meaningful, and set something "in motion."

Likewise, I disagree with Downie's position that the utterance "I forgive you" does not set normative machinery in motion. To consider just one example, I return to Simon Wiesenthal's experience as a concentration camp inmate, related in *The Sunflower*, wherein a dying Nazi soldier asks his forgiveness for war crimes done to others. The soldier who asked Simon Wiesenthal for forgiveness didn't seem to be asking for a report of how Wiesenthal felt. It was critical to him that someone express something like forgiveness to him for his war crimes before he died.[40] Wiesenthal says it was a source of anxiety that he did not express forgiveness to Karl, although he does not indicate regretting the decision; in his symposium, he invited the participants to answer the question, "What would I have *done?*"[41] Wiesenthal does not ask his respondents what he ought to have felt, or reported feeling. Although it is only implied, Wiesenthal seems aware that the expression of forgiveness would itself have been a moral act (if not necessarily the right one).

In addition, consider Judith Boss's argument that women who forgive their unrepentant abusers fail to challenge the patriarchal structures that allow abuse, or Cheshire Calhoun's discussion of forgiveness that sends a message of condonation.[42] These examples are enriched by seeing the expression of forgiveness as a performative utterance; their concerns turn on what normative machinery we set in motion if we express forgiveness to the wrongdoer. Imagine that we were to experience a change of heart but never convey it aloud, and further imagine that we move away so that our future behavior cannot indicate our forgiving feelings. In this case, no message could be sent by one's forgiveness, and discussions of whether or not forgiveness condones a wrong would be moot. Arguments that forgiveness, when conveyed to a wrongdoer, sends a message indicate that the expression of forgiveness sets moral machinery in motion. (Whether it is done rightly or wrongly is another story.)

Third, Downie argues that expressions of forgiveness are, to use Austin's own terms, merely reportive; they describe or report, in verifiably true or false ways, some inward spiritual act of, say, overcoming resentment. For this reason, many contemporary theorists argue that it is incorrect to give forgiveness too soon, and some argue it is incorrect when one is still harboring negative feelings, but intends to overcome them. Margaret Holmgren, for example, argues that forgiveness is "genuine and true" only after one completes the task of responding to wrongdoing by working through the emotional processes involved in overcoming resentment.[43]

This position gives rise to an epistemological difficulty which could be resolved by considering the utterance as a performative and an instance of forgiveness. The epistemological problem has been raised by different theorists and is best explored by H.J.N. Horsbrugh: How does one know when one has forgiven?[44] If I won't know until much later that I still feel inward spikes of anger at the thought of the injury, then the "completed" position seems hampered by the possibility that no one ever really forgives, because we can't know now if we will feel renewed resentment in the future. At best we could report what we currently believe to be our emotional states, but this seems unsatisfying, especially if the granting of forgiveness is necessary to continue a particular relationship. Horsbrugh argues that on the "genuine" account, we can never be sure that we have eradicated and overcome all our negative feelings toward wrongdoers, and if we suppose we have but years later feel those negative feelings again, we were mistaken to think we ever "really" forgave. I suggest that hanging the genuineness or truth of our forgiveness on complete discharge of negative feelings implies that anything short of this is "false," which connotes something needlessly bad about what most people do in saying, "I forgive you." For reasons similar to this, Horsbrugh argues instead that forgiveness is a process, and that we can meaningfully say we forgive another before we have accomplished all the emotional work involved.

He concludes, however, that we have "complete forgiveness" only when we really overcome the last drop of resentment. As I have argued, this is limited to describing only one dimension of forgiveness, and I avoid using such terms as "complete" to refer to forgiveness if doing so implies the inferiority of giving the performative before one has accomplished the shift in attitude. In some cases, such as the example of Meyer forgiving her children, the speech act may even be morally required before one feels an absence of negative feelings, and I wish to resist characterizing doing the morally best thing as incomplete. As Pettigrove says, "The wrongdoer's ability to make a fresh start would be undermined if she could not know from one day to the next if she were forgiven," and I add that as children, we depend on parenting figures to forgive us, provide us a trustable world, whether or not they've eliminated their angry feelings.[45] Certainly we can describe a forgiver as having completed the emotional process involved in changing one's attitude with respect to one's wrongdoer, but forgiveness has a richer multidimensional meaning than Horsbrugh's account of complete forgiveness might imply. Perhaps one could defend the idea of complete forgiveness by pointing to an example of forgiving a very minor wrong, but this doesn't seem like it would serve as a case of overcoming the last drop of resentment, so much as one which it is easy not to resent. That Horsbrugh's complete forgiveness is best illustrated with easy forgiveness seems to point to a problem with the concept. The imagined perfection of a state in which one overcomes the last drop of one's anger seems counter to experiences with serious wrong, and perhaps amounts to an undesirable goal. Robin Dillon makes a similar argument about self-forgiveness, that it "does not require extinguishing all self-reproach, for it is not really about the presence or absence of negative feelings and judgments; it's about their power."[46] She distinguishes between overcoming and eliminating the negative emotions, arguing that forgiving means "not that one no longer experiences" resentment or reproach, but that "one is no longer in bondage to it . . . so that one can now live well enough."[47] If Dillon's characterization is correct, then the speech act is not dependent upon a report of a robustly different attitude.

More often than not, philosophers simply argue that forgiveness is essentially an emotion and therefore cannot be a speech act. Most notably, Jeffrie Murphy says more than once that "forgiveness is primarily a matter of changing how one feels with respect to a person who has done one an injury." This is meant as strongly as it sounds; he adds "[Jean] Hampton sees this as a prelude to forgiveness; I see it as the very thing."[48] Such reasoning relieves us of the necessity to consider that forgiveness has another dimension if we can stipulate that forgiveness, by definition, must refer only to the change of heart important to Murphy. But such a move is unnecessary; to see forgiveness as at times a performative utterance adds to definitions of forgiveness as an emotional transformation, and need not compete with them.

In her book on pardons, Kathleen Dean Moore argues, with Downie and Murphy, that forgiveness is not performative, and she contrasts this with pardons, which she agrees have a performative dimension. On her account, "in part because of the institution-bound nature of a pardon, pardoning is normally performative . . . when uttered by an appropriate person in an appropriate setting."[49] The contrast Downie and Moore draw, however, presumes that forgiveness itself is never part of an institutional response to wrongdoing, that it is instead necessarily personal and interpersonal. Moore's reasons for thinking it necessarily interpersonal stem from her reliance on Murphy's account of forgiveness as "primarily a matter of how I feel about you," which prevents us from seeing forgiveness as something institutions take part in; an institution has no feelings.[50] As I argue above, this account of forgiveness is limited and incomplete. It does not provide us a reason to think that forgiveness does not have a speech act dimension. Forgiveness can sometimes be the work of institutions as well as individuals, since institutions can issue statements that act as performatives.

Moore concludes that "saying 'I forgive' (even under the appropriate circumstances) is not a sufficient and, for that matter, not even a necessary condition for forgiving."[51] Insofar as I have argued that forgiveness is multidimensional, so that the requirements for forgiveness as an emotional process are not identical to the requirements for performative forgiveness, Moore's point is trivially true that the statement of the latter is neither necessary nor sufficient for the former. I disagree, however, that in the appropriate circumstances, saying "I forgive" is not sufficient to constitute performative forgiveness. Moore's argument here reveals a failure to appreciate what the appropriate circumstances are; Austin's view is that these circumstances include having attitudes that the statement accurately reflects.

Further, even if the circumstances are not appropriate, the performative commits a moral act that counts as forgiveness. To tweak Haber's example of John and Mary, imagine that Mary had rather insincerely said, "I promise I'll never mention this again," and at the next opportunity throws his past wrongdoing in John's face. With John, we would not say that Mary didn't *really* promise anything in the past, even if the circumstances were inappropriate because she had no matching attitude. Certain expressions set normative machinery in motion even in, sometimes unfortunately, the worst of circumstances. In this example and in many like it, the speaker commits something in the very act of saying it that changes her relationship to the listener. Just as "I owe you an apology," no matter how reluctantly said, performs the very thing it reports, "I forgive you" alters the status of the wrongdoer relative to the speaker. Indeed, it might be the very reason it can feel so awkward to say it.

In contexts in which women are expected to forgive, and wish to avoid the anger of others, the power of the illocution provides fresh incentive to avoid it; if stating one's forgiveness alters the relationship in a way that makes one's offender angry, then the safer route to ending angry feelings is to engage in it without saying so. The alternative expressions sound more like excusing than forgiving: That's okay. Don't worry about it. It's no big deal. Philosophers routinely distinguish between excusing and forgiving, trumpeting what seems to be a preference for forgiving as holding wrongdoers responsible, rather than letting them off their hooks, in a nearly universal display of the perspective of administrators of punishment. Yet with a fuller understanding of the motivation some agents may have to avoid the powerful force of illocutionary forgiveness, the distinction between excusing and forgiving now seems highly questionable, at least a very fuzzy boundary. If the set of actions involved in forgiving involves, for some, a locution that sounds more like excusing, need we so vociferously draw the distinction?

Alternative locutions, even those easily mistaken for excusing, may rather serve to change the subject, to signal a release of sorts to wrongdoers, to set something new in motion by diverting both speaker and listener from the topic of the offender's blameworthiness. Hampton captures this when she says, "It is . . . natural . . . to communicate [one's] approval to the wrongdoer and to seek to renew a relationship with him, although circumstances . . . might make that impossible."[52] As Murphy indicates, Hampton identifies the essence of forgiveness as "the decision to see the wrongdoer in a new, more favorable light."[53] Because she describes this decision and its realization as a process, Hampton comes closer than other mainstream theorists to arguing for a multidimensional account of forgiveness. She approaches considering the communication of forgiveness as intrinsic to its definition, but ultimately concludes that its expression isn't uniquely important, because she wishes to reject making its delivery a necessary condition for forgiveness to occur. Hampton's richer account is not limited to necessary and sufficient conditions like overcoming resentment or feeling compassion for wrongdoers, and I retain, in my own model, her idea that forgiveness involves a decision. To see forgiveness as a decision made for a multiplicity of moral reasons makes sense of the disparate occasions I've described for (justifiable and more controversial) forgiveness.

Seeing forgiveness as a process is likewise appealing, although models of process-forgiveness are more often defended in psychological literature than in philosophy. I have in mind Robert Enright's especially influential account in *Forgiveness Is a Choice*, although he apparently rejects the idea that the illocution is itself an occasion of forgiveness. In the course of arguing that forgiveness is a process, Enright observes, "Our research group discovered that simply saying 'I forgive you' is usually not enough. Although the words are said, the angry feelings often return."[54] I have no doubt that the research group is correct about their findings. I imagine that the words, even if intended sincerely, may fail to negate or head off seemingly contrary feelings. Analogously, a wedding vow to be monogamous may similarly not be enough to prevent future feelings for and attractions to others, and an apology be second-guessed if the apologizer later feels they didn't really do wrong after all. Even a bet is only a bet until I produce some cash to be able to back it up. In short, I imagine that most of our words for illocutions are also words for their related processes. Indeed, the moral force of them is due in part to the difficulty of living up to the moral machinery they set in motion. We may go so far as to say performative utterances entail moral processes. Therefore, I find myself persuaded by the process-conceptions, and certainly agree with the implicit ethical argument that the value of the communication is circumstantial and often inadequate to the task. But the set of forgiving acts that we could refer to as the process does not yet indicate that the illocution itself commits nothing.

Potentialities and Problems

I have argued that feminist theory rightly attends to often overlooked personal experience with moral actions. As we can see, many of us have experience with the performative utterance, "I forgive you"—with giving it, as in Meyer's case, refusing to give it, as in Wiesenthal's case, or avoiding it by offering excuse-like alternatives. Univocal accounts of forgiveness that require repentance, or compassion, or similar necessary conditions to be present for the action to "count" as forgiveness, are too limited to capture those occasions when we forgive for other moral reasons. An account of forgiveness that honors the experiences of moral agents must be fluid enough to include these occasions, and multidimensional to include the performative utterance of forgiveness.

In arguing that the first dimension of forgiveness involves a choice, I mean to include in this choice-making the widely shared idea that one has, or wants to have, a change of heart toward one's wrongdoer. Psychiatrist Richard Fitzgibbons calls this the cognitive level of forgiveness, "because the person decides to forgive, thinks it is good to do," but may not initially have all the attendant emotions.[55] With Enright, Fitzgibbons argues that cognitive forgiveness necessarily precedes and helps in the acquisition of the concomitant emotions such as compassion and love for one's offender. My identification of the choice-making dimension intends to include the change of heart that follows, and is intended to capture Hampton's and Horsbrugh's idea that forgiveness is a process. I prefer to call this a choice, rather than Hampton's decision, to capture the sense that forgiveness is chosen over other available moral responses to wrongdoing, a voluntary and risky moral act, and the beginning rather than the end of a process.

In arguing that the second dimension of forgiveness involves a speech act, I wish to convey that the meaning of the performative is dependent upon what the speaker means and what the hearer takes it to do. In other words, I think O'Shaughnessy is correct that the utterance, "I forgive," is intended to, and is sometimes taken to, commit one of a number of related acts; Martha Minow's concern that forgiveness in practice means declining to punish is understandable in light of this aspect of speech acts. This may then explain why philosophers generally resist the idea that forgiveness is also a speech act; perhaps it is controversial not because it is logically impossible, but because it is morally risky if the meaning of the speech act depends partly on what the listener takes it to set in motion. Perhaps we resist the idea that we forgive by expressing, "I forgive you," because we don't want the recipient to mistake the act in which we are engaging. That they can does not disprove the idea that forgiveness is sometimes a performative utterance. It does suggest, however, that the utterance has attendant moral difficulties of its own.

Precisely because I see forgiveness as multidimensional, I do not see it as "best" when both dimensions are employed. One of the reasons it is important to see these dimensions of forgiveness as distinct is to make sense of those times when circumstances such as the death of the wrongdoer make it impossible to express one's forgiveness to them. Another is to better account for those occasions in which it is best to engage in one form of forgiveness and not the other. Especially when we choose to forgive unrepentant wrongdoers, we may be praiseworthy for setting aside our justified feelings of resentment and considering ways to renew or improve our relations to them. However, we may at the same time find it morally blameworthy to express this attitude change to them if in their unrepentance they are still a danger to us or to others. In light of my argument that the meaning of a speech act depends in part on the way the hearer receives it, unrepentant wrongdoers who don't believe their actions were really harmful may take expressed forgiveness as condonation or excuse. Holmgren may be entirely correct that it is morally good for us to see them in a better light and work to overcome our own negative feelings, but this does not entail that it is always praiseworthy to communicate our forgiveness.

Last, as I have said and Meyer's early example indicates, it seems possible to express forgiveness before one has lived up to the choice to overcome one's negative feelings such as resentment. As children, for example, we need to believe our parents won't eternally resent us for our minor offenses and even for culpably wronging them, in order to develop basic senses of trust. Especially in response to the most trivial harms, then, parents may bear special obligations to their children to express forgiveness even before they feel forgiving. As parents grow older and more dependent for care upon their adult children, this need may grow in the other direction. Without disagreeing with Wiesenthal's action in *The Sunflower*, I can also imagine arguments that he should have given the dying Nazi soldier the expression of forgiveness he did not (yet, perhaps) feel.

The ethics involved in granting the performative are more difficult to outline than is the case for its coherence. Most philosophers who write about forgiveness are reluctant to offer hard and fast rules, and in this chapter in particular, I have expended much energy arguing for expanding the scope, types and meanings of forgiveness. From the point of view of feminist ethics, I am familiar with excellent arguments against the tendency in philosophy to laying claim to authority, which usually purports to represent all humans even as it fails to listen to or speak for most of us. I have argued that the meanings and purposes of forgiveness may differ for men and women in our culture. The circumstances for men and women with respect to forgiveness have been different enough that women respond in disproportionate numbers to calls to take part in forgiveness research, and different enough that both men and women expect women to be more forgiving. Because illocutions are interpersonal and recipients' interpretations are unpredictable, because forgiver and forgiven may not share cultural scripts and cannot know how they will feel in the future, every instance of the performative utterance, "I forgive you," is laden with moral risk.

Arguments that forgiveness is a performative, even when they differ, accomplish two worthwhile tasks. First, they offer an alternative to fitting forgiveness into what Haber calls "a straitjacket of necessary and sufficient conditions." If we are correct that forgiveness is, among other things, a performative utterance, then we avoid the conceptual difficulties that plague accounts of forgiveness as, for instance, the overcoming of negative feelings. How do we know when we're done overcoming? Hence, we further avoid having to ascribe the label "not forgiveness" to everything short of those instances that fit into the straitjacket.

The second task, although its logic requires further defense, includes accounting for those occasions when we forgive someone for wrongs done to another, or refuse to forgive in the cases of Wiesenthal and the mother forgiving her son's injurer. Because we are not now limited to proving that the mother resents an injury to herself, we have a way to refer to her act as forgiving. Indeed, it's hard to see what *is* morally problematic about forgiving someone for wrongs done to another unless forgiveness is a speech act; if third-party forgiveness were merely an unexpressed change of heart, then where would be the harm done? The added dimension provides us with a way to identify kinds of third-party forgiveness, and evaluate the choice to have certain attitudes toward others' wrongdoers as well as the expression of the attitude. Similarly, we can now discuss group forgiveness in a sensible way. Although groups cannot have a single change of heart, groups can engage in a collective speech act. My argument that forgiveness can consist in a speech act may go some way toward refuting the logical objections to third-party forgiveness and group forgiveness, but we have only glanced at the moral objections to such acts. Deeper discussion of these objections to such applications of performative forgiveness is the task of the next chapter.

Notes

1. Nick Smith, *I Was Wrong: The Meanings of Apologies* (Cambridge: Cambridge University Press, 2008), 12, 18.

2. Joram Haber, *Forgiveness* (Savage, MD: Rowman & Littlefield, 1991), 52.

3. Peter Digeser, *Political Forgiveness* (Ithaca, NY: Cornell University Press, 2001), 28-33.

4. Trudy Govier, *Forgiveness and Revenge* (London and New York: Routledge, 2002), 88.

5. Glen Pettigrove, "The Forgiveness We Speak: The Illocutionary Force of Forgiving," *Southern Journal of Philosophy* 42 (2004): 371.

6. Linda Ross Meyer, "Forgiveness and Public Trust," *Fordham Urban Law Journal* 27, no.5 (2000): 1515-1540.

7. Meyer (2000), 1523.

8. J.L. Austin, *How to Do Things With Words* (Cambridge, Mass.: Harvard University Press, 1962), 6.

9. Austin (1962), 6-7.

10. Austin (1962), 6-7.

11. Austin (1962), 7; Austin goes into some detail as to his examples in Lecture XII, 147-163.

12. Austin (1962), 11, 13-22.

13. Austin (1962), 10-11.

14. Austin (1962), 16.

15. Austin (1962), 11.

16. Austin (1962), 8.

17. Austin suggests the examples of marrying and betting; the example of unexpressed promising is mine.

18. Meyer (2000), 1523.

19. Meyer (2000), 1523.

20. R.J. O'Shaughnessy, "Forgiveness," *Philosophy* 42 (1967): 340-41.

21. William Neblett, "Forgiveness and Ideals," *Mind* 83 (1974): 270-75.

22. Haber (1991), 52, 40.

23. Haber (1991), 45-48.

24. Haber (1991), 49-50.

25. Pettigrove (2004), 386.

26. Meyer (2000), 1520.

27. Meyer (2000), 1521.

28. See especially Susan J. Brison, *Aftermath: Violence and the Remaking of a Self* (Princeton, N.J.: Princeton University Press, 2002).

29. Meyer (2000), 1523.

30. Laurence M. Thomas, "Evil and Forgiveness: The Possibility of Moral Redemption," forthcoming.

31. Joanna North, "Wrongdoing and Forgiveness," *Philosophy* 62 (1987): 505.

32. North (1987), 505.

33. Annette Baier argues further that the relation between trust and forgiveness works in the other direction; for "a trust relationship to continue," she suggests, there must be "willingness to forgive," Annette Baier, "Trust and Antitrust," *Ethics* 96: 238.

34. Trudy Govier, *Dilemmas of Trust* (Montreal and Kingston: McGill-Queen's University Press, 1998), 203 (emphasis hers).

35. Govier (1998), 203.

36. R.S. Downie, "Forgiveness," *Philosophical Quarterly* 15 (1965), 131.

37. Downie (1965), 131.

38. Downie (1965), 132.

39. Pettigrove (2004), 376.

40. Simon Wiesenthal, *The Sunflower* (New York: Schocken Books, 1969), 37.

41. Wiesenthal (1969), 99, emphasis mine.

42. Boss does not address the performative dimension of forgiveness, and Calhoun argues that "I forgive you" is reportive; my point is not that they share my position but that their concerns make more sense when we use the speech-act distinction. Cheshire Calhoun, "Changing One's Heart," *Ethics* 103 (1992): 77; Judith Boss, "Throwing Pearls to the Swine: Women, Forgiveness, and the Unrepentant Abuser," in *Philosophical Perspectives on Power and Domination*, ed. Laura Duhan Kaplan and Lawrence F. Bove (Amsterdam-Atlanta: Rodopi Press, 1997), 235.

43. Margaret Holmgren, "Forgiveness and the Intrinsic Value of Persons," *American Philosophical Quarterly* 30, no.4 (1993): 342. Later she qualifies this with the observation that forgiveness is only "appropriate" after one completes this task (343), which suggests a moral recommendation as to when to express forgiveness but does not obviously amount to a denial that the utterance is performative—just wrong.

44. Horsbrugh is not alone in arguing for forgiveness as the overcoming of resentment, but he expresses the most explicit concern about knowing when this is accomplished. See H.J.N. Horsbrugh, "Forgiveness," *Canadian Journal of Philosophy* 4 (1974): 278-279.

45. Pettigrove (2004), 381.

46. Robin Dillon, "Self-Forgiveness and Self-Respect," *Ethics* 112 (2001): 83.

47. Dillon (2001), 83.

48. Jeffrie Murphy and Jean Hampton, *Forgiveness and Mercy* (Cambridge: Cambridge University Press, 1988), 167.

49. Kathleen Dean Moore, *Pardons: Justice, Mercy, and the Public Interest* (New York, Oxford: Oxford University Press, 1989), 193.

50. Trudy Govier argues against this compellingly, and I take her refutations up in the next chapter.

51. Moore (1989), 185.

52. Murphy and Hampton (1988), 85.

53. Murphy and Hampton (1988), 85.

54. Robert D. Enright, *Forgiveness Is a Choice* (Washington, D.C.: APA Life Tools, 2001), 11.

55. Richard Fitzgibbons, "Anger and the Healing Power of Forgiveness: A Psychiatrist's View," in *Exploring Forgiveness*, ed. Robert D. Enright and Joanna North (Madison: University of Wisconsin Press, 1998), 65-66.

Chapter Five

Third-Party Forgiveness

Until very recently, philosophers of forgiveness generally assumed that only "direct" victims can forgive wrongs done to themselves, with the much-discussed exception of the mother who forgives a wrong done to her child.[1] Most theorists reject, as logically incoherent, many forms of third-party forgiveness (3PF), by which I mean the act of forgiving a wrongdoer for wrongs done to someone other than the forgiving agent. In previous chapters, I argue that in part, a commitment to such dyadic accounts stemmed from adherence to extreme forms of individualism, which, in turn, are often accompanied by masculinist biases and a preference for the administrative voice. Stipulating a dyadic framework presupposes the existence of direct (vs. indirect) victims and further presupposes the existence of identifiable discreet wrongs limited to one person. Although such circumstances are not impossible, this framework succeeds best with the sorts of wrongs we analytic philosophers tend to enjoy identifying: hypothetical, highly artificial, unproblematic cases, usually involving minor infractions of express contracts between adults of equal power. John Wilson, for example, famously takes the imagined violation of a meeting time between academic coworkers to be his paradigm.[2] This is an inadequate model for the occasions on which 3PF becomes a morally pressing issue, namely, when considering evils that harm multiple people in disparate power relationships. A growing minority of accounts have expanded the boundaries of who stands in a position to forgive. Not coincidentally, many such accounts are motivated by attention to, and sometimes membership in, groups that experience group-based harms, and the role of sympathy or solidarity between group members. Because experiences with oppression and marginalization contribute to senses of solidarity with victims, a feminist perspective can helpfully contribute to elucidation of third-party forgiveness.

In what follows, I argue that third-party (and thus group) forgiveness is logically possible, but not often ethically preferable. Based on feminist arguments that we are selves-in-relation, I argue that in some cases, we can say that they make the choice to (not) forgive and that this choice is followed by the relevant emotional and behavioral work that forgiveness usually involves. I argue that third-party forgiveness is multidimensional like forgiveness by direct victims, and can consist of a change in attitude or a performative utterance; both third-party and group forgiveness can be ethically problematic but powerful moral acts. I conclude that third-party forgiveness from a feminist perspective must consider the function of forgiveness in fostering the autonomy of others, while attending to the complications involved in being perceived to speak for those with whom we have relations of identification. By relations of identification I mean the connections we have with intimates and strangers with whom we identify, as I discussed in more detail in Chapter Two.

Intriguingly, although most philosophers reject the possibility that forgiveness can consist in a speech act, discussions of 3PF tend to focus on the moral machinery set in motion by expression of 3PF; as Alice MacLachlan says, "The most stringent objection to third-party forgiveness (that it negates the victim's agency) assumes the question really arises only when the victim herself refuses to forgive," which she notes needlessly restricts the function of 3PF, and which, I add, suggests that objectors *do* see expression of forgiveness as having a performative dimension.[3] In addition to indicating umbrage at occasions when A expresses forgiveness to B for what he did to C in the absence of C's forgiveness, philosophers also explore the appropriateness of A's refusal of forgiveness of B for what he did to C, when C has forgiven. In both cases the implicit prioritization of subverting victims' choices as *the* philosophical problem with 3PF, although understandable, unfortunately limits the terms of metaphysical and moral discussion of 3PF.

My position is that expression of 3PF is not intended metaphorically, and unless otherwise stated, not usually offered as a substitute for forgiveness by the direct victim, if there is one. As a speech act like victim forgiveness, 3PF communicates something to wrongdoers that sets similar moral machinery in motion. And as a moral choice to take up a certain attitude toward the wrongdoer of another, 3PF is a kind of forgiveness with important applications of its own. It does not replace the forgiveness of other victims. Throughout, I use the phrase "direct victim" in order to engage in the taxonomy already adopted by theorists of forgiveness, but what it means to be a direct victim is clearer on some occasions than others. A victim may be any individual or collective who has suffered harm as the result of a perpetrator's actions or culpable omissions.[4] Philosophers who describe third parties' forgiveness intend to refer to 3PF as forgiving for someone else's suffering rather than one's own. I proceed on the assumption that one may be both a victim and a third-party forgiver at the same time. When third-party forgivers are also victims, one may be tempted to describe them as "really" forgiving merely for their own injury, but as I argue below, this is an overly simplistic reduction of complex cases.

I avoid describing forgiveness as forgiveness "on behalf of" direct victims.[5] Although interceding on behalf of another may merely mean acting in their interest or in order to aid, acting on another's behalf can also denote acting as their representative or proxy, and too many scholars seem to conflate these denotations. Yet survivors who struggle with forgiving murderers of loved ones, for example, do not seem preoccupied with the question as to whether their forgiveness *stands in* for the forgiveness of the deceased; rather, they struggle with their own capacities and with moral questions as to what they ought to do. Likewise, perpetrators who offer their reasons for seeking forgiveness do not generally describe themselves as believing forgiveness from different sources to be interchangeable. The language of seeing 3PF as forgiving on behalf of others seems motivated more by moral questions of fairness or epistemological questions of adequate knowledge of particulars, and not a definitional component of 3PF. Objections to the logic of 3PF tend to include objections to the morality or desirability of 3PF; for that reason, it is difficult to describe arguments for 3PF's incoherence without mentioning the same authors' offense at its practice. I wish to show that 3PF plays a role in the defense of wrongdoers' victims, the community and the relationships between wrongdoers and those who identify with the victims of wrongdoing. I address common objections to 3PF before taking up arguments for its possibility.

The "Mere Metaphor" Objection

H.J.N. Horsbrugh, and with him Joram Haber, argues that 3PF is not logically possible, and that when A speaks of forgiving B for wrongs done to C, A either (i) means it metaphorically or (ii) means to communicate forgiveness for A's own suffering; in other words, A is really expressing forgiveness because A is a victim.[6] As an example of the metaphorical use of 3PF, Horsbrugh considers a speaker (A) who says he refuses to forgive the Nazis for what they did to the Jews, although A is "neither a Jew himself nor a relative nor close friend of any of their victims."[7] In such cases, he suggests, A either misuses the language of forgiveness insofar as he tacitly identifies himself as a victim, or refuses forgiveness only metaphorically, since if he is not a victim he must mean to convey instead that what the Nazis did is unforgivable in principle.

Berel Lang considers a similar common-language use, such as a third party (to be phonetically alliterative, let's call him Theo) saying, "I can't forgive Ralph for what he did to Valerie."[8] Given that he argues for the impossibility of third-party forgiveness on the basis that it violates the neces-

sary condition that only victims forgive, Lang argues that the above statement must not really be third-party forgiveness. Lang says the above statement by Theo seems "a metaphor for condemning someone or holding him
guilty, which is not the equivalent" of victim forgiveness precisely because
"on the conditions cited, the speaker is in no position to forgive."[9]

Aurel Kolnai argues, similarly, that "if Ralph commits moral transgres-
sions which do not infringe on [Theo's] rights and are not even indirectly
calculated to hurt [Theo] . . . [Theo] is not strictly speaking the victim of an
offence and the question of his forgiving or not forgiving does not properly
arise."[10] Philosophers using a Kantian model, including Haber and Jeffrie
Murphy, argue that Theo may feel moral indignation at how Valerie is
treated, but not the moral resentment that forgiveness requires; only victims
of wrongs can be said to resent them.[11] Like Kolnai and Lang, Murphy implies that in the statement above, Theo uses the word "forgive" metaphorically.

Lang may be correct that 3PF is not equivalent to the forgiveness of direct victims, but 3PF need not be equivalent in order to be logically possible. Were they equivalent, we would need no distinction between forgiveness by direct victims and 3PF. Instead, I suggest these are distinct moral
acts, and that both still play a role in responding to wrongdoing. Further,
Lang's objection that the speaker is "in no position" to forgive begs the
question; his statement requires some articulation of the position we need
be in to forgive. In the next section, we will have to consider reasons that
Lang does not explicitly entertain, and Murphy does, for the position that
only victims have standing to forgive.

Last, given my arguments in the previous chapter, we can see how a
discussion of Theo's statement would benefit from seeing it as a performative utterance. Rather than arguing against the logical coherence of 3PF, it
may be more productive to analyze the ways in which the utterance is infelicitous. If Theo doesn't even know Valerie—if he read about her in a
newspaper, or if she's a fictional character in a book—we may argue that
the speaker doesn't have the requisite relation of identification with Valerie
to be able to speak sensibly of forgiving her wrongdoer, and thus the performative is abused. If he is mistaken about the facts of the case, and Ralph
has actually done nothing wrong, then the performative misfires. Charles
Griswold similarly argues for conditions that establish a threshold of standing, including "justifiable indignation (sympathetic resentment), but also . .
. identification with the victim. . . . Identification, however, must be warranted; one cannot simply bestow it on oneself."[12] Warranted identification,
Griswold suggests, includes "ties of care" and robust knowledge of the offense and the victim. Absent some such conditions, a performative can be
badly done, but this does not entail that it is logically incoherent. I next

consider both implicit and explicit arguments for the position that only victims can forgive wrongdoers. I call this the 'strict victim' objection.

The "Strict Victim" Objection

The reasons for holding this position depend, of course, on which model of forgiveness is being followed. On some accounts, forgiveness is incompatible with punishment. John Wilson says that forgiveness means the wrongdoer and victim have resolved their debts and renegotiated their contract, or relationship.[13] If forgiveness is incompatible with or cancels punishment, then the advantage of showing 3PF to be incoherent is that this precludes the possibility that others let off the wrongdoer before the victim considers all the wrongdoer's outstanding debts repaid. In other words, the standard view that only victims forgive is important to this sort of debtor-creditor account because no one ought to be able to co-opt the victim's right to punish. The argument is reminiscent of Martha Minow's objection that, especially in cases of mass violence, "forgiveness often produces exemption from punishment" and "sacrifices justice."[14] 3PF would further be problematic on Wilsonian models in which another necessary condition is that the wrongdoer repent wronging his victim, in order for the victim to forgive. Repentance is described as part of the wrongdoer's payment. (Hence the claim by Aurel Kolnai that forgiveness can be earned.[15]) It makes little sense, then, for wrongdoer Ralph to pay some third party for wrongs done to victim Valerie.

On another kind of account, however, forgiveness is compatible with punishment. Howard McGary refers to these as self-pertaining accounts, so called because forgiveness turns on how the victim, herself, feels about the wrongdoer, regardless of the wrongdoer's payment of his debt to the victim.[16] The essence of forgiveness, from the point of view of a self-pertaining theorist, relies on the victim's overcoming his or her negative feelings about the wrongdoer; for Murphy and McGary, the victim must overcome her resentment for forgiveness to take place. The argument against 3PF from this position must be more indirect. How would one justify that "the person harmed forgives" is a necessary condition of self-pertaining forgiveness? Attraction to the standard view here must turn on something other than a fear that the wrongdoer will not be punished.

In this case, we must remember Murphy's argument that forgiveness essentially requires the victim feel the appropriate way toward the wrongdoer.[17] According to Murphy, the appropriate attitude to wrongs against oneself is resentment, and only when this is felt and overcome can forgiveness properly be said to have taken place; "we may forgive only what it is proper to resent."[18] Murphy credits Bishop Joseph Butler with being the first to identify resentment as the feeling forgiveness involves, but adds to Butler's account that only the victim of a wrong can feel resentment toward a wrongdoer. Others who feel for the victim may be moved to indignation toward the wrongdoer, but cannot be said to resent him because the function of resentment is self-defense, and "the primary value defended by the passion of resentment is self-respect."[19] Murphy concludes that only victims have the proper "standing" to resent and to forgive.[20] No one else is in a position to feel the restored self-respect of the victim, and no one else is thus in a position to feel the victim's overcoming of her resentment.

He does not clearly indicate, although perhaps he should, how marked a departure this is from Butler's own account of resentment. In the eighth of his *Fifteen Sermons*, Butler does not distinguish, as Murphy does, between "resentment" and "indignation." He frequently uses these terms interchangeably, and identifies resentment at one's own injuries as a feeling "exactly the same in kind" as one's resentment at wrongs to others, just "in a higher degree."[21] He describes the appropriate attitude to moral wrongdoing as "a resentment against injury and wickedness in general; and in a higher degree when towards ourselves," and suggests this "fellow feeling" is "one of the common bonds, by which society is held together."[22] In "Sermon Nine: Upon Forgiveness of Injuries," Butler notes that he will address only resentment at personal injury in his defense of the precept to forgive, but adds that this is simply because if resentment at personal injury tends to come in higher degrees, then it is most likely to result in "excess and abuse" of resentment—that is, revenge and retaliation.[23] (He does not argue the converse, that resentment at the wrongdoers of others cannot lead to excess and abuse.) Last, Butler notes that one can feel the highest degrees of resentment on behalf of "himself, or one whom he considers as himself."[24]

With his reference to "one whom he considers as himself," Butler seems to suggest that we identify with some individuals in meaningful ways. This is reminiscent of Haber's and Murphy's accounts of the mother who resents on behalf of her son. In refuting the implications of their positions, I argued for relations of identification, by which I mean that we psychologically identify with others in ways that allow us to resent and forgive their wrongdoers without losing the sense of our agency as distinct from the agent's.

As Murphy himself has noted, "There is enormous individual variation, of course, in the degree to which people are psychologically identified with others—even strangers."[25] He concludes that we thus forgive wrongs against those with whom we identify because we are then ourselves victims. As I have argued in previous chapters, this mistakes one's identification with the victim of wrongdoing for identification as the victim of wrongdoing.

At the same time, Murphy's and Butler's insights have pointed to a reason to think that we have relations of identification with those we've never met, perhaps because we can have connections with the otherwise-strangers that are important to our identities. In *The Sunflower*, Wiesenthal says of the Jews he'd never met but were told had burned alive, "I could have been one of the Jews carrying the petrol cans into the house."[26] Trudy Govier argues compellingly for seeing wrongdoing as productive of primary, secondary, and tertiary victims; in material ways, she concludes, Wiesenthal counts as all three:

> Obviously, Simon was not one of the people [Karl] killed: in this respect he was not a primary victim of [Karl] and his particular group. Yet as a starved and brutalized prisoner, Wiesenthal was personally and directly a victim of the Nazis more generally. . . . Simon was also a secondary victim of the Nazis: many of his relatives, including his mother, were killed. He was a Jew . . . so clearly he was also a tertiary victim of the Nazis. If it is victims who are in a position to forgive, then Simon was in a position to forgive.[27]

That a person can be in a position to identify with those who were killed, for the very reasons that they were killed, suggests that we can "think of another as ourselves" whom we have never encountered. Butler's account, as opposed to Murphy's, provides us with a compelling reason to think we resent a wrongdoer to a higher degree when the cruelty or injustice is practiced against someone whose interests we take as seriously as we take our own interests.

I have argued against Wilson's debtor-creditor model that forgiveness need not preclude punishment, although 3PF may carry with it special obligations to attend to serving justice for the victims. Against the self-pertaining model, I suggest that the feelings of those who psychologically identify with victims are relevant and not excluded from consideration. As I argued in Chapter Two, we are selves-in-relation, and constituted in part by our chosen and unchosen relationships with other people. For this reason, we psychologically identify with some others and can feel resentment against their wrongdoers. As Horsbrugh says, many can be hurt when a wrongdoer harms a victim.

Of course, Horsbrugh's answer is that in each instance of wrongdoing there are many victims *simpliciter*; in the case of a mother forgiving the person who wrongs her son, he says the mother really forgives the wrongdoer for causing her to suffer. This brings us to consideration of the objection that we are really discussing forgiveness by victims, and need not distinguish between forgiveness and 3PF.

The Argument for Many Victims

Horsbrugh and Haber argue that sometimes when A speaks of forgiving B for wrongs done to C, A means to communicate forgiveness for A's own suffering. I described this argument against 3PF, that it is really used to convey forgiveness or its refusal for one's own suffering, in Chapter Two with Haber's example of the mother forgiving someone for wronging her son. Haber argues in that case that an injury to the son is just an injury to the mother, because she psychologically identifies with her son, and so she really forgives the wrongdoer for the wrong done to her.[28] Horsbrugh argues similarly that close personal relationships "make it inevitable that someone other than the immediate victim sustains a serious injury," so the mother can forgive the wrongdoer for the harms she suffers as a mother; unlike Haber, Horsbrugh makes a point of adding that the wrongdoer is still not forgiven by the child.

Haber and Horsbrugh conclude that this kind of 3PF collapses into forgiveness *simpliciter*, since the mother, as a victim, forgives the wrongdoer for the harms she suffers. To return to Lang's example, Horsbrugh's analysis may suggest there is a sense in which Theo expresses moral resentment of his own. Perhaps he's personally affronted by Ralph's wrongdoing. For example, if Ralph was guilty of infidelity to Valerie, Theo could be expressing his personal disgust with infidelity.

As I argued in Chapter Two, however, Haber's interpretation of the mother-son example mistakes the mother's act because it describes her as identifying as her son, rather than with her son, in a way that loses the sense of her own agency. Horsbrugh's interpretation is limited in the other direction, since it misconstrues what the mother is upset about. His argument implies she is in a position to forgive her child's wrongdoer for her motherly suffering; I wish to show the opposite, that she experiences suffering because her child was wronged in a way that makes her anger and forgiveness of the wrongdoer appropriate.

Horsbrugh argues that the mother, like Theo, is really expressing some "first-party" reactive attitude, like personal offense at Ralph's infidelity. I resist this characterization because the objection seems to rest on something like a version of psychological egoism. I have previously suggested that because we are selves-in-relation, we may psychologically identify with those victims if we have personal relationships with them, or if we identify with their interests or the reasons they are suffering, and can resent and forgive on their behalf. In further defense of this position, I wish to argue now that doing this does not mean we forgive the wrongdoer instead of, or for, the victim. To show this, I return to another of Butler's *Fifteen Sermons*, in order to appeal to a form of Butler's argument in refutation of psychological egoism; just as egoists may confuse the subject with the object of one's desires, I argue that opponents to third-party forgiveness may confuse the subject of the refusal to forgive (Theo) with the object of his refusal (to defend Valerie's worth).

In the eleventh of his *Fifteen Sermons*, Butler considers the argument of psychological egoists that we are incapable of benevolence—that is, we are incapable of desiring the happiness of others.[29] Butler refers to the position of psychological egoism, the idea that all we can desire is our own happiness, as a "general mistake," and observes, "people are so very much taken up with this one subject that they seem from it to have formed a general way of thinking, which they apply to other things that they have nothing to do with. Hence, in a confused and slight way, it might well be taken for granted that" all we desire is gratification of our general desire for our own happiness.[30] Butler argues against this, saying that we have, in addition to a general desire for our happiness, particular desires for objects external to us, such as the desire for the good of another.

Butler acknowledges that there are those who assume that furthering the good of others is merely done to further our general desire for our own good; however, he suggests that those who confuse all desires for the good of others with desires for our own good are confusing the subject of desire with the object of desire. While I am the subject of all my desires, Butler concludes, I am not the object of all my desires, nor is my happiness the object of all my desires. A desire for the good of others is a particular desire with an object external to me. Although benevolence is compatible with my wanting my own happiness, I do not desire the good of others merely as a means to achieving my own happiness. If I did, then the satisfaction of any of my desires should be sufficient to give me happiness, and my desire for benevolence in particular would be inconsequential.[31]

In light of what Butler says, Theo's refusal to forgive Ralph for wrongs done to Val could be seen as a desire on Theo's part for Val's well-being. If this is the case, then it seems Theo is not merely expressing his own personal offense at Ralph's conduct as an injury to his sensibilities, for the object of Theo's benevolence is Val's happiness and not his own. Were Theo expressing mere personal offense at an injury to himself ("I can't forgive Ralph because infidelity repulses me,") then perhaps Ralph could simply make enough reparations to Theo to substitute for making reparations to his victim, the woman to whom he promised fidelity.

However, it matters, in our example, that the wrong was done "to Valerie." What makes Theo the third party and not the first party here is that he does not identify himself as the victim of wrongdoing. He clearly identifies Valerie as the victim of wrongdoing; it is her interests at stake, and not Theo's. If Butler is correct that we can have as the object of our desires the well-being of another person, then it seems consistent to hold that we can resent a wrong done to another for reasons other than that we are also victims of wrongdoing. If we can resent wrongs done to others for reasons that go beyond the extent to which we ourselves are victims, then we are in a position to give or refuse forgiveness to the wrongdoer.

This may be why Butler himself does not distinguish between resentment and indignation the way contemporary philosophers do. He argues that resentment is a passion we feel on behalf of anyone suffering injustice, "a resentment against injury and wickedness in general," and its natural object is anyone "who has been in a moral sense injurious either to ourselves or others."[32] Although philosophers who base their analyses of forgiveness on Butler's draw a very strong distinction between resentment, on one's own behalf, and indignation on behalf of others, Butler himself draws no such clear distinction.[33] Alice MacLachlan prefers a different approach, moving away from the language of resentment rather than expanding it, adding, "Insofar as forgiveness does frequently involve a shift in angry feelings, there is something question-begging in predicating it—by definition—on a version of anger that is only self-pertaining, then concluding that we can only forgive injuries to ourselves."[34]

However, in arguing that 3PF is possible and distinct from forgiveness by direct victims, I do not wish to imply that 3PF is always appropriate to express. Although I am unconvinced by those arguments that 3PF is logically impossible, I can understand why so many philosophers find it undesirable. The arguments against its desirability are the subject of the next section.

The Presumptuous Position

Minow objects, against amnesty by government officials, that "public forgiveness in particular runs the risk of signaling to everyone the need to forget." Noting Aryeh Neier's objection that 3PF may "usurp the victim's exclusive right to forgive his oppressor," Minow argues that third parties "thereby fail to respect fully those who have suffered."[35] Similarly, respondents to Wiesenthal's dilemma argue that 3PF ought not to be extended to Karl. Abraham Heschel posits that "no one can forgive crimes committed by other people. It is therefore preposterous to assume that anybody alive can extend forgiveness for the suffering of any one of the six million people who perished."[36] Another, after quoting Dryden's dictum "Forgiveness, to the injured doth belong," asks, "How can you possibly forgive monsters who burned people alive in public?"[37]

Like many philosophers, Peter Twambley reveals his suspicion of third-party forgiveness when he says, "We quite naturally stigmatize the presumption of one who offers to forgive a person who has not offended him by declaring that he has no right to forgive."[38] And Piers Benn says, "For third parties to declare that offenders need no longer feel they are objects of [the victim's] rightful resentment . . . is to bypass the victim's right to assert his moral standing."[39] One of the assumptions underlying the above statements is that third-party forgiveness is intended to take the place of forgiveness on the part of the victim of wrongdoing. How dare anyone do that, the theorists ask from both the debtor and self-pertaining points of view. Only the victim of wrongdoing knows whether she has been sufficiently repaid, on the debtor conception. And only the victim can feel and overcome the appropriate negative emotion (usually resentment), on the self-pertaining conception. For a third party to extend forgiveness to her wrongdoer is to wrongly presume to know what the victim should do, and further, to take that choice out of her hands.

However, it is not obvious that all third-party forgiveness is intended as a substitute for forgiveness on the part of the victim. Trudy Govier locates different varieties of skepticism at work in such responses; she and Eve Garrard identify double standards in holding principled or pessimistic views of forgiveness when the reverse does not seem true: "We certainly seem prepared to countenance third party *refusals* to forgive."[40]

Twambley and Benn may be attacking a straw figure in arguing only against those occasions of 3PF which proceed from an arrogant presumption that forgiveness by the third party will substitute for forgiveness by the victim. I infer that philosophers opposed to third-party forgiveness also fear that the wrongdoers may take expressed 3PF to be a substitute (even if it's not intended as such), and be led to dismiss the needs of their victims as a result. But this seems a problem with insensitive wrongdoers grasping at straws, and not proof that third-party forgiveness inherently wrongly substitutes in for the forgiveness of victims.

Let's take another look at Lang's example of third-party refusal of forgiveness: "I can't forgive Ralph for what he did to Valerie." One cannot tell from this statement whether the victim herself has forgiven Ralph. This sentence does not refer to what Valerie should or shouldn't do. And it does not say, "No matter what Valerie does, Ralph should consider himself unforgiven." The speaker [Theo] does not say that his judgment stands in for Val's or supercedes it. But Theo is saying something about his sense that the victim's worth is threatened by Ralph's wrongdoing. It matters to Theo that this wrong was done to her, and expresses Theo's regard for Valerie. Analogously, the statement, "Val is too good for him," could be an expression of Theo's high esteem for Val, and is not intended to prevent Val from considering Ralph her equal; to say Val is too good for Ralph is compatible with holding that no one deserves Val, and cannot substitute for Val's own "reactive attitude."

With this distinction in mind, let's return our attention to the objections from Part I. The first was that third-party forgiveness violates a necessary condition of the possibility of forgiveness listed in the two dominant definitions of forgiveness, namely the condition that only the victim of wrongdoing is in a position to forgive. The possible justifications for this exclusionary condition, however, rest on a presumption that third-party forgiveness cannot substitute for that of the victim. As I argue above, third-party forgiveness does not necessarily attempt to substitute for that of the victim; it can be, instead, non-substitute 3PF. And this objection can work in both directions; the forgiveness of the victim cannot substitute for the forgiveness of third parties. Theo could coherently say, "Valerie may have forgiven Ralph for treating her so awfully, but I certainly don't forgive him."

I suggested earlier that objections to 3PF from the point of view of the debtor conception could rest on some fear that 3PF co-opts the victim's right to reparation. Now it seems this is a variation of what I have described as the assumption that 3PF is intended as a substitute for victim forgiveness. However, it is not the case that if, in our example, Ralph makes reparations to Theo then he need not make reparations to the woman he wronged. Likewise, the self-pertaining account may also rest on some fear of substituting 3PF, if I am right that the objection rests on the idea that only the victim can be said to overcome the requisite resentment and recover her sense of self-worth. But in response to the self-pertaining account, I suggest that Theo is not expressing any judgment as to how Valerie feels about her sense of self-worth; he is rather expressing his own moral judgment about Valerie's dignity and Ralph's blameworthiness.

Articulating the Scope of 3PF

I have argued for the logical possibility of 3PF, but this does not show its ethical preferability. The objections against co-optation may not prove expressions of 3PF are incoherent, but what they say gives us pause when we consider the moral implications of such expressions. The moral objection to co-opting the victim's choice to forgive is compelling. Philosophers opposed to 3PF also indicate that both wrongdoers and witnesses may take expressed 3PF to be a substitute, even if it's not intended as such, and be led to dismiss the needs of victims as a result. Last, as Eve Garrard observes, objections to 3PF in response to crimes so heinous as to be unforgivable have both metaphysical and epistemological valences, although she argues that neither turn out to preclude forgiveness. The "claim that the Holocaust was too great a crime to be forgiven," Garrard argues, "begs the question at issue," and the related argument that the evils of the Holocaust are too incomprehensible to be forgiven worrisomely implies that forgiveness is almost always prevented, because "there is something difficult to understand about all wrongdoing."[41] I would add that the question as to how anyone can forgive monsters evokes the sense that on occasion, forgiveness is inappropriate whether the forgiver is a direct victim or not. This may well be true, but does not constitute an ontological objection to 3PF per se.

With Garrard, I see these objections as ethical rather than ontological; co-opting victims' responses and derailing restitution are certainly possible and at the same time morally wrong. Moreover, the ethical objection is not always warranted; it is not the case that all 3PF is intended as a substitute for forgiveness on the part of the victim. Yet certainly it is possible for someone to say he extends 3PF as a substitute for the forgiveness of the victim. Consider the following example: Ralph bemoans his lot to Sam, saying, "I've apologized to Val, sent her flowers, promised I'll never cheat again and groveled in the dirt, but she still won't forgive me." Sam responds, "Don't even worry about this anymore, because you've done everything you could. If you ask me, you've more than made up for your mistakes, and Val really should forgive you. I know I thought I'd never forgive you for what you did, but I've come around after seeing you suffer this long." In performing the preceding, Sam not only takes Ralph off the moral hook, in a clearly intentional way, but he also urges Ralph not to worry about doing any more for Val. This is the sort of occasion that gives us legitimate reason to worry that 3PF not only may unintentionally come across as substituting for forgiveness by the victim, but may be tendered by the speaker himself as intending to substitute for her forgiveness.

Rather than concede that this is metaphorical and not forgiveness, I suggest that substitute 3PF is, quite simply, very likely morally wrong. This does not seem controversial to me, given that first-party forgiveness could also be wrong, on occasion. Norvin Richards suggests that at times one is wrong not to hold on to her resentments, if it is at the cost of protecting herself from evildoers.[42] Haber and Murphy argue similarly that the victim of wrongdoing is morally required to respect herself and that it is dangerous to forgive too readily.[43] That 3PF may be morally wrong even more so than hasty forgiveness by victims is due to its potential to involve harm to others, since Sam's forgiveness above may undercut Val's need to assert her self-worth by withholding forgiveness from Ralph.

Even if the speaker doesn't intend for 3PF to substitute for the victim's forgiveness, this doesn't relieve all our concerns. In Chapter Three I argued that the power of performative utterances lies in part in what the listener receives; performatives set moral machinery in motion precisely because the hearer interprets such statements in meaningful ways. As Minow puts it, the process forgiveness sets in motion "depends upon a script that must be shared by the forgiven and the forgiver," and perhaps unfortunately, "many people do not share this script."[44] We can see that although possible, performative 3PF is morally problematic because in employing it the speaker takes a moral risk. There are some things we ought not to express even if we've taken up the new attitude toward the wrongdoer that sees him in a better light. Some moral machinery is wrong to set in motion, even if, as I've argued, we are in a position to do so.

However, because of this power performatives have, there may be occasions when it is morally incumbent upon us to refuse forgiveness for the wrongdoers of those with whom we have relations of identification. If I am right that the statement on Theo's part expresses his moral resentment of an injury done to Valerie, this raises the possibility that the refusal of 3PF may be the morally praiseworthy thing to do. Murphy wrote that resentment and the refusal of first-party forgiveness is a way for the victim to assert her moral worth against her wrongdoer.[45] On my account, the refusal of third-party forgiveness could be seen as a way for others to affirm the worth of the victim. Murphy argues that in injuring us, a wrongdoer indicates that he does not respect us and consequently may undermine our own self-respect. If so, one resource in recovering one's own self-worth is to have it affirmed by others; the moral resentment of third parties at wrongs done to us may assist us in recognizing that we have been wronged and resent the wrong as a way of affirming our self-respect.

If third parties can assist an injured person by affirming her worth, then it may be the case that third parties have an obligation to communicate this to her wrongdoer. The refusal of third-party forgiveness is one way to affirm that the victim is entitled to respect. It is meaningful in a way that saying, "Your victim ought not to forgive you," is not. Communicating to the wrongdoer that the victim ought not to forgive her injury may indicate nothing about the degree to which the wrongdoer ought to be morally condemned. Saying the victim ought not to forgive her injury is compatible with believing that the wrongdoer is deserving of forgiveness, but the victim is most likely too vulnerable right now. To say the victim ought not forgive is also compatible with holding that we do not find the wrongdoer merits our own moral condemnation. I may believe that Ralph didn't err all that badly in finding love in more than one woman, but still see that from his wife's point of view, he ought not to be forgiven for adultery.

The communication of refusal to extend my own forgiveness to a wrongdoer for the injuries of another says something much stronger, however, as we can see from contemporary examples. Descendants of Holocaust victims who assert that they can never forgive Germany's burden of guilt, nor those of countries like Switzerland who enabled the Holocaust, say much more than that the direct victims are dead and they mustn't speak for them, that the time isn't right or that it was wrong from one perspective but not from another. Those who object that they can never forgive are affirming the worth and dignity of the dead and their willingness to defend other potential victims from future holocausts.

It could be argued that the fact that they are descendants means they act as agents for their ancestors, and in this sense really are taking on the role of first-party victims; many of us without such intimate connections to the Holocaust appeal to no personal policy of nonforgiveness. However, this doesn't raise serious conceptual difficulties for 3PF. Granted, those who are closer to victims of wrongdoing are more likely to be moved to moral resentment of the wrongdoer. If they are outraged and strangers are not, it may be because they are rightly paying attention, or have the ties of care that Griswold considers important.

Ties of Care and Knowledge

Having greater opportunity to be moved to defend a victim does not, in itself, render one a victim, or the agent of a victim. The scope of appropriate 3PF in such cases may be limited to those who have relations of identification with the victims of wrongdoing. What makes 3PF seem so presumptuous to Horsbrugh and Downie in a case where I say, "I can't forgive the Nazis for what they did to the Jews," could have more to do with our suspicion that it is disrespectful to those related to the victims for me to claim a relation of identification where none exists. One may argue that it's possible for many people to empathize with the victims of the Holocaust, but such an argument would have to establish that many of us understand, from similar experience, the situation the victims found themselves in. This is intuitively implausible, and ethically suspect.

Particular responsibilities for caregiving or attention provide added justification for 3PF, where imaginative empathy alone may not suffice. It is surprising that Griswold would require ties of care for warranted 3PF, yet neglect to mention the extensive feminist literature on the moral valence of caring relationships. In calling attention to the moral significance of ties of care, feminist philosophers reject care as autonomic, "natural" in the sense of being unreflective and therefore nonmoral; instead, we call attention to care as a moral activity. Eva Kittay and Diana Meyers famously describe "a morality of responsibility and care," which "begins with a self who is enmeshed in a network of relations to others, and whose moral deliberation aims to maintain these relations."[46] The responsibility to give care inherently includes being in a position of power to provide care, and so the ties of care are also power relations; care providers can have both "power to" and "power over"—that is, capacities to act and in addition social positions that allow them to exert their will to act in the interests of the cared-for. As I argued in Chapter Three, ties of care are also particular; it is not the case that just anyone has the responsibility or the opportunity to check on us when we're sick, meet with our students, provide for our dependents, or serve as trustees for our parents. Despite advances in gender equity, women in the U.S. are still more often than not the primary sources of house- and child-care, and so these ties of care may proliferate in gendered ways. Such robust and pervasive responsibilities for caregiving would therefore seem to add to the sorts of standing, warrant, or authority that philosophers require for third-party forgiveness.

Standing does not entail forgiving, but does give rise to the responsibilities inherent in any relationship in which one is in a position to attend and listen in helpful ways. Sarah Hoagland articulates an ethic of attending, according to which "I am present to you, I engage with you. I focus my energy on you. . . . I become a witness."[47] Attending, on Hoagland's account, fosters responses attuned to "power from within" rather than "power over," a necessity in horizontal relationships which both respects and brings about relations of equality; she has argued against Nel Noddings's portrayal of caring, which focuses on unequal relations and the sometimes overarching power of maternal caregivers, in ways which permit views of care as unidirectional and deprioritize the desirability of equal relationships.[48] Their accounts share a resistance to impartial principles which ignore the responsibilities created by relational ties. Yet as Hoagland notes, a resistance to impartiality need not entail insular or parochial attitudes toward others; resistance to oppression also requires attention to "political reality, material conditions, and the social structure of the world."[49] Susan Brison captures the sense of identification inherent in sociopolitical ties of care, when she identifies the roles of testimony, witnessing, and group-based narratives in constructing moral agents and memories. Her own experiences with trauma and recovery reinforced her "view of autonomy as fundamentally dependent upon others. . . . The right sort of interactions with others can be seen to be essential to autonomy."[50] Moreover, which individuals with whom we identify can change, depending on the functions of different testimonies and narratives. "The groups with which I identify expand (from rape survivors to all trauma survivors), contract (victims of attempted sexual murder), expand in other ways (hate crime survivors), contract (rape survivors), and so on," Brison says, moving her to suggest "we also need to question common assumptions about identity and acknowledge our multiple, shifting, intersecting identities."[51]

Identifying primary, secondary, and tertiary victims may help to clarify with whom one identifies on some occasions; in light of Brison's insights above, they may also be beside the point with respect to with whom one identifies, and why, on other occasions. As Margaret Walker notes, there are many situations in which one is faced with "whether to remain in a position of grievance and demand with respect to the wrongdoer."[52] I add that the impulse to identify that which is unforgivable reveals our mixed responses to the possibility that we stand to grant or withhold third-party forgiveness, as we decide how best to assist the aggrieved. When we are in a position to extend attention or care to victims by participating in reacting to their wrongdoers, we must come to terms with our relationships to wrongdoers and victims, negotiating relationships in a way which enhances recognition of agency and correct self-perception.

At times, the moral decision to defend victims may require that we refuse 3PF. If victims of wrongdoing could be assisted by having their worth affirmed by third parties, then refusing 3PF could be a moral obligation. Perhaps it is incumbent upon us to affirm a victim's worth most especially when she declines to show respect for herself. Whether or not her forgiveness of someone who still presents a threat to her is "genuine" is not especially important here. Someone whose self-respect was never great to begin with may genuinely believe that she feels no worse than before injury was done her, and thus forgive her wrongdoer insofar as she feels sufficiently reconciled to him. In a more extreme example, a child who does not fully appreciate the enormity of a wrong done to him may forgive an adult wrongdoer. It could be argued that here again, the third party actually acts as an agent for the child, but it isn't obvious why this is so. If the third party feels moral outrage although the child is the victim, this seems like a clear candidate for a case of 3PF.

Group Forgiveness as a Form of 3PF

The ethics of group forgiveness have been discussed at greater length by other philosophers, most notably Trudy Govier, and I will not rehearse all her arguments here. However, what she says in defense of its logical possibility is supported by my arguments for 3PF. Govier rightly notes that "the philosophical literature on forgiveness . . . deals almost exclusively with individuals," but argues that "we must be willing to apply" discussion of forgiveness to groups if our work is to be "relevant in political contexts."[53] The project of applying philosophies of forgiveness to groups is helped by seeing forgiveness as at times a performative utterance which groups could endorse and issue. Accounting for 3PF is also important to defending the logic of group forgiveness, since in political contexts not every member of the forgiving group is always directly wronged by every member of the groups who are the objects of their statements.

Yet here we also find one source of resistance to the idea that the possibility of 3PF entails the possibility of group forgiveness. To appropriately forgive whole groups, we must be able to appropriately blame whole groups. If, however, one denies that we can do the latter, then one may understandably object to the former. A white congressional representative who hears that the president considers apologizing for slavery on behalf of the entire U.S. government may say, "I've never owned slaves. Why should my group need forgiveness?" The argument may be that if all members of the forgiven group did not harm all members of the forgiving group, then there is nothing to be forgiven for.

It is outside the scope of this chapter to refute all objections to collective responsibility. I will limit myself to suggesting that whole groups can indeed be appropriately blamed, if said groups are in positions in which they can take responsibility for harms and apologize. Philosophers have done much work to establish that groups can be blamed non-distributively; in other words, it need not be the case that each member of a group is equally to blame in order for the entire group to be responsible as a collective.[54] Peter French argues that rather than focus on the extent of each member's responsibility within a collective, we should attend to the power the members have in their group to be able to move a group to action or inaction.[55] That is, instead of demonstrating a lack of responsibility for past harms, group members should demonstrate a lack of power to rectify or call attention to those harms. In the above example, the congressional representative would, I submit, have a hard time showing he has no such power.

The argument against group forgiveness that groups cannot have attitudes of resentment as a group is, I hope I have shown, unconvincing. One can feel resentment for one's own hurts and the hurts of those with whom one is intimately connected. Donald Shriver said of his experience in the civil rights movement "that group resentments against other groups often have deep roots in memories of a traumatic past," which is complicated by the difficulties in identifying individual wrongdoers in society-wide oppression.[56] And Govier argues that groups can teach cultural distrust of each other, which forgiveness can be a part of resolving.[57]

Last, resistance to the idea that groups forgive may stem from a fear, like Minow's, that some powerful members of the group will speak for those less powerful members in a way that denies their agency. While Minow's objection is a serious ethical concern for anyone recommending a group's forgiveness, it does not constitute an argument that groups cannot forgive. It's entirely possible that a group, or its spokespeople, go about expressing such performatives in ways that are morally risky, even morally wrong. Yet to suggest they cannot logically be said to forgive at all seems to deny the agency of victims in another way.

I have argued that 3PF is not identical with forgiveness *simpliciter*; it is a distinct, though related, moral act with similar dimensions. 3PF, as distinct from forgiveness *simpliciter*, does not collapse into forgiveness by victims, but can play a role in the defense of the victim or the wider community. For example, refusing 3PF to someone whom a victim forgave even though he continues to be a threat to her self-worth could be a moral obliga-tion. Granting group forgiveness, which may entail 3PF, can be a part of resolving groups' cultural distrust of each other. Yet 3PF should not be lightly recommended. We are well-advised to take seriously those concerns that 3PF may be morally wrong when it is granted on the assumption that it can substitute for the forgiveness of the victim. It gives us further pause to consider that the speech act involved in giving 3PF may be received by the hearer as substituting for the forgiveness of victims even if we intend no such substitution. 3PF turns out to be a logically possible, but morally risky, act.

Notes

Some portions of this chapter appeared in rough early forms in "Why Self-Forgiveness Needs Third-Party Forgiveness," in *Forgiveness: Probing the Boundaries*, e-book, Oxford: Inter-Disciplinary Press, 2008. My thanks to editors and reviewers for their helpful comments on those incarnations.

1. As Charles Griswold (*Forgiveness: A Philosophical Exploration*, Cambridge and New York: Cambridge University Press, 2007, 117) succinctly observes, it is "taken for granted by almost all authors on the subject that only the injured party may forgive." Examples in philosophy tend to be found most often in earlier works; see R.S. Downie, "Forgiveness," *Philosophical Quarterly* 15 (1965): 128-34; H.J.N. Horsbrugh, "Forgiveness," *Canadian Journal of Philosophy* 4 (1974): 269-282; Aurel Kolnai, "Forgiveness," in *Ethics, Value and Reality* (London: Athlone Press, 1977), 211-224; Jeffrie Murphy and Jean Hampton, *Forgiveness and Mercy* (Cambridge: Cambridge University Press, 1988); Berel Lang, "Forgiveness," *American Philosophical Quarterly* 31, no.2 (1994): 105-117. The intuition that only direct victims forgive is more easily found today in popular and press accounts; see especially the outpouring of responses to the news story of the English vicar who, in 2006, quit her job when she couldn't forgive those responsible for her daughter's death in the London bombings of July 7, 2005. For an excellent discussion of the nuances of this view, see Trudy Govier and W. Verwoerd, "Forgiveness: The Victim's Prerogative," *South African Journal of Philosophy* 21, no.1 (2002): 97-111.

2. John Wilson, "Why Forgiveness Requires Repentance," *Philosophy* 63 (1988): 534-535.

3. Alice MacLachlan, "Forgiveness and Moral Solidarity," in *Forgiveness: Probing the Boundaries*, e-book (978-1-904710-62-2) (Oxford: Inter-Disciplinary Press, 2008).

4. In defining victims this way, I borrow the language of the United Nations' Declaration of Basic Principles of Justice for Victims of Crime and Abuse of Power (A/RES/40/34), 29 November 1985: "'Victims' means persons who, individually or collectively, have suffered harm, including physical or mental injury, emotional suffering,

economic loss or substantial impairment of their fundamental rights, through acts or omissions that are in violation of criminal laws. . . . A person may be considered a victim, under this Declaration, regardless of whether the perpetrator is identified, apprehended, prosecuted or convicted and regardless of the familial relationship between the perpetrator and the victim. The term 'victim' also includes, where appropriate, the immediate family or dependants of the direct victim and persons who have suffered harm in intervening to assist victims in distress or to prevent victimization."

5. Griswold (2007), 117.

6. Horsbrugh (1974), 274.

7. Horsbrugh (1974), 275.

8. Lang borrows the example of common usage from Downie (1965), 128; Lang uses symbols rather than proper names, and Downie's example is "I can't forgive the Nazis for what they did to the Jews." I took the liberty of inserting proper names into this example because I am also drawing on Aurel Kolnai, who uses phonetically alliterative names such as 'Ralph' for the wrongdoer. I use 'Valerie' to refer to the victim and 'Theo' to refer to the third party involved. See Lang (1994), 107.

9. Lang (1994), 107.

10. Kolnai (1974), 212.

11. As noted in Chapter Two, it is my position that we have good reasons to think more than one person is in a position to resent.

12. Griswold (2007), 112.

13. Wilson (1988), 534-535.

14. Martha Minow, *Between Vengeance and Forgiveness* (Boston: Beacon Press, 1999), 15.

15. Kolnai (1974), 102.

16. Howard McGary, "Forgiveness," *American Philosophical Quarterly* 26 (1989): 343.

17. Murphy (1988), 21.

18. Murphy (1988), 20.

19. Murphy (1988), 16.

20. Murphy (1988), 21.

21. Bishop Joseph Butler, Sermon IX, "Upon Forgiveness of Injuries," *Fifteen Sermons* (Charlottesville, VA: Ibis Publishing, 1987, edition previously published by Robert Carter & Brothers, New York, 1860), 75.

22. Butler (1860/1987), 75.

23. Butler (1860/1987), 80-81.

24. Butler (1860/1987), 80-81.

25. Murphy (1988), 21n9.

26. Simon Wiesenthal, *The Sunflower* (New York: Schocken Books, 1969), 15.

27. Trudy Govier, *Forgiveness and Revenge* (London and New York: Routledge, 2002), 109.

28. Joram Haber, *Forgiveness* (Savage, MD: Rowman & Littlefield, 1991), 49.

29. Butler (1860/1987), 164-83.

30. Butler (1860/1987), 167.

31. Butler (1860/1987), 178-180.

32. Butler (1860/1987), 74-75.

33. See esp. Murphy (1988) and Haber (1991) for evidence of this strong division. Butler may, in this respect, be undercommitted while those philosophers, including Mur-

phy, Haber, Strawson, and Rawls, who distinguish between resentment and indignation are overcommitted. See P.F. Strawson, *Freedom and Resentment and Other Essays*, Oxford: Methuen, 1974; Rawls, "The Sense of Justice," in *A Theory of Justice* (Cambridge, Mass: Harvard University Press, 1971).

34. MacLachlan (2008), n.8.

35. Minow (1999), 17.

36. Heschel, in Wiesenthal (1969), 131.

37. Mark Goulden, in Wiesenthal (1969), 119.

38. P. Twambley, "Mercy and Forgiveness," *Analysis* 36 (1976): 89.

39. Piers Benn, "Forgiveness and Loyalty," *Philosophy* 71 (1996): 376.

40. Eve Garrard, "Forgiveness and the Holocaust," in *Moral Philosophy and the Holocaust*, ed. Eve Garrard and Geoffrey Scarre (Burlington, VT: Ashgate Publishing Co., 2003), 232; on moral skepticism, see Govier (2002), 79, 92-95.

41. Garrard (2003), 234.

42. Norvin Richards, "Forgiveness," *Ethics* 99 (1988), 77-97.

43. Haber (1991), 88-108. Murphy (1988), 24-29.

44. Minow (1999), 18-19.

45. Murphy (1988), 19-25.

46. Eva Feder Kittay and Diana T. Meyers, "Introduction," *Women and Moral Theory*, ed. Kittay and Meyers (Totowa, NJ: Rowman and Littlefield, 1987), 10.

47. Sarah Hoagland, *Lesbian Ethics: Toward New Value* (Palo Alto, Cal.: Institute of Lesbian Studies, 1988), 127.

48. Sarah Hoagland, "Some Thoughts About 'Caring,'" in *Feminist Ethics*, ed. Claudia Card (Lawrence, Kan.: University Press of Kansas, 1991), 246-253.

49. Hoagland (1991), 260.

50. Susan J. Brison, *Aftermath: Violence and the Remaking of a Self* (Princeton, N.J.: Princeton University Press, 2002), 61.

51. Brison (2002), 94-95.

52. Margaret Urban Walker, *Moral Repair: Reconstructing Moral Relations after Wrongdoing* (Cambridge and New York: Cambridge University Press, 2006), 163.

53. Trudy Govier, "Forgiveness and the Unforgivable," *American Philosophical Quarterly* 36, no.1 (1999): 1n.

54. Accounts of collective responsibility include David Cooper, "Collective Responsibility," *Philosophy* 43 (July 1968), pp. 258-268; Virginia Held, "Can a Random Collection of Individuals be Morally Responsible?" in *Journal of Philosophy* 67 (70): 471-480; Larry May, *The Morality of Groups* (Notre Dame, Ind.: University of Notre Dame Press, 1987); Gregory Mellema, *Collective Responsibility* (Amsterdam: Rodopi, 1997); Richard Swinburne, *Responsibility and Atonement* (Oxford: Clarendon Press, 1989); and Peter French, *Responsibility Matters* (Lawrence, Kan.: University Press of Kansas, 1992).

55. French (1992), 71.

56. Donald Shriver, *An Ethic for Enemies: Forgiveness in Politics* (Oxford: Oxford University Press, 1995), ix.

57. Trudy Govier, *Dilemmas of Trust* (Montreal and Kingston: McGill-Queen's University Press, 1998), 194-195.

Chapter Six

Self-Forgiveness

Despite my best efforts, I cannot ignore the mistakes I made at the interrogation facility in Fallujah. I failed to disobey a meritless order, I failed to protect a prisoner in my custody, and I failed to uphold the standards of human decency. Instead, I intimidated, degraded and humiliated a man who could not defend himself. I compromised my values. I will never forgive myself.

Eric Fair, "An Iraq Interrogator's Nightmare"

I am working on forgiving myself, but when I think about my past behavior, I feel guilty all over again.

Women's substance abuse treatment group member

When faced with our own errors, the sense that we cannot forgive ourselves can feel so pronounced that it is hard to believe the phenomenon is in doubt. Yet philosophers rarely discuss self-forgiveness, and a surprising number exhibit skepticism or ambivalence about self-forgiveness, perhaps because paradigms of forgiveness usually entail harming easily identified, external victims who are in a position to both feel and enact extension of forgiveness to the wrongdoer. I suggest that self-forgiveness is both possible and often morally preferable. In saying this, I rely on feminist and non-feminist arguments that we are fragmentary, rather than unified, selves-in-relation. I argue that the fragmented nature of the self, especially the traumatized self, is one that supports and enables the possibilities of self-inflicted evil and self-forgiveness. Perhaps not surprisingly, the fragmented self is also the source of obstacles to self-forgiveness, as is the unpredictability of memory. I argued in previous chapters for a view of forgiveness as, at times, necessitating continual recommitment, given the epistemological impossibility of knowing whether external victims will continue to recommit to forgiveness in the future. The parallel is true of self-forgiveness; although some occasions of self-forgiveness may be easy, our own internal unpredictabilities permit ongoing reassessment of ourselves.

Self-forgiveness may be a response to one's harming others, or to harming oneself. Difficulties involved in both overlap, but differences in their complexities bear investigation separately. Both varieties of self-forgiveness face theoretical objections. Against the possibility of forgiving oneself for harming others, objections to third-party forgiveness recur for those who believe only victims forgive. Against the possibility of forgiving one's self-harm, objections to the possibility that one can either wrong oneself or make amends to oneself require some refutation. Beyond their logical possibility, forms of self-forgiveness evoke ethical resistance, as those identifying with external victims rather than self-forgivers find just cause to be skeptical of the worth or desert of self-forgiving perpetrators. At times when just punishment is not possible, the awareness that wrongdoers may let themselves off internal hooks can seem odious to victims with no hope of justice, and to administrators burdened with the frustrated awareness that none of their remedial actions will be adequate, as well as those of us who identify with victims and administrators.

Yet surely we can all identify with wrongdoers to some extent. We are none of us innocents; even good people living uneventful lives occasionally err. It may be less likely for some people than others to struggle with self-condemnation, but I presume most readers have had the experience of self-blame to a degree with which external others would not agree, or berating oneself either voluntarily or involuntarily, or regret which brings home whole new appreciation for the expression, "I could kick myself." At times when self-condemnation is upon us, the reassurances of others seem off the mark. It can feel as though no one knows how truly at fault we are, as though anyone who would assure us our self-blame is uncalled for simply doesn't have our inside information. Occasions for self-forgiveness are occasions for self-perception, and reveal the extent to which we are complex and divided, rather than unified selves.

Fragmented Selves

The longstanding debate in philosophy as to whether the self is unified is complicated, to put it mildly. Traditionally, Euro-American analytic philosophers have tended toward the view that the self is unified and can be identified by essential characteristics; feminist philosophers have generally opposed this view. With the attention to complexities of cognition in twenty-first-century philosophy, more theorists have come to agree with views of the self as structurally fragmented. The increased diversity of philosophers and attention to the complexities of moral and sociopolitical lives has led to more theorists advancing views of the moral agent as socially fragmented. Parallel developments in psychology have included debates as to the importance of self-complexity, whether this refers to differentiation of compositional elements of the self, integration of self-perceptions, or some balance thereof.[1] Postmodern accounts of the self do not sharply distinguish between fragmented composition or structure and fragmented social perceptions; Judith Butler, for example, argues that the fragmented self is composed by interacting in social situations.[2] The emerging subfield of gender studies adds to accounts of the self as structurally and socially fragmented; Anne Fausto-Sterling, for one, argues that bodies, genders, and identities are indefinitely subject to change, and never finally stable. Gender and sexuality become "somatic facts," bodily realities.[3]

When I describe the self as fragmented, I intend to refer to the structure or composition of the self as well as the multiplicities of self-perceptions and social perceptions. I take recognition of the existence of fragmented selves to be compatible with projects of integrity; descriptions of our inward multiplicity are not intended as arguments against the value of integrating our self-perceptions. Further, fragmentation admits of differences in kind and differences in degree; to say we are all fragmented selves, while true, scarcely approaches accounting for the sorts of fragmentation of those who suffer from schizophrenia, dissociative identity, and other disorders involving deep psychological disconnections, victims of trauma with conflicting or divorced self-conceptions, and oppressed people with the heightened self-consciousness born of looking at themselves through others' eyes. Put this way, fragmentation may seem so ubiquitous as to be uninteresting, but feminist theorists are persuasive that attending to fragmentedness is philosophically important. The nature of the self has implications for what it means to count as a self socially, politically, and morally, and implications for health and well-being, knowing oneself, living with oneself, and developing integrity—that is, a self-conception consistent enough that one may avoid being "an interpersonal chameleon . . . fitfully reacting in all ways to all people."[4]

Examples of individuals with extreme structural fragmentation may move some to argue that it is possible some selves are fragmented, without making it true that all selves are fragmented. One may allow for the possibility of multiple personalities, more recently designated as dissociative identity disorder (DID), and see it as proof that to the extent one is not so disordered, one is not, therefore, fragmented.[5] The tradition of philosophizing about rational moral agents as opposed to the nonrational, or unified agents as opposed to the exceptional few who are not unified, lends itself to seeing persons as divided into the larger class of individuals who are normal, rational, and unified (or capable of integrity) and the smaller class of abnormal, less than rational, fragmented individuals. Although I can imagine points at which to establish thresholds of rationality or integrity which support locations of moral responsibility, I suggest that it is no longer useful or accurate to describe humans as either unified or fragmented. Much evidence compels us to acknowledge that fragmentation comes in varieties and degrees.

Descriptions of DID are revealing of that variation. Stephen Matthews identifies two possible interpretations of "the individuation of persons with DID," which he refers to as the "multiple person thesis" and the "single person thesis."[6] On the former, DID can be interpreted to mean that one body literally contains multiple persons. On the latter, "individuals with DID have a disorder that has the effect of fragmenting one's existing personality. . . . The alleged alter personalities are not to be thought of as literally separate persons, but rather states in which patients lose control . . . and are globally deceived about who they are."[7] In either case, Matthews says, the person suffers from a "paucity of psychological connections between the alter states."[8]

Although most of us do not suffer from DID, I find Matthews's characterization of DID helpful in thinking about fragmentation as, in part, a paucity of psychological connections. In the cases of constrained but less radically fragmented persons, connections between past, current, and future selves are sometimes intentionally severed, sometimes unintentionally. Matthews's attention to patients' being "globally deceived about who they are" is likewise instructive, because it calls to mind the similar, though less radical, fragmentation caused by conflicting self-concepts, which are possible for many people, and notably reported by victims of trauma. Susan Brison, both a philosopher and a survivor of a brutal attack, describes conflicting self-concepts as obstacles to overcoming trauma, and argues that they reveal the relational nature of the self, "one of the positive aspects of a kind of multiple consciousness."[9] "That survivors gain the ability to reconnect with their former selves by empathizing with others . . . suggests that healing from trauma takes place by a kind of splitting off of the traumatized self which one then is able to empathize with, just as one empathizes with others."[10]

It is certainly possible to point to valuable evidence that victims of serious harms both self-report and demonstrate varieties of fragmentation. Diagnoses of survivors of abuse share elements with diagnoses of post-traumatic stress disorder (PTSD).[11] Unlike DID patients, sufferers of PTSD may not be globally deceived about who they are, but a sudden awareness of their conflicting assumptions and unreflective self-deceptions can be painful. Brison concludes, "The literature on trauma does seem to support the view, advocated by Derek Parfit, that the unitary self is an illusion and that we are all composed of a series of successive selves."[12] Trauma fragments selves (more than usual) because it disrupts the narratives we tell ourselves about our past, present, and future, dashing plans, focusing our attention on our vulnerabilities, and maintaining a state of alertness to danger which prevents integrating beliefs about a self-in-control with awareness of one's uncontrollable responses to new fears.

Self-image discrepancy is likewise reported in high correlation with eating disorders, which are, not coincidentally, more likely to be found in victims of domestic abuse and similar traumas.[13] Psychologists note that marked "disparity between the real self-image (the self as one currently is) and the ideal self-image (the self one would like to be)" is coupled with a very low real self-image.[14] The fragmentation of the self in eating disorders takes the form of divorced self-concepts in addition to conflicting concepts; perceptions of how one looks relative to others, and how one thinks of one's past and future selves, are so (literally and figuratively) disproportionate that victims are considered to be radically, pathologically self-deceived. Therapists' concerns include the seeming inability of patients with anorexia to relate the nearness of death with starving behaviors. Patients often exhibit belief in basic truths ("Starvation causes death," "I'm not eating"), and disconnection between them at the same time ("It won't kill me"). Such contradiction is evidence of Matthews's "paucity of psychological connection"; the falsity of the belief that anorexia isn't fatal is clearer when one reflects that one in 10 women hospitalized with anorexia dies of the disorder.[15] Feminist attention to victims of domestic violence and to women and girls with eating disorders has culminated in an appreciation of self-deception and the social self as a product of structural fragmentation and fragmented, conflicting self-perceptions.

Claudia Card notes similarly that self-conceptions are relationally informed, saying, "If attachments are the source of our fundamental norms and values, some selves may not be very unified; we may have conflicting self-conceptions."[16] This observation occurs in her discussion of "doubling," defined by Robert Lifton as the fairly extreme dissociation of Nazi doctors, who "develop a 'second self' to avoid having to confront inconsistencies in one's own values and behavior."[17] In later passages she cites W.E.B. DuBois's description of "'twoness,' having two selves;" "one self he called 'American,' and one he called 'Negro.' He also described this 'double-consciousness' as a sense of 'always looking at oneself through the eyes of others.'"[18] Although she discusses doubling and the double-consciousness of twoness separately, I take them to be forms of fragmentation which lie on a spectrum defined by degrees of dissociation and self-awareness. The double-consciousness described by DuBois, the habit of looking at oneself through the eyes of others, also typifies the other-directedness of femininity. When raised to the extreme of divorced self-conception described above, other-directedness is a hallmark of eating disorders.

The intentional and unintentional disconnections people make between their self-conceptions and their chronological selves is also a predominant theme of self-forgiveness literature. Robin Dillon attends to practices of self-condemnation which involve renouncing oneself, or one's previous selves, in an effort to reconcile conflicting self-conceptions, noting that "wrongdoing is not all that might call for self-forgiveness. Wrong feeling, wishing, wanting, thinking, reacting, and especially wrong *being* may bring it into play as well."[19] She suggests that "our view of ourselves . . . is always double: we see ourselves both as we think we are and as we would have ourselves be."[20] This sense of double consciousness is amplified in some with unmanageable remorse. She cites psychologists' interviews with subjects seeking self-forgiveness who struggle with "a sense of 'brokenness,' an estrangement from self and others that is deeply painful . . . 'beating oneself up,' . . . 'internal battle' with 'the enemy within'"; in short, Dillon says, "one is alienated from oneself."[21] I add to her account that it is important to note the complexity of this stance toward oneself, which has both controllable and uncontrollable aspects. Surely anyone who has beaten themselves up inwardly can recall the almost involuntary repetitiveness with which we do so, and yet, other forms of self-condemnation or self-distancing can be thoroughly reflective and deliberate, even, as Dillon says, "a mark of one's decency," as one renounces past wrongs.[22] Renouncing the self that could choose wrong acts may act as a negative connection when it does not result in the sense of alienation.

As I have characterized it so far, the fragmented self can become literally disintegrated by a paucity of psychological connection, by intentional or unintentional distancing between selves, by other-oriented views which take oneself as an object, and by conflicting self-conceptions and divorced self-conceptions, as well as other sources. Fragmentation can be structural, perceptual, or both. Fragmentation is not merely temporal, on my account, although the concept of a fragmented self includes the difference between chronological, "successive" selves; fragmentation is also intended to capture the multiplicity of selves inherent in conflicting self-conceptions and double-consciousness. Not all persons suffer from such fragmentation, or rather, all persons are fragmented but in ways which do not always result in suffering, especially if these sources of fragmentation are mild or rare. The fragmented selves I have discussed so far are victims of more basic harms. Those of us who have lived with such harms are also well-documented as likely to be self-blaming and self-punishing, excessively so.[23] Whether we are right to consider ourselves culpable is a separate question.

Self-Perception and Culpability

Those who suffer are sensibly identified as victims, and culpability is rightly assigned to others who cause such suffering, when identifiable external wrongdoers inflict basic losses and exacerbate psychological disconnections. Consequently, many accepted therapeutic treatments involve dissuading victims from self-blame and self-punishment. It is not ordinarily appropriate to hold up their culpability to the victims who suffer so. "To be culpable," as Card says, "we ought to have acted differently," which presupposes that we have the requisite capacities and opportunities to act differently.[24] Feminists have documented the ways in which victims of domestic abuse and those who suffer eating disorders are deprived of options by factors outside of their control; certain capacities may be limited. In cases of domestic abuse, abusers sometimes intentionally arrange the choices of the abused, the better to control them, and others interested in upholding institutions of law, marriage, family, private property, and so on wittingly or unwittingly assist in limiting those choices. In cases of eating disorders, therapeutic practitioners describe their patients' own pathological misapprehension of their bodies as limiting their capacities to correctly choose how to eat and live; others interested in reinforcing the requirements of femininity, masculinity, social affirmation, cultural hegemony, and so on wittingly or unwittingly assist in limiting the capacities of disorderly minds.

As power comes in degrees, then, so does culpability, and with reduced freedom comes reduced culpability. Yet some victims of evils are also articulate about the sorts of decisions involved in living with evils by adopting forms of compliance with evildoers. Unlike those victims of the Holocaust who chose death rather than bow to their captors, Primo Levi says, those who survived by perpetrating evils on others inhabit a "gray zone" in which they are "rightful owners of a quota of guilt."[25] Although resistant to misappropriating the experience of the Holocaust to discuss the experience of women, Card notes the relationship between Levi's sense of guiltiness and Andrea Dworkin's argument against battered women's innocence; as Dworkin says, "I don't know any innocent adult women. Life is harder than that for everyone. But adult women who have been battered are especially not innocent. Battery is a forced descent into hell and you don't get by in hell by moral goodness."[26]

In discussing both Primo Levi's and Andrea Dworkin's rejections of uncomplicated innocence, Card focuses on their concern with victims harming external others. Card concludes that women suffering the evils of misogyny and oppression inhabit "gray areas," which do not always entail the severe life-or-death stresses of Levi's gray zones, but which share important features of gray zones: "First, its inhabitants are victims of evil. Second, these inhabitants are implicated through their choices in perpetrating some of the same or similar evils on others who are already victims like themselves."[27] Misogyny and oppression, Card says, "complicate women's choices," and she notes that feminist philosophers, like many philosophers who grapple with evils, "have long struggled with the question of how ethically responsible agency is possible under oppression."[28] Like Card, I rely on the evidence that even in some of the worst gray zones, victims report making ethical choices, even when those choices are so complicated. To attempt moral agency and, potentially, break chains of evils requires seeing oneself as responsible, which, itself, requires at least partially correct self-perception.

The extent to which anyone has correct self-perception is usually presumed to be fallible, even when discussing healthy agents with uneventful lives. Whether damaged victims perceive themselves correctly and have first-person authority is in even more doubt in the cases I'm most interested in considering. The very suffering that renders agents victims also compromises their agency, and it is impossible to know exactly how accurate their self-perceptions are. The complicated nature of gray-zone victims' self-knowledge results in the bind that Brison identifies for victims of being perceived as a "credible, but (or because) sick, victim-witness;" in other words, damaged agents are "trustworthy (about their felt suffering), and untrustworthy (about what they could do)."[29] The epistemic difficulties inherent in self-perception are reflected in Hannah Arendt's account of "the deepest reason . . . nobody can forgive himself:"

[In being forgiven,] as in action and speech generally, we are dependent upon others, to whom we appear in a distinctness which we ourselves are unable to perceive. Closed within ourselves, we would never be able to forgive ourselves any failing or transgression because we would lack the experience of the person for the sake of whom one can forgive.[30]

Arendt's suggestion that we are "closed within ourselves" certainly evokes some of the self- and other-deception, even the secrecy, with which gray agents live. Yet on Arendt's account, self-knowledge amounts to a contradiction; knowledge is shared, public, relationally verified. Only action and speech reveal our inner natures: "In acting and speaking, men show who they are. . . . This disclosure of 'who' can almost never be achieved as a willful purpose. . . . On the contrary, it is more than likely that the 'who,' which appears so clearly and unmistakably to others, remains hidden from the person himself."[31] Secrets hide us from ourselves as much as from others.

However, precisely because inhabitants of gray areas are often in oppressively lonely and unacknowledged straits, I doubt that we are entirely "dependent upon others, to whom we appear in a distinctness which we ourselves are unable to perceive." In accounts of those who have been both victims and perpetrators of evils, sometimes the gray agent has the most information about the wrongs done and their magnitude. Card evokes the difficulty and complexity of gray agents "fighting oppression from within," saying, "The evil done to them is one that neither perpetrators nor victims are eager to acknowledge publicly."[32] Surely the evils done *by* them are not clearest to others, either. In one of Levi's painful examples of his morally gray choices, he recounts a day in which he and fellow concentration camp victims are close to dying of thirst during forced labor, when he finds a pipe containing a small amount of water.[33] Only Levi knows of the pipe, and therefore bears the awful responsibility as to whether to share it, and with whom, a close friend, or the worst-off among them. Until he shared the details in his memoirs, it seems that no one knew Levi's choices as well as he did himself. In suggesting he appeared to himself more distinctly than he did to others, I do not mean to suggest that his self-apprehension was either perfect or complete. Nor is the situation of his own making. Yet choices present themselves, even in the grayest zones. Where one bears the responsibility for making them, one may bear some of the responsibility for the foreseeable sufferings that result.

The capacity for the fragmented self to "appear to oneself distinctly" is less than perfect, but it is demonstrable, especially in examples of self-condemnation for harming others. In the epigraph opening this chapter, a former interrogator perceives at least some of his own culpable wrongdoing, and it is not necessary to our purposes to know if he has perfect or even nearly perfect self-knowledge. To the extent he recognizes the decisions over which he had control, Eric Fair blames himself, and denies himself forgiveness. Dillon defends the understandability of self-condemnation for harming others, even in the absence of control. She points to examples such as "accidentally backing a car over and killing a child, leaving one's invalid mother behind to get the rest of the family to safety when the murdering soldiers sweep down on one's village," and committing an aging, unwilling parent to a nursing home, as occasions for guilt over one's responsible actions, "even though one did, objectively or in one's own mind, nothing wrong."[34] Dillon follows philosophers including Jeffrie Murphy and Herbert Morris in being refreshingly skeptical of the claim that where there wasn't objective wrong, there isn't "really" forgiveness, arguing, "In fact we do speak of not being able to forgive ourselves in cases like these;" with Murphy, she resists regarding the feeling of "self-hatred even when one has done nothing wrong as merely inappropriate or irrational or neurotic."[35] Consistent with this view, Card notes that "self-forgiveness makes sense as a renunciation of self-condemnation or self-blame," in the absence of an external wrongdoer to "resent."[36]

Self-Forgiveness for Harming Others

Self-forgiveness for harming others comes in for more moral and logical skepticism than does self-forgiveness for self-harm. This is understandable, since skeptics tend to identify with victims who have not yet extended forgiveness of their own. I defend self-forgiveness for one's wronging others for the same reasons that I defend the coherence of many forms of third-party forgiveness (3PF). Consider the case of someone who exclaims, "I'll never forgive myself for hurting you!" Discussions of self-forgiveness often involve one's refusal to forgive one's own harming of another; that is, one refuses to forgive though someone else is the victim. Surprisingly, philosophers rarely notice that self-forgiveness for harming others is a form of 3PF, even as most philosophers contend that 3PF is either impossible or imperfect.[37] I am moved to wonder if so many philosophers would be comfortable ruling out 3PF if they realized that doing so ruled out varieties of self-forgiveness as well. Self-forgiveness is a form of third-party forgiveness which simultaneously supports the likelihood that 3PF is possible and benefits from its defense. Recall that self-pertaining accounts often rely on a strict distinction between resentment and indignation, arguing that we resent injuries done to ourselves, and feelings for all others, no matter how dear to or distant from us, are feelings of "indignation," not resentment. As I have argued, sentiments do not sharply divide into resentment versus indignation, and the world is not neatly divided into self versus everyone else. We are selves in relation and are constituted not only by our connections to intimate others but also by our relations of identification to those we have never met. When we "understand another person's situation . . . intensely," we engage in a kind of empathy with another which gives rise to the personal feeling of resentment on behalf of the other.[38] In cases of self-condemnation and self-forgiveness, it is even clearer that we are not just relational, we are also fragmented selves; in holding up our own blameworthiness, we identify more with our victims than with our wrongdoing selves. I suggest that because we are fragmented and relational, we may psychologically identify with our victims, especially when we have personal relationships with them, or identify with their interests or the reasons they are suffering. Therefore, we can resent and forgive ourselves as their wrongdoers, in ways which recognize victims' sufferings.

Yet we all know this is more easily done at some times than others. When we cannot reconcile with ourselves, when efforts at integrating new information about ourselves fail, the effects of self-alienation can be profound. Instead of guilt at particular acts, which may motivate wrongdoers to recompense or account for them, self-alienation can easily lead to shame, which, unlike guilt, "often motivates people to hide their flaws or to lash out defensively against anything (or anyone)."[39] Taking responsibility for the well-being of one's victims entails seeing oneself as capable of responsiveness; self-alienation is not a hallmark of capability, and instead of looking to the future, mires one in the past, horrified at one's own deeds or faults. Claudia Card seems to share this view when she says, "Some willingness to forgive oneself, even for evil deeds, may be needed to sustain motivation to fulfill our obligations and avoid repeated wrongs."[40]

Severe self-condemnation is even more likely as a response to serious harm, and it is neither unlikely nor usually desirable that victims forgive such harms quickly. Although victims' forgiveness, as I said, would facilitate self-forgiveness, wrongdoers with the power to do something about their victims' suffering have no right to demand their forgiveness and, even more, may be morally wrong to wait for it before allowing self-forgiveness to begin. This seems a painful bind; the very decency that renders one appalled at one's actions also calls for one to move toward capable responsibility taking. Severe self-reproach is not entirely under one's control, however, if one feels so broken and alienated. How are senses of integrity and worthiness to be recovered in wrongdoers who would do better to act in recompensing their victims?

Here, I return to the possibilities inherent in the logic of third-party forgiveness. As Eve Garrard notes, "We certainly seem prepared to countenance third-party *refusals* to forgive."[41] She argues that third-party refusals are only sensible if third-party forgiveness is possible. I suggest that third parties, including witnesses, bystanders, and political leaders, have a role to play in wrongdoers' self-forgiveness, which is only possible because third parties can forgive; however, my argument is not that third parties ought to forgive wrongdoers, especially before victims forgive. Instead, I argue that third parties' recognition of wrongdoers as moral agents with capacities for responsibility may promote the sense that the wrongdoer, although not yet forgiven, is still a part of the moral community. Research on political amnesty suggests that moral responses such as recognition, apology, and clear understanding of past harms are positively correlated with senses of responsibility and future-oriented acts, even if they are not correlated in any consistent way with forgiveness. In short, I suggest that even express refusals of forgiveness, by third parties, would accomplish forms of recognition and respect which may promote wrongdoers' capacities for guilt (instead of shame) and action (instead of alienation). I hope I have shown that 3PF and self-forgiveness are at least coherent concepts and logically possible, especially for those who have relations of identification with victims.

I do not wish to ignore those occasions on which 3PF and self-forgiveness are morally wrong, arrogant or intended to substitute for victims' forgiveness in order to let wrongdoers off their moral hooks. Yet sus-

picion of morally wrong 3PF seems well represented in philosophy already
for at least the past fifty years. The epistemic difficulties inherent in knowing the inner heart of wrongdoers moves Hannah Arendt to argue that we
cannot properly forgive ourselves at all; citing her view, Charles Griswold
says, more recently, "Self-forgiveness is rightly suspected of abuse," although he makes more room for its possibility and usefulness than does
Arendt.[42] And the most public occasions for reflecting on the possibility of
3PF at group or national levels are those involving great atrocities, after
which all moral responses are likely inadequate. Rather than concede that
3PF and self-forgiveness in such cases are merely metaphorical or not forgiveness, I suggest that offering 3PF as a substitute for the forgiveness of
victims is morally wrong, when it distorts the agency of others or abdicates
one's own responsibilities. When it does not, say, on those occasions when
victims are dead and 3PF is the only available variety of forgiveness, we
are best off biting the bullet and accepting that 3PF is the best available
response even as it is also "unquestionably imperfect."[43] Its imperfection
does not weigh against self-forgiveness or 3PF as forms of forgiveness, on
my account, since no form of forgiveness is perfect. Even those tenderings
of forgiveness that adhere to idealistic descriptions are risky, since we are
subject to change, to memory, to reversal, and to the interpretations and
misinterpretations of others.

Despite its imperfections, 3PF and self-forgiveness have important
moral functions. In discussing the evils people suffer, we are forced to accept moral remainders that cannot be neatly discharged; memories and feelings linger and come to constitute identities. 3PF is just one response to
suffering, and it will not be an adequate response, even at those times when
it is the best available. These are even greater problems for self-
forgiveness, precisely because self-forgiveness centrally involves the sorts
of remainders with which we struggle to live. Not everyone succeeds, and
some end the struggle without forgiving themselves.

Self-forgiveness does not always require great internal struggle, of
course. For example, self-forgiveness for a trivial wrong which the victim
has already quickly forgiven and forgotten may not require any reflection at
all, so much as mere rest and recovery; renewing one's connections facilitates self-forgiveness even more swiftly, and when it is anterior to victim
forgiveness, it may even be a morally unimportant achievement. I have in
mind more complicated occasions, however, as I continue to resist taking
unproblematic and trivial cases as paradigmatic. Self-forgiveness is morally
at issue when we struggle with ourselves, our very desire to continue living
with ourselves, and when others are not yet forgiving of us or entirely decided about continuing to live with us. In other words, self-forgiveness is
significant when it intersects with our capacities for taking responsibility,
for our own well-being, and for the well-being of victims. Because morally

pressing occasions involve self-reproach and varieties of self-renunciation, self-forgiveness becomes important in the course of recovering moral integrity. Although we may be capable of living without integrity, lacking it may be conducive to neglecting our responsibilities, our own moral ideals, and work against such basic goods as hope and trust.

Self-Forgiveness for Self-Harm

Our responsibilities to others may require, as Dillon says, renouncing oneself in ways that put distance between one's remorseful and harming selves, as a mark of one's decency or a motivation to change and make recompense to one's victims. It is more difficult to establish culpability for self-inflicted evils. Philosophers have occasionally doubted self-inflicted evils are even possible, except in prudential senses. Card cites Hobbes's related objection that there are no duties to oneself "because [a man] can release himself at his own pleasure," and refers to Marcus Singer's objection that self-release "would surely be nonsense;" like Hobbes, Singer says "alleged duty to oneself would be a 'duty' from which one could release oneself at will, which is self-contradictory."[44]

Yet the evidence of the excessive self-condemnation of fragmented selves would seem to provide exceptions to these views, at a minimum. Were we rationally self-interested calculators and unified selves, we may indeed be best off releasing ourselves from disproportionate senses of responsibility. Instead, however, we exhibit capacities for fragmentation, self-punishment, and dissociation, in both controllable and uncontrollable ways. The uncontrollable forms of self-harm may be amoral, or symptoms of illness, but controllable forms of self-harm may be moral harms when our practices demean us, damage our capacities, or limit the opportunities of our future selves.

Moral self-harm is most often defended by pointing to the requirements of self-respect. Dillon and Card both point to the demands of self-respect as engendering duties to oneself.[45] Bernard Boxill and Laurence Thomas argue that servility under the oppressive practices of racism can degrade one's character over time, and self-respect may require a form of protest which asserts one's worthiness as a person.[46] That racism and misogyny are evils is not in dispute, of course; it is understandable that living with evils confronts us with daily choices about how to get by. These choices often involve compromise and sometimes involve damaging our own self-respect, or undermining our senses of self-worth. Although understandable, the self-infliction of evils in such circumstances may still be culpable. In saying one who self-inflicts is culpable, I am not arguing he or she is an evil person, or maliciously embraces evil motives; following Card, I hold that evils are characterized by the severity of their foreseeable and basic deprivations, and not by the diabolical wills of perpetrators.

Further, I am compelled to point out that not all the choices of victims of self-inflicted evils are equally culpable. As I have said, culpability admits of degrees correlative with the freedom of one's choices. Whether to stay in a room or attempt to leave when one has been threatened with violence is painfully constrained. Whether to tell someone about it at a gathering the next day is different, and survivors can attest to the storm inside as they weigh which truths to tell. No options feel like good ones in a world in which reporting abuse is seen as a reflection on one's choices of relationships in the first place, or likely to increase the abuse if the report is mishandled. Similarly, the choices of eating disorder patients to deprive themselves of food stem from recognized illnesses, but the further choices involved in keeping their behaviors, their self-hatred, and their deprivations secret are more robust. When they take the form of ending relationships, deceiving others, or declining opportunities for meaningful work, those who self-inflict incur costs for which their current and future selves may hold them accountable.

So far, I have argued that it is logically possible to establish the culpability of self-inflicted evil. It is equally important to consider ethical objections to identifying self-infliction. Dangers include (1) detracting attention from blame rightly assigned to external perpetrators, and (2) victim-blaming in a way that feeds classic responses to domestic abuse ("why don't they leave") and eating disorders ("eat something and get over it"), which place too much of the blame on victims, and neglect the responsive powers and responsibilities of witnesses, groups, institutions, and nations.[47] Card cites the impulse toward feminist solidarity that motivates "refraining from judging women who give in" to complicity with evil and harming fellow women.[48] Such motivations might be even more compelling in refraining from judging self-damaging self-compromise. One who self-inflicts evils has by definition suffered, and locating any culpability may add to her suffering. When victims in gray areas are prone to self-punishment, sensitive people hesitate to add to their burdens.

Yet crediting victims with (occasionally) accurate self-reproach may restore agency to damaged agents, opening up the possibility that victims engage in some rational forms of self-blame, and assisting those who self-inflict in limiting excessive self-condemnation by locating where self-blame is appropriate (and where it is not appropriate). To begin the process of what Brison describes as empathizing with oneself or other one-selves, we have to be able to see ourselves, recognizing ourselves as both agents and victims. External others would do well to listen to our stories of, as Arendt would have it, appearing to ourselves distinctly. Given the somewhat secretive lives gray-area inhabitants often live, victims are sometimes the only ones who know the extent of their choices involved in living with evils. As Card says, "The realization of women's—or any victim's—capacity to compromise with evil is disillusioning."[49] I would add that many of us who have inhabited these gray areas realized this about our capacities for compromise in the course of living with evils, and so the confrontation with what she calls "myths of female innocence" can be disorienting. One way to assist victims in recovering agency may be for others to cooperate in our confrontation of our responsibilities to our past and present selves, and, as Card says, "overcome the moral traps that oppression sets for us."[50]

In rejecting the possibility of self-forgiveness, Arendt may have presupposed an indistinct and unified self in her early work, yet she captures the difficulty with self-forgiveness as a process "closed within ourselves." Self-reproach is a function of memory, and self-inflicted evils such as self-degradation, sacrifice of plans and hopes, and taking on another's unworthy image of oneself as one's own, linger long. Like the evils Card focuses on, they come with moral remainders that are not simply discharged like debts, nor always resolved with the long processes that therapy and self-forgiveness involve. Card refers to self-forgiveness as an achievement.[51] Because of the way memory uncontrollably recurs, however, I prefer to describe self-forgiveness as an ongoing commitment, much like the commitments involved in long-term relationships. Given my adherence to the ontology of the fragmented self, I see forgiveness as a commitment to the ultimate long-term relationship: the set of relationships between one's past, current, and future selves.

Not everyone manages this relationship with equal ease. I recall a student who asked me, "Does forgiveness require reconciliation?" At the time, given our discussion of interpersonal and political forgiveness, I told her that theoretically, it did not necessarily entail reconciliation, but that in practice it was difficult to do without it. Persons can make efforts to sever relationships, for example, but find they are constrained to remain in the same communities, relational circles and geographical locations. Nations can divide, establishing new borders, building walls and declaring themselves independent from each other, but continue to share land and people with affective ties and ongoing hatreds. Therefore, varieties of reconciliation may become necessary for the sake of continued persistence. Likewise, self-forgiveness requires reconciliation with oneself so that one may go on living, or living well. I have come to agree with psychologist Marjorie Baker's saying that "one must, of necessity, reconcile with oneself if one is to forgive oneself."[52]

Not everyone continually decides to reconcile with their many selves. Primo Levi seemingly chose not to continue to live with his memories, and wrote that he would lightheartedly absolve those whose compulsions were greatest and perpetations minimal just months before apparently taking his own life.[53] Brison provides us reason to think that reconciliation with one-self and one's world is not always necessary, or even rational or morally best:

> It is not a moral failing to leave a world that has become morally unacceptable. I wonder how some can ask, of battered women, "Why didn't they leave?" while saying, of those driven to suicide by the brutal and inescapable aftermath of trauma, "Why didn't they stay?" . . . as if such an explanation were needed. Those who have survived trauma understand well the pull of that solution to their daily Beckettian dilemma, "I can't go on, I must go on," for on some days the conclusion "I'll go on" cannot be reached by faith or reason.[54]

Therefore, unlike Singer and Hobbes, who reject duties to oneself because it is "nonsense" to think that we could release ourselves from our obligations at our own pleasure, I have the opposite concern. Closed within our fragmented, not entirely controllable selves, we don't always see the renewal of self-blame coming, the intrusive memories, the fresh act of self-deprivation that reminds us we are not perfectly healed. With such worrisome unpredictabilities of the human mind, self-forgiveness is in danger of becoming an infinitely receding point, if self-forgiveness entails release.

Attention to Dillon's distinctions between different kinds of self-forgiveness suggests possible long-term responses. Dillon distinguishes between transformative self-forgiveness and preservative self-forgiveness, and of the two, transformative self-forgiveness is more centrally involved in the early work of overcoming particular self-inflicted evils.[55] Transformative self-forgiveness overcomes a negative stance toward oneself, not just one's negative evaluation of one's own wrongdoing but fundamentally one's shame; "even when the stance is prompted by wrongdoing or the terrible consequences of one's actions, its object is oneself."[56] Dillon locates the difficulty of self-forgiveness for serious harms in the senses of self-worth and moral self-identity, "how one assumed one was and believed one should be."[57] Transformative self-forgiveness, on this account, is necessary when one's self-conceptions are constituted by one's past acts; it is backward-looking and assesses one's attitude toward how one has lived so far.

Preservative self-forgiveness, in contrast, is forward-looking, allowing for what Dillon refers to as "a margin for error or shortcoming," and comprised of an attitude toward oneself which is realistic and accepting; preservative self-forgivers "see themselves as basically decent and aiming to be good, capable of moral self-improvement . . . and, on the other hand, as inherently fallible and liable to get even far off track."[58] Dillon uses the analogy of a forgiving surface that allows one to drop a glass without its shattering; the idea is that one will still make errors, which can be accommodated rather than felt to be irreversibly damaging.[59] Dillon notes that this relies on a self-conception that is "not dominated by standards they must not fail to meet."[60] In the context of living with self-inflicted evils, the self-conception may be benefitted by accurately seeing oneself as fragmented and not entirely in control of one's memories and habits of self-reproach. Accepting that one's own moral remainders make continually releasing oneself difficult eases the high standards of one's long-term relationship with oneself.

The work of preservative self-forgiveness need not be done by a victim in isolation. Brison persuasively argues that the recovery of autonomy is interdependent and relational.[61] The recognition of others provides us with options, sources of control, and assists us in integrating our self-narratives; the denial of recognition can leave us trapped within ourselves. If Arendt's note that we are "closed within ourselves" is all too true, I take comfort in Brison's insight that we can re-integrate ourselves through dialogue and narrative, because "*saying* something about a traumatic memory *does* something to it."[62] Our most basic capacities for self-acceptance and self-respect rely on the perceptions of our worth on the part of others as well as our own self-perception. Recovering from self-inflicted evils requires more than the confidence of the Cartesian assertion, "I think, therefore, I exist," if one's thoughts include the old threat that one ought not to exist. The relational nature of autonomy then bears out Card's observation, "Perpetrators need the sense that they are worth the effort that self-improvement will require. Some self-forgiveness may be requisite to that sense of self-worth."[63] As the logic of her statement reveals, self-forgiveness may need to begin before self-worth is recovered. Being valued and affirmed by others makes sense as a part of self-forgiveness.

Card sees limits on that which forgiveness can accomplish, including the extent to which it prevents regret. She describes some regret as a "moral remainder" and "primarily a sense of loss."[64] Most philosophers of forgiveness conclude that forgiveness is not the end of the story, accomplishing, instead, a change in how the story might continue. For some of us, regret may be inevitable, but reconnecting with others and engaging in forward-looking preservative forgiveness are acts of hope that affirm the possibility that one will continue even in the presence of regret. It is difficult to recommend that one look forward in the full knowledge that the future contains intrusive memories, yet acceptance of oneself includes acceptance of one's uncontrollable parts. The commitment to persist includes the commitment to continue the work of self-forgiveness despite oneself. Brison reminds us, "By constructing and telling a narrative of the trauma endured, and with the help of understanding listeners, the survivor begins not only to integrate the traumatic episode into a life with a before and an after, but also to gain control over the occurrence of intrusive memories."[65] This does not mean that we can control their recurrence, but by developing empathy for one's own past self, one may come to see oneself as worthy of self-improvement. Self-forgiveness, like all forgiveness, is optimistic, hoping and trusting that one's future selves will continue the commitment to be kind.

Notes

Epigraphs to this chapter are drawn from the following sources: Eric Fair, "An Iraq Interrogator's Nightmare," *Washington Post*, Friday, February 9, 2007, Page A19; anonymous participant in a substance abuse treatment group for women, quoted in Baker (2008), 70. Portions of this chapter are drawn from ideas first expressed in "The Limits of Forgiveness," *Hypatia*, Vol. 24, no. 1 (Winter 2009); "Why Self-Forgiveness Needs Third-Party Forgiveness," in *Forgiveness: Probing the Boundaries*, e-book, Oxford: Inter-Disciplinary Press, 2008. My thanks to editors and reviewers for their helpful comments on those incarnations.

1. In using the term, "self-complexity," I am relying on P.W. Linville's well-known account, in which he said that "[self-]complexity can be thought of in a number of ways, depending on one's choice of representation. . . . The concept is multifaceted, model-specific, and sometimes fuzzy;" see P.W. Linville, "Affective consequences of complexity regarding the self and others," in *Affect and cognition: The 17th Annual Carnegie Symposium on Cognition*, ed. M. S. Clark & S. T. Fiske (Hillsdale, NJ: Lawrence Erlbaum Associates, Inc., 1982), 79–109. I draw from more recent surveys of the extant literature examining his account; see especially Eshkol Rafaeli-Mor and Jennifer Steinberg, "Self-Complexity and Well-Being: A Review and Research Synthesis," *Personality and Social Psychology Review* 6, no. 1 (2002): 31–58. Although it is still the subject of some debate, "psychologists have recognized that the self is multifaceted and context–dependent rather than unitary in nature" (Deidra J. Schleicher and Allen R. McConnell, "The Complexity of Self–Complexity: An Associated Systems Theory Approach," *Social Cognition* 23, no. 5 (2005): 387-416; see also R. F. Baumeister, "The Self," in *Handbook of Social Psychology* (4th ed., Vol. 1), ed. D. T. Gilbert, S. T., Fiske, and G. Lindzey (New York: McGraw–Hill, 1998), 680–740; P.W. Linville and D.E. Carlston, "Social cognition perspective on self," in *Social cognition: Contributions to classic issues in social psychology*, ed. P. G. Devine, D. L. Hamilton, and T. M. Ostrom (New York: Springer–Verlag, 1994), 143–193.

2. Judith Butler, *Gender Trouble: Feminism and the Subversion of Identity* (New York: Routledge, 1990); see especially Chapter One, section V, "Identity, Sex, and the Metaphysics of Substance," 22-32.

3. Anne Fausto-Sterling, *Sexing the Body* (New York: Basic Books, 2000), 235.

4. J. Block, "Ego identity, role variability, and adjustment," *Journal of Consulting Psychology* 25 (1961): 392.

5. American Psychiatric Association, *Diagnostic and Statistical Manual of Mental Disorders*, Fourth Edition (Washington, DC: American Psychiatric Association, 1994), 161.

6. Steve Matthews, "Establishing Personal Identity in Cases of DID," *Philosophy, Psychiatry, & Psychology* 10, no.2 (2003): 143.

7. Matthews (2003), 144.

8. Matthews (2003), 149.

9. Susan J. Brison, *Aftermath: Violence and the Remaking of a Self* (Princeton, N.J.: Princeton University Press, 2002), 137n44.

10. Brison (2002), 63.

11. M. Harway and M. Hansen, *Spouse abuse: Assessing and treating battered women, batterers, and their children*, 2nd ed. (Sarasota, FL: Professional Resource Press, 2004); Edward S. Kubany, "Cognitive Trauma Therapy for Battered Women With PTSD," *Journal of Consulting and Clinical Psychology* 72, no.1 (2004); Stephanie A. Eisenstat and Lundy Bancroft, "Domestic Violence," *New England Journal of Medicine* 341, no.12 (1999): 886-892.

12. Brison (2002), 49.

13. Eisenstat and Bancroft (1999), 886; Brison (2002), 46; Maria P. Root, "Persistent, disordered eating as a gender-specific, post-traumatic stress response to sexual assault," *Psychotherapy: Theory, Research, Practice, Training* 28, no.1 (Special issue: Psychotherapy with victims) (1991): 96-102.

14. Carrie E. Landa and Jane A. Bybee, "Adaptive Elements of Aging: Self-Image Discrepancy, Perfectionism, and Eating Problems," *Developmental Psychology* 43, no.1 (Jan 2007): 84, 91.

15. Sharon K. Farber, Craig C. Jackson, Johanna K. Tabin, and Eytan Bachar, "Death and annihilation anxieties in anorexia nervosa, bulimia, and self-mutilation," Psychoanalytic Psychology 24, no.2 (2007): 289-305; for fatality rates of anorexia, see APA (1994).

16. Claudia Card, *The Atrocity Paradigm: A Theory of Evil* (Oxford: Oxford University Press, 2002), 91.

17. Qtd. in Card (2002), 89.

18. Card (2002), 215.

19. Robin Dillon, "Self-Forgiveness and Self-Respect," *Ethics* 112 (2001): 59.

20. Dillon (2001), 67.

21. Dillon (2001), 62, 63.

22. Dillon (2001), 60.

23. Helen M. Pettinati, Violet Franks, and Julie H. Wade, "Distinguishing the role of eating disturbance from depression in the sex role self-perceptions of anorexic and bulimic inpatients," *Journal of Abnormal Psychology* 96, no.3 (1987): 280-282; D.G. Dutton and S. Painter, "The battered woman syndrome: Effects of severity and intermittency of abuse," *American Journal of Orthopsychiatry* 63 (1993): 614–621.

24. Card (2002), 18.

25. Primo Levi, *The Drowned and the Saved*, translated by Raymond Rosenthal (New York: Vintage, 1989), 49.

26. Qtd. in Card (2002), 220.

27. Card (2002), 224.

28. Card (2002), 228, 234.

29. Brison (2002), 70.

30. Hannah Arendt, "Irreversibility and the Power to Forgive," *The Human Condition* (Chicago: University of Illinois Press, 1958/1998), 243.

31. Arendt (1958/1998), 179.

32. Card (2002), 213.

33. Levi (1989), 80-82.

34. Dillon (2001), 60.

35. Dillon (2001), 60, n.18.

36. Card (2002), 176.

37. Charles Griswold provides a welcome exception, noting that 'self-forgiveness for injuries done to others is peculiarly similar to third party forgiveness;' Charles Griswold, *Forgiveness: A Philosophical Exploration* (Cambridge and New York: Cambridge University Press, 2007), 123. Although we arrived at this insight separately, I am grateful for the corroboration provided by Griswold's account.

38. Linda Ross Meyer, "Forgiveness and Public Trust," *Fordham Urban Law Journal* 27, no.5 (2000): 1523.

39. M. Fisher and J. Exline, "Self-Forgiveness versus Excusing: The Roles of Remorse, Effort, and Acceptance of Responsibility," *Self and Identity* 5 (2006): 129.

40. Card (2002), 176.

41. Eve Garrard, "Forgiveness and the Holocaust," in *Moral Philosophy and the Holocaust*, ed. Eve Garrard and Geoffrey Scarre (Burlington, VT: Ashgate Publishing Co., 2003), 232.

42. Griswold (2007), 122.

43. Griswold (2007), 119.

44. Hobbes, qtd. in Card (2002), 19; Marcus G. Singer, "Duties and Duties to Oneself," *Ethics: An International Journal of Social, Political, and Legal Philosophy* 73 (January 1963): 133.

45. Dillon (2001), 56-71; Card (2002), 19, 176-177.

46. Bernard R. Boxill, "Self-Respect and Protest," in *Philosophy Born of Struggle: Anthology of Afro-American Philosophy from 1917*, ed. Leonard Harris (Dubuque, Iowa: Kendall/Hunt Publishing Co., 1983), 266-274; Laurence M. Thomas, "Self-Respect: Theory and Practice," in *Philosophy Born of Struggle*, 174-189.

47. This example was bravely provided by Joann Phillips, as an attitude she held with others until her own daughter began visibly wasting away from anorexia; see P. Tyre, "Fighting Anorexia: No One to Blame," *Newsweek*, December 5, 2005, 50-59.

48. Card (2002), 217.

49. Card (2002), 218.

50. Card (2002), 218.

51. Card (2002), 176.

52. Marjorie Baker, "Self-Forgiveness: An Empowering and Therapeutic Tool for Working with Women in Recovery," in *Women's Reflections on the Complexities of Forgiveness*, ed. Wanda Malcolm, Nancy DeCourville, and Kathryn Belicki (New York: Routledge, 2008), 64.

53. Levi (1989), 54.

54. Brison (2002), 65-66.

55. Dillon (2001), 54-65.

56. Dillon (2001), 63.

57. Dillon (2001), 64.

58. Dillon (2001), 72.

59. Dillon (2001), 72n52.
60. Dillon (2001), 72.
61. Brison (2002), 49-66.
62. Brison (2002), 56, emphasis hers.
63. Card (2002), 176.
64. Card (2002), 180.
65. Brison (2002), 53-54.

Selected Bibliography

American Psychiatric Association. *Diagnostic And Statistical Manual Of Mental Disorders*, fourth edition. Washington, DC: American Psychiatric Association, 1994.

Annis, David B. "The Meaning, Value, and Duties of Friendship." *American Philosophical Quarterly* 24, no. 4 (1987): 349-56.

Arendt, Hannah. *The Human Condition*. Chicago: University of Illinois Press. 1958/1998.

_____. *The Origins of Totalitarianism*. New York: Harcourt Brace Jovanovich. 1951/1973.

Aristotle. *Nicomachean Ethics*. Translated by Terence Irwin. Indianapolis, Ind.: Hackett Publishing, 1985.

Augustine, Saint. "Faith and the Creed [De Fide et Symbolo]." In *Augustine: Earlier Writings*, edited and translated by John H. S. Burleigh. Philadelphia: Westminster Press, 1953.

_____. "On the Liturgical Seasons." In *The Works of Saint Augustine: Sermons*. Vol. III., Book 7, edited by John E. Rotelle, O.S.A., and translated by Edmund Hill, O.P. New Rochelle, NY: New City Press, 1993.

_____. "On the New Testament." In *The Works of Saint Augustine: Sermons*. Volume III, Book 1, edited by John E. Rotelle, O.S.A., and translated by Edmund Hill, O.P. Brooklyn, NY: New City Press. 1991.

Austin, J.L. *How to do Things With Words*. Cambridge, Mass.: Harvard University Press, 1962.

Baier, Annette. *Postures of the Mind: Essays on Mind and Morals*. Minneapolis: University of Minnesota Press, 1985.

_____. *Moral prejudices: Essays on Ethics*. Cambridge, Mass.: Harvard University Press, 1994.

_____. "Trust and Antitrust." *Ethics* 96 (1986): 231-61.

Baker, Marjorie. "Self-Forgiveness: An Empowering and Therapeutic Tool for Working with Women in Recovery." Pp. 61-74 in *Women's Reflections on the Complexities of Forgiveness*, edited by Wanda Malcolm, Nancy DeCourville, and Kathryn Belicki. New York: Routledge, 2008.

Barbieri, Paula. *The Other Woman*. New York: Little, Brown & Co, 1997.

Baumeister, R. F. "The self." Pp. 680–740, in *Handbook of social psychology* (4th ed., Vol. 1), edited by D. T. Gilbert, S. T., Fiske, and G. Lindzey. New York: McGraw–Hill, 1998.

Becker, Dana. *Through the Looking Glass*. Boulder, CO: Westview Press, 1997.

Belicki, Kathryn, Jessica Rourke, and Megan McCarthy. "Potential Dangers of Empathy and Related Conundrums." Pp.165-186, in *Women's Reflections on the Complexities of Forgiveness*, edited by Wanda Malcolm, Nancy DeCourville, and Kathryn Belicki. New York and London: Routledge, 2008.

Bem, S. L. *The lenses of gender: Transforming the debate on sexual inequality*. New Haven, CT: Yale University Press, 1993.

Benn, Piers. "Forgiveness and Loyalty." *Philosophy* 71 (1996): 369-83.

Biehl, Linda. Stories: Linda Biehl & Easy Nofemela, from The Forgiveness Project. URL: http://www.theforgivenessproject.com/stories/linda-biehl-easy-nofemela. Accessed February 19, 2008. First published 2004.

Block, J. "Ego identity, role variability, and adjustment." Journal of Consulting Psychology 25 (1961): 392–397.

Boss, Judith. "Throwing Pearls to the Swine: Women, Forgiveness, and the Unrepentant Abuser." Pp. 235-248, in *Philosophical Perspectives on Power and Domination*, edited by Laura Duhan Kaplan and Lawrence F. Bove. Amsterdam-Atlanta: Rodopi Press, 1997.

Boxill, Bernard R. "Self-Respect and Protest." Pp. 266-274, in *Philosophy Born of Struggle: Anthology of Afro-American Philosophy from 1917*, edited by Leonard Harris. Dubuque, Iowa: Kendall/Hunt Publishing Co., 1983.

Brison, Susan J. *Aftermath: Violence and the Remaking of a Self*. Princeton, N.J.: Princeton University Press, 2002.

_____. "The Use of Narrative in the Aftermath of Violence." Pp. 210-255, in *On Feminist Ethics and Politics*, edited by Claudia Card. Lawrence, Kan.: University Press of Kansas, 1999.

Butler, Bishop Joseph. *Fifteen Sermons*. Charlottesville, VA: Ibis Publishing, 1987. Edition previously published by Robert Carter & Brothers, New York, 1860.

Butler, Judith. *Gender Trouble: Feminism and the Subversion of Identity*. New York: Routledge, 1990.

Calhoun, Cheshire. "Changing One's Heart." *Ethics* 103 (1992): 76-96.

Cantacuzino, Marina. The Forgiveness Project: A journalist's storytelling experiment. From *The Storyteller and the Listener online: Essays on the role of story and narrative in peacemaking, bridge building, healing and reconciliation*. http://storyteller-and-listener.blog-city.com/marina_cantacuzino.htm. Accessed Feb. 19, 2008. First published 2007.

_____. Stories of Forgiveness. From Dart Center for Journalism and Trauma: Personal Stories, at: http://www.dartcenter.org/articles/personal_stories/cantacuzino_marina.html. Accessed Feb. 19, 2008.

Card, Claudia. *The Atrocity Paradigm: A Theory of Evil*. Oxford: Oxford University Press, 2002.

_____. "The Atrocity Paradigm Revisited." *Hypatia* 19, no.4 (2004): 210-220.

_____. "Caring and Evil." *Hypatia* 5, no.1 (Spring 1990): 101-08.

_____. "Pluralist Lesbian Separatism." Pp. 125-142, in *Lesbian Philosophies and Cultures*, edited by Jeffner Allen. Albany: State University of New York Press, 1990.

_____. "Rectification and Remainders." In *Routledge Encyclopedia of Philosophy*, edited by Edward Craig. London and New York: Routledge, 1995.

_____. *The Unnatural Lottery: Character and Moral Luck*. Philadelphia: Temple University Press, 1996.

Climbié, Berthe. Stories: Francis & Berthe Climbié, from The Forgiveness Project. URL: http://www.theforgivenessproject.com/stories/francis-berthe-climbie. Accessed Feb. 19, 2008. First published 2004.

Code, Lorraine. "Voice and Voicelessness: A Modest Proposal?" Pp. 204-230 in *Philosophy in a Feminist Voice: Critiques and Reconstructions*, edited by Janet A. Kourany. Princeton, N.J.: Princeton University Press, 1998.

Coleman, Paul W. "The Process of Forgiveness in Marriage and the Family," in *Exploring Forgiveness*, edited by Robert Enright and Joanna North. Madison, WI: The University of Wisconsin Press, 1998.

Cox, Brian. "Television: The Face of Evil," *Guardian* (London). May 21, 2001, Features, 16.

Cox, Deborah L., Sally D. Stabb and Karin H. Bruckner. *Women's Anger: Clinical and Developmental Perspectives*. Philadelphia: Brunner-Routledge, 1999.

Darwall, Stephen. Two Kinds of Respect. *Ethics* 88, no.1 (1977): 36-49.

Davion, Victoria. "How Feminist is Ecofeminism?" Pp. 278-284 in *The Environmental Ethics and Policy Book*, edited by Donald Van de Veer and Christine Pierce. Belmont, Cal.: Wadsworth Publishing, 1997.

DeCourville, Nancy, Kathryn Belicki and Michelle M. Green. "Subjective Experiences of Forgivenes in a Community Sample: Implications for Understanding Forgiveness and Its Consequences." Pp. 1-20 in *Women's Reflections on the Complexities of Forgiveness*, edited by Wanda Malcolm, Nancy DeCourville, and Kathryn Belicki. New York and London: Routledge, 2008.

Digeser, Peter. *Political Forgiveness*. Ithaca, NY: Cornell University Press, 2001.

Dillon, Robin. "Self-Forgiveness and Self-Respect." *Ethics* 112 (2001): 53-83.

Downie, R.S. "Forgiveness." *Philosophical Quarterly* 15 (1965): 128-34.

Dutton, D. G., & Painter, S. "The battered woman syndrome: Effects of severity and intermittency of abuse." American Journal of Orthopsychiatry 63 (1993): 614–621.

Eaton, Judy, Laurier Wilfrid, C. Ward Struthers, and Alexander G. Santelli. "The Mediating Role of Perceptual Validation in the Repentance-Forgiveness Process." *Personality and Social Psychology Bulletin* 32, no.10 (2006): 1389-1401.

Eisenstat, Stephanie A. and Lundy Bancroft. "Domestic Violence." New England Journal of Medicine 341, no.12 (1999): 886-892.

Enright, Robert D. *Forgiveness is a Choice*. Washington, D.C.: APA LifeTools, 2001.

Enright, Robert D. and Joanna North, eds. *Exploring Forgiveness*. Madison, WI: The University of Wisconsin Press, 1998.

Enright, Robert D., Suzanne Freedman, and Julio Rique. "The Psychology of Interpersonal Forgiveness." Pp. 46-62 in *Exploring Forgiveness*, ed. by Enright and North. Madison: The University of Wisconsin Press, 1998.

Epstein, Barbara L. *The Politics of Domesticity*. Middletown, CT: Wesleyan University Press, 1981.

Farber, Sharon K., Craig C. Jackson, Johanna K. Tabin, and Eytan Bachar. "Death and annihilation anxieties in anorexia nervosa, bulimia, and self-mutilation." *Psychoanalytic Psychology* 24, no.2 (2007): 289-305.

Fausto-Sterling, Anne. *Sexing the Body*. New York: Basic Books, 2000.

Feder, Ellen K., and Eva Feder Kittay, eds. *The Subject of Care: Feminist Perspectives on Dependency*. Lanham, MD: Rowman & Littlefield, 2002.

Ferguson, Ann. "Feminist Communities and Moral Revolution." Pp. 367-98 in *Feminism and Community*, edited by Penny Weiss and Marilyn Friedman. Philadelphia: Temple University Press, 1995.

Ferguson, T.J., and S.L. Crowley. "Gender differences in the organization of guilt and shame." *Sex Roles* 37 (1997), 19-44.

Fineman, Martha. "Masking Dependency: The Political Role of Family Rhetoric." Pp. 215-244 in *The Subject of Care: Feminist Perspectives on Dependency*. Lanham, MD: Rowman & Littlefield, 2002.

Fisher, M. and J. Exline. "Self-Forgiveness versus Excusing: The Roles of Remorse, Effort, and Acceptance of Responsibility." *Self and Identity* 5 (2006): 127–146.

Fitzgibbons, Richard. "The Cognitive and Emotive Uses of Forgiveness in the Treatment of Anger." *Psychotherapy* 23 (1986): 629-32.

_____. "Anger and the Healing Power of Forgiveness: A Psychiatrist's View." Pp. 63-74 in *Exploring Forgiveness*, edited by Enright and North, 1998.

Flanigan, Beverly. "Forgivers and the Unforgivable." Pp. 95-105 in *Exploring Forgiveness*, edited by Enright and North, 1998.

Forward, Susan. *Toxic Parents*. New York: Bantam Books, 1989.

French, Peter. *Responsibility Matters*. Lawrence, Kan.: University Press of Kansas, 1992.

Friedman, Marilyn. "Autonomy and Social Relationships: Rethinking the Feminist Critique." Pp. 40-61 in *Feminists Rethink the Self*, edited by Diana T. Meyers. Boulder, CO: Westview, 1997.

_____. *What Are Friends For?* Ithaca, N.Y.: Cornell University Press, 1993.

_____. "The Social Self and the Partiality Debates." Pp. 161-179 in *Feminist Ethics*, edited by Claudia Card. Lawrence, Kan.: University of Kansas Press, 1991.

Frye, Marilyn. *The Politics of Reality: Essays in Feminist Theory*. Freedom, CA: Crossing Press, 1983.

Garrard, Eve. "Forgiveness and the Holocaust." Pp. 231-45 in Moral *Philosophy and the Holocaust*, edited by Eve Gerrard and Geoffrey Scarre. Burlington, VT: Ashgate Publishing Co., 2003.

Gilligan, Carol. *In a Different Voice: Psychological Theory and Women's Development*. Cambridge: Harvard University Press, 1982.

_____. "Joining the Resistance: Psychology, Politics, Girls and Women." *Michigan Quarterly Review* 29 (1990): 501-536.

Gomberg, E. "Shame and guilt issues among women alcoholics." *Alcoholism Treatment Quarterly* 4 (1987): 139-155.

Govier, Trudy. *Dilemmas of Trust*. Montreal and Kingston: McGill-Queen's University Press, 1998.

_____. *Forgiveness and Revenge*. London and New York: Routledge, 2002.

_____. "Forgiveness and the Unforgivable." *American Philosophical Quarterly* 36, no.1 (1999): 59-75.

Govier, Trudy and W. Verwoerd. "Forgiveness: The Victim's Prerogative." *South African Journal of Philosophy* 21, no.1 (2002): 97-111.

Grace-Odeleye, Beverlyn E. "An examination of the role of forgiveness in the leadership practices of women leaders in higher education." *Dissertation*

Abstracts International (Section A: Humanities and Social Sciences), 64, no.5-A (2003): 1550.

Griffin, Susan. *Woman and Nature: The Roaring Inside Her.* New York: Harper & Row, 1978.

Griffiths, Morwenna. *Feminisms and the Self: The Web of Identity.* New York: Routledge, 1995.

Grimshaw, Jean. *Philosophy and Feminist Thinking.* Minneapolis: University of Minnesota Press, 1986.

Griswold, Charles. *Forgiveness: A Philosophical Exploration.* Cambridge and New York: Cambridge University Press, 2007.

Gusterson, Hugh. *People of the Bomb.* Minneapolis: University of Minnesota Press, 2004.

Haaken, Janice. "The Good, the Bad, and the Ugly: Psychoanalytic and Cultural Perspectives." Pp. 172-91 in *Before Forgiving,* ed. by Sharon Lamb and Jeffrie Murphy. Oxford: Oxford University Press, 2002.

Habe, Hans. Symposium response, in *The Sunflower,* written and edited by Simon Wiesenthal. New York: Schocken Books, 1976.

Haber, Joram. "Forgiveness and Feminism." Pp. 141-150 in *Norms and Values: Essays on the Work of Virginia Held,* edited by Joram Graf Haber and Mark S. Halfon. Lanham: Rowman and Littlefield Publishers, 1998.

_____. *Forgiveness.* Savage, MD: Rowman & Littlefield Publishers, 1991.

Harway, M., and M. Hansen. *Spouse abuse: Assessing and treating battered women, batterers, and their children* [2nd ed.]. Sarasota, FL: Professional Resource Press, 2004.

Hekman, Susan J. *Moral Voices, Moral Selves: Carol Gilligan and Feminist Moral Theory.* University Park, Penn.: Pennsylvania State University Press, 1995.

Held, Virginia. *Feminist Morality: Transforming Culture, Society and Politics.* Chicago: University of Chicago Press, 1993.

Helm, Barbara. "Combating Misogyny?: Responses to Nietzsche by Turn-of-the-Century German Feminists." *Journal of Nietzsche Studies* 27 (2004): 64-84.

Hieronymi, Pamela. "Articulating an Uncompromising Forgiveness." *Philosophy and Phenomenological Research* 62, no.3 (2001): 529–555.

Hoagland, Sarah. "Some Thoughts About 'Caring.'" Pp. 246-263 in *Feminist Ethics,* edited by Claudia Card. Lawrence, Kan.: University Press of Kansas, 1991.

_____. "Some Concerns About Nel Noddings' 'Caring.'" *Hypatia* 5, no.1 (1990): 108-13.

_____. *Lesbian Ethics: Toward New Value.* Palo Alto, Cal.: Institute of Lesbian Studies, 1988.

_____. "Why Lesbian Ethics?" Pp. 199-209 in *Adventures in Feminist Philosophy,* edited by Claudia Card. Bloomington, Ind.: Indiana University Press, 1994.

Hoffman, Rose Marie, and L. DiAnne Borders. "Twenty-five years after the Bem sex-role inventory: A reassessment and new issues regarding classification variability." *Measurement & Evaluation in Counseling & Development* 34, Issue 1 (2001): 39-56.

Holmgren, Margaret. "Forgiveness and the Intrinsic Value of Persons." *American Philosophical Quarterly* 30, no4 (1993): 341-352.

_____. "Forgiveness and Self-Forgiveness in Psychotherapy." Pp. 112-135 in *Before Forgiving*, edited by Sharon Lamb and Jeffrie Murphy. Oxford: Oxford University Press, 2002.

hooks, bell. *Feminist Theory: From Margin to Center*. [2nd edition.] Cambridge, Mass.: South End Press, 2000.

Horsbrugh, H.J.N. "Forgiveness." *Canadian Journal of Philosophy* 4 (1974): 269-282.

Houston, Barbara. "Caring and Exploitation." *Hypatia* 5, no.1 (1990): 115-119.

Jack, Dana. *Silencing the Self: Depression and Women*. Cambridge, Mass.: Harvard University Press, 1991.

Jacoby, Susan. *Wild Justice: The Evolution of Revenge*. New York: Harper & Row, 1983.

_____. *Freethinkers: A History of American Secularism*. New York: Metropolitan Books, 2004.

Jaeger, Marietta. "The Power and Reality of Forgiveness: Forgiving the Murderer of One's Child." Pp. 9-14 in *Exploring Forgiveness*, edited by Enright and North, 1998.

Jaggar, Alison. "Feminist Ethics: Projects, Problems, Prospects." Pp. 78-104 in *Feminist Ethics*, edited by Claudia Card. Lawrence, Kan.: University of Kansas Press, 1991.

James, Kerrie. "The interactional process of forgiveness and responsibility: A critical assessment of the family therapy literature." Pp. 127-138 in *Hope and despair in narrative and family therapy: Adversity, forgiveness and reconciliation*, edited by Carmel Flaskas, Imelda McCarthy, and Jim Sheehan. New York: Routledge/Taylor & Francis Group, 2007.

Jones, Sandra S. *Forgiveness and its relationship to personality, spirituality, and well-being: The question of incremental validity*. Dissertation Abstracts International: Section B: The Sciences and Engineering, Vol 67(4-B), pp. 2269. 2006.

Kant, Immanuel. *The Metaphysical Elements of Justice*. New York: Bobbs-Merrill. First published 1780. 1965.

_____. *Observations on the Feeling of the Beautiful and the Sublime*. Trans. John T. Goldthwait. Berkeley: University of California Press. First published 1764. 1960.

_____. *Religion within the Limits of Reason Alone*. Translated by Theodore M. Greene and Hoyt H. Hudson. New York: Harper & Row. First published in 1792. 1960.

Katz, Eric. *Nature as Subject: Human Obligation and Natural Community*. Lanham, MD: Rowman & Littlefield, 1996.

Kellaway, Kate. "Could you forgive the unforgivable?" *Observer*, June 25, 2006.

Kesten, Hermann. Symposium response, in *The Sunflower* by Simon Wiesenthal. New York: Schocken Books. 1969.

Kittay, Eva Feder. *Love's Labor: Essays on Women, Equality, and Dependency*. New York: Routledge, 1999.

_____. "When Caring is Just and Justice is Caring: Justice and Mental Retardation." Pp. 257-276 in *The Subject of Care: Feminist Perspectives on Dependency*, edited by Ellen Feder and Eva Feder Kittay. Lanham, MD: Rowman & Littlefield, 2002.

Kittay, Eva Feder and Ellen Feder, eds. *The Subject of Care: Feminist Perspectives on Dependency.* Lanham, MD: Rowman & Littlefield, 2002.

Kittay, Eva Feder and Diana T. Meyers, eds. *Women and Moral Theory.* Totowa, NJ: Rowman and Littlefield, 1987.

Kolnai, Aurel. "Forgiveness." Pp. 211-224 in *Ethics, Value and Reality.* London: Athlone Press, 1977.

Konrad, Alison M., and Claudia Harris. "Desirability of the Bem Sex-Role Inventory items for women and men: A comparison between African Americans and European Americans." *Sex Roles* 47, no. 5/6 (2002): 259-272.

Konstam, Varda, Miriam Chernoff, and Sara Deveney. "Toward Forgiveness: The role of shame, guilt, anger, and empathy." *Counseling and Values* 46, no.1 (2001): 26-40.

Konstam, Varda, Fern Marx, Jennifer Schurer, Nancy Emerson Lombardo and Anne K. Harrington. "Forgiveness in Practice." Pp.54-71 in *Before Forgiving,* edited by Lamb and Murphy, 2002.

Kubany, Edward S. "Cognitive Trauma Therapy for Battered Women With PTSD." *Journal of Consulting and Clinical Psychology* 72, no.1 (2004): 81-91.

Laitinen, Arto. "Interpersonal Recognition: A Response to Value or a Precondition of Personhood?" *Inquiry* 45, no.4 [Symposium on Axel Honneth and Recognition] (2002): 463-478.

Lamb, Sharon. "Women, Abuse, and Forgiveness: A Special Case." Pp. 155-71 in *Before Forgiving,* edited by Lamb and Murphy, 2002.

Lamb, Sharon, and Jeffrie Murphy, eds. *Before Forgiving.* Oxford: Oxford University Press, 2002.

Landa, Carrie E., and Jane A. Bybee. "Adaptive Elements of Aging: Self-Image Discrepancy, Perfectionism, and Eating Problems." *Developmental Psychology* 43, no.1 (Jan 2007): 83-93.

Lang, Berel. "Forgiveness." *American Philosophical Quarterly* 31, no.2 (1994): 105-117.

Lawler-Row, Kathleen A., and Kimberly A. Reed. "Forgiveness and Health in Women." Pp. 75-92 in *Women's Reflections on the Complexities of Forgiveness,* edited by Wanda Malcolm, Nancy DeCourville, and Kathryn Belicki. New York and London: Routledge, 2008.

Lawler-Row, Kathleen A. and Rachel L. Piferi. "The forgiving personality: Describing a life well lived?" *Personality and Individual Differences* 41, no.6(Oct 2006): 1009-1020.

Levi, Primo. *The Drowned and the Saved.* Translated by Raymond Rosenthal. New York: Vintage, 1989.

Lewis, Janet L. "Forgiveness and psychotherapy: The prepersonal, the personal, and the transpersonal." *The Journal of Transpersonal Psychology* 37, no.2 (2005): 1-24.

Lewis, M. *Shame: The exposed self.* New York: Free Press, 1992.

Linville, P.W. "Affective consequences of complexity regarding the self and others." Pp.79–109 in *Affect and cognition: The 17th Annual Carnegie Symposium on Cognition,* edited by M. S. Clark & S. T. Fiske. Hillsdale, NJ: Lawrence Erlbaum Associates, Inc., 1982.

Linville, P. and D. E. Carlston. "Social cognition perspective on self." Pp. 143–193 in *Social Cognition: Contributions To Classic Issues In Social Psychology,* edited by P. G. Devine, D. L. Hamilton, and T. M. Ostrom. New York: Springer-Verlag, 1994.

Luskin, Frederic. *Forgive for Good*. New York and San Francisco: Harper Collins/Harper San Francisco, 2003.

Macaskill, Ann, John Maltby, and Liza Day. "Forgiveness of self and others and emotional empathy." *Journal of Social Psychology* 142, no.5 (2002): 663-665.

MacIntyre, Alasdair. *After Virtue*, 2nd ed. Notre Dame, Ind.: University of Notre Dame Press, 1984.

MacLachlan, Alice. "Forgiveness, Feminism, and the Diversity of Women's Experiences," online, Society for Women's Advancement in Philosophy 2005 Conference for Topics of Diversity in Philosophy, http://conference2005.swapusa.org/papers/maclachlan/ (First presented at the first meeting of the Society for Women's Advancement in Philosophy, Tallahassee, Florida, April 2005).

————. "Forgiveness and Moral Solidarity." *Forgiveness: Probing the Boundaries*, e-book [978-1-904710-62-2]. Oxford: Inter-Disciplinary Press, 2008.

Malcolm, Wanda, Nancy DeCourville, and Kathryn Belicki, eds. *Women's Reflections on the Complexities of Forgiveness*. New York: Routledge, 2008.

Mathias-Riegel, Barbara. "Discovering the Bliss Of Forgiveness." *Washington Post*, July 14, 1997, C5.

Matthews, Steve. "Establishing Personal Identity in Cases of DID." *Philosophy, Psychiatry, & Psychology* 10, no.2 (2003): 143-151.

May, Larry and James Bohman. "Sexuality, Masculinity, and Confession." *Hypatia* 12, no.1 (1997): 138-154.

McCullough, Michael E., Kenneth Pargament, and Carl E. Thoresen, eds. *Forgiveness: Theory, Research and Practice*. New York: The Guilford Press, 2000.

McFall, Lynne. "What's Wrong with Bitterness?" Pp. 146-160, in *Feminist Ethics*, edited by Card, 1991.

McGary, Howard. "Forgiveness." *American Philosophical Quarterly* 26 (1989): 343-351.

Meyer, Linda Ross. "Forgiveness and Public Trust." *Fordham Urban Law Journal* 27, no.5 (2000): 1515-1540.

Minow, Martha. *Between Vengeance and Forgiveness*. Boston: Beacon Press, 1999.

Moody-Adams, Michelle M. "Self/other." Pp. 255-262 in *A Companion to Feminist Philosophy*, edited by Alison M. Jaggar and Iris Marion Young. Malden, Mass.: Blackwell Publishers, 1998.

Moore, Kathleen Dean. *Pardons: Justice, Mercy, and the Public Interest*. New York, Oxford: Oxford University Press, 1989.

Morris, Allison. "How could you ever forgive the evil killers?; As grieving vicar quits, we ask other victims' relatives." *Mirror*, March 13, 2006, 13.

Munthit, Ker. "Khmer Rouge leaders say they're sorry about deaths." *Chicago Sun-Times,* Wed., Dec. 30, 1998, News, p. 26.

Murphy, Jeffrie G. "Forgiveness in Counseling: A Philosophical Perspective." Pp.41-53 in *Before Forgiving*, edited by Lamb and Murphy, 2002.

————. *Getting Even: Forgiveness and its Limits*. Oxford: Oxford University Press, 2003.

_____. "Jean Hampton on Immorality, Self-Hatred, and Self-Forgiveness." *Philosophical Studies* 89 (1998): 215-236.

_____. "Kant's Theory of Criminal Punishment." Pp. 434-441 in *Proceedings of the Third International Kant Congress*, edited by Lewis White Beck, Dordrecht, Holland: D. Reidel Publishing, 1972.

Jeffrie G. Murphy and Jean Hampton. *Forgiveness and Mercy*. Cambridge: Cambridge University Press, 1988.

Neblett, William. "Forgiveness and Ideals." *Mind* 83 (1974): 269-284.

Nedelsky, Jennifer. "Reconceiving Autonomy." *Yale Journal of Law and Feminism* 1, no.1 (1989): 7-36.

Nelson, Hilde Lindemann. *Damaged Identities, Narrative Repair*. Ithaca, N.Y.: Cornell University Press, 2001.

Neu, Jerome. "To Understand All is to Forgive All – Or is it?" Pp.17-38 in *Before Forgiving*, ed. by Lamb and Murphy, 2002.

Newberry, P.A. *Forgiveness and Emotion*. Doctoral Dissertation, Claremont Graduate School, Claremont, Cal. 1995.

Nietzsche, Friedrich. *Beyond Good and Evil*, first published 1886. Pp. 179-435 in *Basic Writings of Nietzsche*, translated and edited by Walter Kaufmann. New York: The Modern Library, 1992.

_____. *The Gay* Science, translated and edited by Walter Kaufmann. New York: Vintage, 1974.

_____. *On the Genealogy of Morality*. First published 1887. Trans. M. Clark and A. J. Swensen. Indianapolis, IN: Hackett. 1998.

Noddings, Nel. *Caring: A Feminine Approach to Ethics and Moral Education*. Berkeley: University of California Press. 1984.

_____. "Coping with Violence." *Educational Theory* 52, no.2 (2002): 241-253.

_____. *Women and Evil*. Berkeley: University of California Press, 1989.

Nofemela, Easy. Stories: Linda Biehl & Easy Nofemela, from The Forgiveness Project. URL: http://www.theforgivenessproject.com/stories/linda-biehl-easy-nofemela. Accessed Feb. 19, 2008. First published 2004.

Norlock, Kathryn J. "Self-inflicted Evils and Self-Forgiveness." Forthcoming.

_____. "Why Self-Forgiveness Needs Third-Party Forgiveness," in *Forgiveness: Probing the Boundaries*, e-book [978-1-904710-62-2]. Oxford: Inter-Disciplinary Press, 2008.

Norlock, Kathryn J. and Jean Rumsey. "The Limits of Forgiveness." *Hypatia* 24, no. 1 [Special Issue: Oppression and Agency: Claudia Card's Feminist Philosophy] (2009).

North, Joanna. "The 'Ideal' of Forgiveness: A Philosopher's Exploration." Pp.15-34 in *Exploring Forgiveness*, ed. by Enright and North, 1998.

_____. "An Obligation to Forgive?" *The World of Forgiveness: An International Forgiveness Institute Periodical* 4, no.2, Issue 14 (2001): 25-35.

_____. "Wrongdoing and Forgiveness." *Philosophy* 62 (1987): 499-508.

O'Shaughnessy, R.J. "Forgiveness." *Philosophy* 42 (1967): 336-352.

Oswald, Patricia A. "An examination of the current usefulness of the Bem sex-role inventory." *Psychological Reports,* Part 2, 94, Issue 3 (2004): 1331-1336.

Pedhazur, E. J. and T. J. Tetenbaum. "Bem Sex Role Inventory: A theoretical and methodological critique." *Journal of Personality and Social Psychology* 37 (1979): 996-1016.

Pettigrove, Glen. "The Forgiveness We Speak: The Illocutionary Force of Forgiving." *Southern Journal of Philosophy* 42 (2004): 371-392.

Pettinati, Helen M., Violet Franks, and Julie H. Wade. "Distinguishing the role of eating disturbance from depression in the sex role self-perceptions of anorexic and bulimic inpatients." Journal of Abnormal Psychology 96, no.3 (1987): 280-282.

Plumwood, Val. *Feminism and the Mastery of Nature*. London and New York: Routledge, 1993.

Potter, Nancy. "Is Refusing to Forgive a Vice?" Pp. 135-150 in *Feminists Doing Ethics,* edited by Joanne Waugh. Lanham: Rowman & Littlefield, 2001.

Rafaeli-Mor, Eshkol and Jennifer Steinberg. "Self-Complexity and Well-Being: A Review and Research Synthesis." *Personality and Social Psychology Review* 6, no. 1 (2002): 31–58.

Rawls, John. *A Theory of Justice*. Cambridge, Mass: Harvard University Press, 1971.

Reed, B.G. "Developing women-sensitive drug dependence treatment service: Why so difficult?" *Journal of Psychoactive Drugs* 19 (1987): 151-164.

Reed, Gayle L. and Robert D. Enright. "The Effects of Forgiveness Therapy on Depression, Anxiety, and Posttraumatic Stress for Women After Spousal Emotional Abuse." *Journal of Consulting and Clinical Psychology* 74, no.5 [Special issue: Benefit-Finding] (October 2006): 920-929.

Reimer, Susan. "Forgiveness: Healing the heart and mind." *Baltimore Sun*, August 3, 1996, City Section, 4.

Richards, Norvin. "Forgiveness." *Ethics* 99 (1988): 77-97.

Ritchie, Joy S. "Confronting the 'Essential' Problem: Reconnecting Feminist Theory and Pedagogy." *Journal of Advanced Composition* 10, no.2 (1990): 249-71.

Root, Maria P. "Persistent, disordered eating as a gender-specific, post-traumatic stress response to sexual assault." *Psychotherapy: Theory, Research, Practice, Training* 28, no.1 [Special issue: Psychotherapy with victims.] (1991): 96-102.

Rosenfeld, Megan, and Brooke A. Masters. "The Ultimate Team Player." *Washington* Post, September 26, 1997, C1.

Rousseau, Jean-Jacques. *Emile*. Trans. Allan Bloom Jackson, Tenn.: Basic Books, 1979. First published 1762.

Ruddick, Sara. *Maternal Thinking*. New York: Ballantine Books, 1989.

Rumsey, Jean P. "Some Feminist Questions on Forgiveness." Conference presentation, Society of Women in Philosophy, Antioch College, Yellow Springs, Ohio, October 2000.

_____. "Ways to Think About Dying." Pp. 329-349 in *On Feminist Ethics and Politics*, edited by Claudia Card. Lawrence, Kan.: University Press of Kansas, 1999.

Schleicher, Deidra J. and Allen R. McConnell. "The Complexity Of Self–Complexity: An Associated Systems Theory Approach." Social Cognition 23, no. 5 (2005): 387-416.

Schott, Robin May. "The Atrocity Paradigm and the Concept of Forgiveness." *Hypatia* 19, no.4 (2004): 202-209.

_____. "War Rape and the Political Concept of Evil." Forthcoming.

Schrift, Alan. "On the Gynecology of Morals: Nietzsche and Cixous on the Logic of the Gift." Pp. 210-229 in *Nietzsche and the Feminine*, edited by Peter J. Burgard. Charlottesville: University of Virginia Press, 1994.

Scobie, Geoffrey E.W., Enid D. Scobie, and Alexandros K. Kakavoulis. "A cross-cultural study of the construct of forgiveness: Britain, Greece, and Spain." *Psychology: The Journal of the Hellenic Psychological Society* 9, no.1 (2002): 22-36.

Shackelford, Todd K., David M. Buss, and Kevin Bennett. "Forgiveness or breakup: Sex differences in responses to a partner's infidelity." *Cognition and Emotion.* 16, no.2 (2002): 299-307.

Shriver, Donald. *An Ethic for Enemies: Forgiveness in Politics.* New York: Oxford University Press, 1995.

_____. "Is There Forgiveness in Politics?" Pp. 131-149, in *Exploring Forgiveness,* edited by Enright and North, 1998.

Sidgwick, Henry. *The Methods of Ethics.* 7th edition. Indianapolis, Cambridge: Hackett Publishing Co. , 1981. First published 1907.

Singer, Marcus G. "Duties and Duties to Oneself." *Ethics* 73 (January 1963): 133-142.

Smith, Nick. *I Was Wrong: The Meanings of Apologies.* Cambridge: Cambridge University Press, 2008.

Strawson, P.F. *Freedom and Resentment and Other Essays.* Oxford: Methuen, 1974.

Switanowsky, Irene. "Sympathy and Empathy." *Philosophy Today* 44, no.1 (2000): 86-92.

Thomas, Kevin. "'Journey into Day' Tells of Apartheid Horror." *Los Angeles Times*, Friday, March 9, 2001, Home Edition; F8.

Thomas, Laurence M. "Evil and Forgiveness: The Possibility of Moral Redemption." Forthcoming.

_____. (1983) "Self-Respect: Theory and Practice." Pp. 174-89 in *Philosophy Born of Struggle*, edited by Leonard Harris. Dubuque, Iowa: Kendall/Hunt, 1983.

Tirrell, Lynne. "Sexual Dualism and Women's Self-Creation: On the Advantages and Disadvantages of Reading Nietzsche for Feminists." Pp. 158-182 in *Nietzsche and the Feminine*, edited by Peter J. Burgard. Charlottesville: University Press of Virginia, 1994.

Tuana, Nancy. *The Less Noble Sex: Scientific, Religious, and Philosophical Conceptions of Woman's Nature.* Bloomington, Ind.: Indiana University Press, 1993.

_____. *Woman and the History of Philosophy.* New York: Paragon House, 1992.

Tutu, Desmond. *No Future Without Forgiveness.* Los Angeles: Image Publishing, 1999.

Twambley, P. "Mercy and Forgiveness." *Analysis* 36 (1976): 84–90.

Tyre, P. "Fighting Anorexia: No One to Blame," *Newsweek*, December 5, 2005 (146), 50-59.

Vandenberg, Donald. "Caring: Feminine Ethics or Maternalistic Misandry?" *Journal of Philosophy of Education* 30, no.2 (1996): 253-269.

Walker, Margaret Urban. *Moral Repair: Reconstructing Moral Relations after Wrongdoing.* Cambridge and New York: Cambridge University Press, 2006.

_____. "Diotima's Ghost: The Uncertain Place of Feminist Philosophy in Professional Philosophy." *Hypatia* 20, no.3 (2005): 153-164.

_____. *Moral Understandings: A Feminist Study in Ethics*. New York: Routledge, 1998.

Warren, Karen. "The Power and the Promise of Ecological Feminism." Pp. 257-270 in *The Environmental Ethics and Policy Book*, edited by Donald Van de Veer and Christine Pierce. Belmont, Cal.: Wadsworth Publishing, 1997.

Welch, Bud. Stories: Bud Welch, from The Forgiveness Project. URL: http://www.theforgivenessproject.com/stories/bud-welch. Accessed Feb. 19, 2008. First published 2004.

Weldon, Fay. *Female Friends*. London: Heinemann, 1975.

Wiesenthal, Simon. *The Sunflower*. New York: Schocken Books, 1969.

Wilson, John. "Why Forgiveness Requires Repentance." *Philosophy* 63 (1988): 534-535.

Woolf, Virginia. "Professions for Women." *Collected Essays*. London: Hogarth Press, 1966.

Worthington, Everett L., Jr., Steven J. Sandage, and Jack W. Berry. "Group Interventions to Promote Forgiveness." Pp.228-253 in *Forgiveness: Theory, Research and Practice*, edited by Michael E. McCullough, Kenneth Pargament, and Carl E. Thoresen. New York: The Guilford Press, 2000.

Worthington, Everett L. and Michael Scherer. "Forgiveness is an emotion-focused coping strategy that can reduce health risks and promote health resilience: theory, review, and hypotheses." *Psychology and Health* 19, no. 3 (June 2004): 385–405.

Zimmerman, Michael J. *The Concept of Moral Obligation*. Cambridge: Cambridge University Press, 1996.

_____. "Rethinking the Heidegger-Deep Ecology Relationship." *Environmental Ethics* 15, no. 3 (Fall 1993): 195-224.

Index

About the Author

Kathryn Norlock is an associate professor of Philosophy at St. Mary's College of Maryland, and affiliated faculty with the Women, Gender and Sexuality Studies and Environmental Studies programs. She received her Ph.D. from the University of Wisconsin-Madison in 2001. She is the co-editor of a collection of essays on *The Atrocity Paradigm*, forthcoming with Lexington Books, and has written and spoken widely on feminism, forgiveness, environmental ethics, and the uneasy connections between all three.